Mike Meyers' Network+® Guide to Managing and Troubleshooting Networks Lab Manual

Mike Meyers
Martin Acuña

Mc Graw Hill **Technology Education**

McGraw-Hill Technology Education

Boston   Burr Ridge, IL   Dubuque, IA   Emeryville, CA   Madison, WI   New York
San Francisco   St. Louis   Bangkok   Bogotá   Caracas   Kuala Lumpur   Lisbon
London   Madrid   Mexico City   Milan   Montreal   New Delhi   Santiago   Seoul
Singapore   Sydney   Taipei   Toronto

Technology Education

1333 Burr Ridge Parkway
Burr Ridge, Illinois 60527
U.S.A.

Mike Meyers' Network+® Guide to Managing and Troubleshooting Networks Lab Manual

For information on translations or book distributors outside the U.S.A., please see the International Contact Information page immediately following the index of this book. Some ancillaries, including electronic and print components, may not be available to customers outside the United States.

5 6 7 8 9 0 QPD QPD 0 1 9 8

ISBN 978-0-07-225564-5
MHID 0-07-225564-1

Sponsoring Editor
Christopher Johnson

Developmental Editor
Pamela Woolf

Technical Editor
Brian Schwarz

Project Editor
Mark Karmendy

Copy Editor
Mike McGee

Proofreader
Susie Elkind

Indexer
Claire Splan

Composition
Maureen Forys, Happenstance Type-O-Rama

Series Design
Maureen Forys, Happenstance Type-O-Rama

Cover Series Design
Tom Slick

This book was composed with QuarkXPress 4.11 on a Macintosh G4.

*To the Most Perfect Woman in the Universe, Allison;
to the Greatest Daughter in Existence, Emily; and to
IPv6. (I'm not kidding! This stuff is awesome!)*

—Mike Meyers

*I dedicate this book with chongo-sized love to the
beauteous Acuña womenfolk, wife Anne, and daughter Isabella. I would also like to acknowledge the love
and support given by my two families. I thank my
parents, Ed Sr. and Margaret, brothers Mike and Ed
Jr., and sisters Elida, Elia, and Eloisa. I thank all
of my in-laws, Lester and Rhoda Nimsker; Claudia,
Cliff, Rachael, and Kiel Van Wagner; Marilee, Joe,
and Tori Urbanczyk; Ian Hamelin; Joe, Leslie, Cullen;
and Mackenzie Fleming. Next time you visit, I'll try
not to spend the whole time in front of the computer
(note that I said try).*

—Martin Acuña

Contents

Acknowledgments

Thanks to the whole crew at Total Seminars for assistance and support and for not getting too upset when we kick you off the network during our mad experiments: Dudley Lehmer at the helm; Janelle Meyers keeping things running; Kathy Yale, spreading the word; Scott Jernigan, editing, writing, planning, and generally multitasking like Rick Wakeman during an extended solo; and all the rest—Edit Grrl Cindy Clayton, Roger Conrad (on the road again), David Biggs, David Dussé, Lloyd Jeffries, Brandy Taylor, Emily Meyers, Shannon Lehmer, Mike Smyer, and Bambi "I could kill you with my thumb" Thibodeaux.

On the McGraw-Hill/Osborne side, a hearty thanks to the gang who made this book possible and such a pleasure to produce: Gareth Hancock, our sponsoring editor; Pamela Woolf, developmental editor extraordinaire; Mark Karmendy, the "take no prisoners" project editor; Brian Schwarz, master technical editor; Mike McGee, copyeditor; Susie Elkind, proofreader; and the good folks at Happenstance for another excellent job.

About the Authors

Mike Meyers is the industry's leading authority on Network+ Certification. He is the president and founder of Total Seminars, LLC, a major provider of PC and network repair seminars for thousands of organizations throughout the world, and a member of CompTIA.

Mike has written numerous popular textbooks, including the best-selling *Mike Meyers' A+® Guide to Managing & Troubleshooting PCs*, *Mike Meyers' A+® Guide to PC Hardware*, and *Mike Meyers' A+® Guide to Operating Systems*. If you have any questions or problems, feel free to send an e-mail to Mike at michaelm@totalsem.com.

Martin Acuña is a network engineer, writer, and instructor in Houston, Texas. Martin has designed, deployed, and managed networks of all sizes and platforms in the business, retail, industrial, and non-profit arenas; has authored a successful online MCSE certification course series; and is the co-author of *Mike Meyers' A+ Certification Passport, Second Edition* (McGraw-Hill/Osborne, 2004). Martin holds A+, Network+, MCP, MCSA, and MCSE certifications, an FCC third-class broadcasting license, and HAZMAT certification from the Texas DOT.

Information Technology Skill Standards and Your Curriculum

NATIONAL WORKFORCE CENTER
for EMERGING TECHNOLOGIES

Students in today's increasingly competitive IT career market are differentiated not only by their technical skills, but by their communication, problem solving, and teaming skills. These professional skills are the ones that guarantee career longevity and success. The *National Workforce Center for Emerging Technologies* (NWCET) and McGraw-Hill Technology Education have partnered in an effort to help you build technical *and* employability skills in the classroom.

Skill standards–aligned curriculum is becoming a de facto requirement for schools everywhere in the United States today. Programs are required to be standards aligned in order to show clearly that students are being taught and assessed consistently to an agreed upon set of skill and content standards. For those programs preparing students to enter the workforce, skill standards provide an excellent skeleton upon which to build courses.

Research has shown improved learning and retention of knowledge when learning takes place in a rich learning context. Students that learn in a real-world context are also better equipped to transfer their skills to the real world. IT skill standards provide the kind of real-world data that educators can use. Educators can draw from the skill standards to develop contextually rich assignments that help students to situate their learning in specific work contexts with complex and real-world problems to solve.

IT skill standards provide a common language between industry and education so that building bridges between these two groups can be more efficient. The more industry recognizes what educational programs are doing, the easier it is for education to gain industry support. Schools that use a skill standards–aligned program are better prepared to gain support from industry for technical advisory boards, student internships, job shadows, faculty internships, and a host of other support resources.

IT skill standards provide increased portability of skills because of the common language. Other institutions can clearly identify the content and skills that graduates of a skill standards–aligned curriculum have acquired. Programs that are skill standards–based will effectively oil the wheels of articulation between programs that traditionally may have difficulty agreeing on what has been taught and assessed.

NWCET and McGraw-Hill in Partnership

McGraw-Hill Technology Education and the NWCET have partnered with the goal of helping IT educators meet these demands by making the IT skill standards more easily available and ready to use. McGraw-Hill Technology Education and the NWCET have developed different products that will help you to address the IT skill standards in your network design and administration programs and courses:

A summary crosswalk highlights the IT skill standards addressed by the McGraw-Hill *Mike Meyers' Network+ Guide to Managing and Troubleshooting Networks* textbook.

Chapter 1	**Chapter 2**	**Chapter 3**	**Chapter 4**	**Chapter 5**
None	A5—Research technical alternatives and analyze technical options	A5—Research technical alternatives and analyze technical options	A5—Research technical alternatives and analyze technical options	A5—Research technical alternatives and analyze technical options
Chapter 6	**Chapter 7**	**Chapter 8**	**Chapter 9**	**Chapter 10**
A5—Research technical alternatives and analyze technical options	A5—Research technical alternatives and analyze technical options	C7—Install hardware	A5—Research technical alternatives and analyze technical options	A5—Research technical alternatives and analyze technical options
Chapter 11	**Chapter 12**	**Chapter 13**	**Chapter 14**	**Chapter 15**
A5—Research technical alternatives and analyze technical options	C2—Implement new system configuration	C2—Implement new system configuration	C2—Implement new system configuration	A5—Research technical alternatives and analyze technical options
Chapter 16	**Chapter 17**	**Chapter 18**	**Chapter 19**	**Chapter 20**
A5—Research technical alternatives and analyze technical options	G1—Gather and document security requirements	A5—Research technical alternatives and analyze technical options	B2—Identify, analyze, and evaluate infrastructure and network vulnerabilities	F5—Troubleshoot and maintain client, server, and network systems

- A detailed crosswalk listing Technical Knowledge, Employability Skills, and Performance Indicators addressed by the compliant curriculum (textbook, lab manual, and learning activities in the instructor pack CD)

- Twenty skill standards–based activities with associated assessment tools

- A training document that helps instructors understand and use the features of teaching a skill standards–aligned curriculum

NWCET IT Skill Standards–Compliant Curriculum

When you use *Mike Meyers' Network+® Guide to Managing and Troubleshooting Networks Lab Manual* designed to accompany the textbook *and* the 20 NWCET IT skill standards–based student learning activities included on the Instructor Pack (look for NWCET Skill Standards in the menu on the Instructor CD), you are teaching an IT skill standards fully aligned curriculum. What does that mean? Compliant curriculum assures that your students are getting technical, foundation, and professional or soft skills that successful people have.

When you use the McGraw-Hill/NWCET–compliant materials, your students will learn current business processes and how IT skills fit into the larger business context. They will learn how to perform actual job tasks that network technicians perform on the job. NWCET-compliant materials achieve these goals because the NWCET engages in ongoing research of the IT industry and what it demands of its workers.

NWCET Background and Mission

In 1995, the National Science Foundation (NSF) designated and funded the NWCET as a National Center of Excellence in Advanced Technological Education. The Center was created to advance IT education and improve the supply, quality, and diversity of the IT workforce.

The National Workforce Center for Emerging Technologies has since become a leader in new designs for IT education developing products, services, and best practices that provide timely, relevant, and lasting solutions to meet the needs of IT educators and the IT workforce. The NWCET translates the rapidly changing demands of the technology workplace into programs, curricula, courseware, and assessments that prepare students for current and future IT careers.

The NWCET is perhaps best known for its IT skill standards. Skill standards provide an agreement of what is expected to be successful in a given career area. They provide a validated, industry-derived framework upon which educators can build curricula. Using industry skill standards as the foundation for curricula will result in a closer alignment between educational programs and workplace expectations and result in a better-skilled workforce.

To support new and innovative IT programs and degrees, the NWCET (www.nwcet.org) provides other professional development opportunities for high school teachers and community college and university faculty. The Educator-to-Educator Institute (E2E) (http://e2e.nwcet.org), the training branch of the NWCET, is dedicated to helping IT educators achieve excellence in IT instruction. CyberCareers (www.cybercareers.org) is a website oriented toward middle and high schools students and teachers and provides a wide variety of career education materials such as job descriptions and an IT Interest Inventory.

Instructor and Student Website

For instructor and student resources, check out www.mhteched/mikemeyers/networkplus.com. You'll find all sorts of stuff that will help you learn more about troubleshooting and fixing computers.

Chapter 1
Introduction

Lab Exercises

Let me be the first to congratulate you on your decision to get certified. Don't let anybody kid you—IT certification is a big deal, and the CompTIA Network+ certification is one of the most respected in the IT industry. The fact that you've got the *Mike Meyers' Network+® Guide to Managing and Troubleshooting Networks* and this lab manual in your hands shows that you're serious about earning that certification. That's a smart move!

Understand, however, that you've got your work cut out for you. The Network+ exam will tax your networking skills to their utmost, so you need to be ready for it. This chapter will show you how to prepare for the Network+ exams, while the lab will take you through the steps needed to start studying for them. First, you'll make certain that you understand the important details of the certification itself. Next, you'll look at how Network+ applies toward other IT industry certifications. Then you'll formulate a study plan. Finally, you'll schedule your Network+ exam. So, let's get started!

 60 MINUTES

Lab Exercise 1.01: Understanding Network+

CompTIA's Network+ is a vendor-neutral certification denoting basic networking skills. Network+ is to network techs what A+ is to PC techs: it's your "driver's license" that tells clients and employers that you possess the technical skills and knowledge to implement and maintain computer networks on a variety of hardware and software platforms. To achieve this certification, you must pass the Network+ exam (a single exam, unlike the two exams needed to get A+) at an approved exam administration center. You're already sold on the value of the Network+ certification, but what does the exam actually entail? The good folks at CompTIA don't simply throw you to the wolves with a random barrage of networking questions. Instead, the Network+ exam is defined by a documented list of exam objectives called *domains*. Each domain counts toward a percentage of the exam's total scoring. These domains are organized into four categories: Media and Topologies, Protocols and Standards, Network Implementation, and Network Support.

Hands-on support of networking technologies is given the most weight on the exam, followed by knowledge of network protocols and standards, implementation, and then media and topology. It's important to understand what's required of you for the Network+ exam, so you should now research the exam objectives to develop that understanding. Detailed descriptions of each exam domain can be found on the CompTIA web site.

Learning Objectives

In this lab, you will visit the CompTIA web site to view the latest Network+ exam objectives. By the end of this lab, you will be able to:

- Understand the objectives being tested on the Network+ exam

Lab Materials and Setup

The only thing needed for this lab is a PC with Internet access.

Getting Down to Business

Too many techs make the mistake of pursuing a certification without knowing whether or not the certification is beneficial to their career goal. You won't make a very good Network+ candidate if you don't understand what the Network+ certification is all about. To develop your understanding of the Network+ certification's requirements, spend some time researching the exam domains listed on the CompTIA web site.

Step 1 Fire up your web browser and head over to www.comptia.org/certification/Network/objectives.asp to view the latest Network+ exam objectives. You can follow the links to view each of the four objective domains individually, or you can download the whole list as a .PDF file.

Step 2 Summarize the Network+ exam objective domain 1.0, Media and Topologies.

_____

_____

Step 3 Summarize the Network+ exam objective domain 2.0, Protocols and Standards.

_____

_____

Step 4 Summarize the Network+ exam objective domain 3.0, Network Implementation.

_____

_____

Step 5 Summarize the Network+ exam objective domain 4.0, Network Support.

_____

_____

 30 MINUTES

Lab Exercise 1.02: Related Certifications

In addition to the value of the Network+ certification itself, the IT industry recognizes that the skill sets defined by the Network+ objective domains overlap those of other established IT certifications. Thus, the Network+ certification counts directly toward the requirements of certifications from several of the IT industry's major vendors, including Microsoft and Novell. That's right! Passing the Network+ exam means that you have one less exam to take in order to get certain certifications from other IT industry giants. Slick!

Because of the broad base of networking skills that it covers, achieving Network+ certification will also give you a leg up on IT certifications, even those for which it doesn't directly fulfill certification requirements.

Learning Objectives

In this lab, you'll explore the benefits of Network+ certification as it applies toward other IT industry certifications.

At the end of this lab, you will

- Understand how the Network+ certification applies toward other IT certifications

- Map out a certification path beyond Network+

Lab Materials and Setup

The only material you'll need for this lab is a PC with Internet access.

Getting Down to Business

The CompTIA Network+ certification is vendor-neutral. This means that the broad skill base encompassed by Network+ lends itself to a number of related IT industry certifications from vendors such as Microsoft and Novell.

Step 1   Head to the CompTIA Network+ certification FAQ web site at www.comptia.com/certification/ Network/faqs.asp. Which other IT certifications accept the CompTIA Network+ certification as partial fulfillment of their requirements?

_____

_____

Step 2   Visit Microsoft's certification web site at www.microsoft.com/learning/mcp/default.asp and explore the requirements for the Microsoft Certified Professional (MCP), Microsoft Certified Systems

Administrator (MCSA), and Microsoft Certified Systems Engineer (MCSE) certifications. How do you think the Network+ certification will benefit an IT tech pursuing these certifications?

_____

_____

Step 3 Now do the same for Novell's Certified Novell Administrator (CNA) and Certified Novell Engineer (CNE) certifications at www.novell.com/training/certinfo/. How does the Network+ certification benefit an IT tech pursuing these certifications?

_____

_____

Step 4 Now that you've seen the more common certifications that relate to Network+, what do you think will be a natural certification progression for you?

_____

_____

 25 MINUTES

Lab Exercise 1.03: Study Preparation

If you're like most techs, you know someone who claims to have breezed through some certification exam or other without _any_ preparation or effort. I'll let you in on something: those people are _lying!_ The CompTIA Network+ exam is very thorough, very detailed, and very in-depth. Hey, I just said three words that all mean the same thing, didn't I? Let's just say that, in short, the Network+ exam is extremely tough. No matter how much networking experience and skill you possess, without preparation you won't have much chance of passing the exam!

With that in mind, your next step is coming up with a plan of attack for the Network+ exam. Preparation is key, so start by identifying what you need to study and how to go about studying.

Learning Objectives

In this lab, you will develop your plan of action for preparing for the Network+ exam. To do this you need to deal with two issues: determining which topics you need to study the most and checking your study habits.

At the end of this lab, you will

- Identify the Network+ topics you need to learn
- Develop a study plan

Lab Materials and Setup

The only thing you will need for this lab is a PC with Internet access.

Getting Down to Business

Having taught Network+ certification for years, I've developed a handy template to give students some idea of what they need to study and how much time they need to devote to preparing for the Network+ exams. This template is essentially the same one that appears in the *Mike Meyers' Network+® Guide to Managing and Troubleshooting Networks* textbook, except that here I've added an extra step to help you determine which topics you need to study.

Step 1 Look at each of the listed skills and then circle the amount of experience you have regarding that skill. Circle any skill where your amount of experience is None or Once or Twice.

Type of Experience	None	Once or Twice	Every Now and Then	Quite a Bit
Installing a wireless (802.11) network	4	2	1	1
Installing network cards	8	7	2	1
Installing RAID devices	4	2	1	1
Building PCs from scratch	4	4	1	0
Installing NetWare using IP	8	8	6	1
Installing 2000/2003 server using IP	8	8	5	1
Configuring a DHCP server	1	1	0	0
Configuring a WINS server	1	1	0	0
Configuring Internet dial-ups	5	4	2	1
Supporting a NetWare network	6	5	3	1
Supporting a UNIX/Linux network	4	4	1	1
Supporting a Windows NT Network	6	5	3	2
Supporting a Windows 9x/Me network	3	3	2	2
Supporting a Windows 2000/2003/XP network	6	6	5	4
Installing/troubleshooting routers/firewalls	3	3	1	1
Installing/troubleshooting hubs/switches	2	2	1	1

Now that you've got a feel for the topics that you need to concentrate on, you need to determine your total study time. Take the total amount of time you've circled and use the following table to add in your experience factor.

Months of Direct, Professional Experience...	To Your Study Time...
0	Add 50 hrs
Up to 6	Add 30 hrs
6 to 12	Add 10 hrs
Over 12	Add 0 hrs

What is the total number of estimated hours you will need to study for the Network+ exam?

_____

Step 2   Now that you know what topics are important to you and how much time they will take, you need to develop your study plan. First of all, take the amount of time you've set aside and determine how many days you will need to prepare. Consider work, holidays, weekends—anything that will affect your study time. (If you're in an instructor-led course, this is easy. Use the end of the course.) Then break down your textbook into manageable chunks. (Again, if you're in a course, your instructor will certainly already have done this for you.) You now have your deadline—the day that you will say *I'm ready to take the test!*

What is your deadline for studying for the Network+ exam?

_____

 15 MINUTES

Lab Exercise 1.04: Scheduling the Network+ Exam

Schedule your exam with one of the approved exam administration centers, Prometric or Pearson VUE. Don't put this off—do it now! Get it out of the way so that so that you'll feel you're working toward a deadline.

Learning Objectives

In this lab, you'll learn how to schedule your Network+ exam with an approved exam administration center.

At the end of this lab, you will be able to:

- Schedule your Network+ exam with an approved test administration center.

Lab Materials and Setup

The materials you need for this lab are

- A PC with Internet access, or a telephone

- Payment method (credit card or voucher number)

- In the United States, your Social Security number (SSN)

Getting Down to Business

There are a lot of very qualified, yet uncertified, techs out there in the IT world. While they may well be able to do the job, they have no way of proving it. To paraphrase Steve Jobs, *real techs certify*. Sure, some scoff and say that certifications are just pieces of paper, but I'll tell you this: without that piece of paper, no sane administrator is going to let you anywhere near his or her network.

Take the plunge! Schedule your exam for the CompTIA Network+ exam right now.

Step 1   Register online for Prometric exams at www.register.prometric.com/menu.asp. Pearson VUE's online exam registration is at www.vue.com/comptia/. You can also register the old-fashioned way by calling them on the telephone. In the United States and Canada, call Prometric at 888-895-6116 or Pearson VUE at 877-551-7587 to locate the nearest testing center and schedule the exam. You'll also find toll-free numbers for test centers on the respective testing organizations' web sites. Prometric's phone numbers are at www.prometric.com/ContactUs/TestTakers. Pearson VUE's toll-free telephone numbers are at www.vue.com/contact/vuephone/. Make sure you have a method of payment (credit card or voucher number) and some form of identification. In the United States, you'll also need your Social Security number.

Here's some great news: You don't have to pay full price for your Network+ exam! Virtually every organization that provides Network+ training and testing also offers discount vouchers. In a nutshell, you pay a CompTIA member a discounted price, and in return you get a unique number that you provide instead of a credit card number when you schedule your exam. One provider of Network+ vouchers is my company, Total Seminars. You can call Total Seminars toll-free from the U.S. or Canada at 800-446-6004, or check the web site: **www.totalsem.com**. If you don't buy your voucher from us, for goodness' sake, buy one from *somebody*!

When are you scheduled to sit for the CompTIA Network+ exam?

✖ Cross-Reference

For details on taking the Network+ test, go to the CompTIA web site (www.comptia.org).

Lab Analysis

1. You are interviewing for a network support position at a large business organization. The hiring officer isn't familiar with the Network+ certification. Can you briefly summarize the value of the Network+ certification for her?

    _____

    _____

2. How can Network+ certification help you achieve the Microsoft Certified Systems Administrator certification?

    _____

    _____

3. How can Network+ certification help you achieve Novell certification(s)?

    _____

    _____

4. What network operating systems are referenced on the Network+ exam?

    _____

    _____

5. Name four popular network protocols referenced on the Network+ exam.

    _____

    _____

Key Terms Quiz

Use the vocabulary terms from the list below to complete the sentences that follow. Not all of the terms will be used.

Approved exam administration center

CNA

CNE

CompTIA

MCP

MCSA

MCSE

Network+

Objective domains

Pearson VUE

Prometric

1. _____ is the organization that offers the Network+ certification.

2. Network+ certification counts toward the Microsoft _____ certification.

3. Network+ certification counts toward the Novell _____ and _____ certifications.

4. Your Network+ exam must be taken at an _____.

5. Prometric and _____ are the two organizations that administer the Network+ exam.

Chapter 2
Defining Networking

Lab Exercises

To understand the present state of the computer networking world, it's important that you appreciate how things came to be. Networking technology didn't spring forth out of the minds of network techs fully formed! It took decades of development for networks to reach their current state of sophistication. It's easy to forget this when you're trying to troubleshoot some obscure networking hardware issue or decipher a nonsensical error message, but it's true.

In this chapter, you'll review the computing developments that led us from the lumbering, text-only networks of yore to the slick, graphically rich networks we have today. You'll also look at the networking goals that have driven the march of network technology, then dive into the two key roles of networked PCs—*servers* and *clients*—and look at the computer services that enable these roles. You'll look at how to share a PC's resources on a network and access resources shared on other PCs. Finally, you'll take a brief look at how you can fine-tune the *permissions* that control the level of access that a user has to a shared resource.

The exercises in this lab assume that you're using Microsoft Windows XP Professional, so the instructions for performing actions reflect the steps for that operating system. If you're using a different OS, the specific steps to perform the same actions may vary slightly. Let's go!

 60 MINUTES

Lab Exercise 2.01: The Birth of Networking

In the PC world, the dinosaur age was only a few decades ago. Colossal mainframes ruled the computing world, and only a select few technicians had the know-how to control them. Networking these monsters together was a gargantuan feat in and of itself, and the results were often far from stellar, at least by today's standards.

Still, it's important for you to appreciate the amazing advancements that went into designing and building the first networks. Let's take a look at how those early networks led to what we have now.

Learning Objectives

In this lab, you will identify and describe networking hardware and software technology from the birth of networking to the present.

At the end of this lab, you will be able to:

- Describe the progression of networking technology from mainframe computers to PC computer networks

Lab Materials and Setup

The only thing you'll need for this lab is a PC with Internet access.

Getting Down to Business

Early computers such as mainframes, minicomputers, and even the first microcomputers—what we now call PCs—had very limited networking capabilities. It's important to understand and appreciate the progression that brought these early systems from the roots of networking to where we are today. To accomplish this, spend some time reviewing the history of modern computer networking.

Step 1   Early mainframe computers lacked any networking capabilities. Describe how multiple users were able to enter data into and retrieve data from mainframe computers at the same time.

_____

_____

Step 2   Name two of the major challenges that had to be overcome to initiate networking on early mainframe computers.

_____

_____

Step 3   How were these challenges met?

_____

_____

Step 4   What is considered to be the first successful implementation of a computer network?

_____

_____

Step 5   What were the two types of data transfer technologies enabled on these early networked main-frame computers?

_____

_____

Step 6   How do modern networked PCs communicate with mainframe computers?

_____

_____

Step 7   Name at least three modern computer operating systems that are capable of networking.

_____

_____

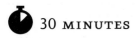 30 MINUTES

Lab Exercise 2.02: Defining the Goals of Networking

One of the mistakes that techs make early in their careers is never developing a clear understanding of the goals of networking. The real power of PCs comes not from raw CPU muscle, massive amounts of RAM, or endless storage space, but from the ability to share resources. Think about how limited your computing world would be if you were unable to connect to a network.

The same goals apply to networking, whether you're accessing a shared resource across the hall or across the globe. Let's examine those goals now to make sure that you're clear on the why's and how's of networking.

Learning Objectives

In this lab, you will examine the goals of computer networking. By its end, you will be able to:

- Define the goals of networking

Lab Materials and Setup

The only thing you'll need for this lab is a PC with Internet access.

Getting Down to Business

One of the many challenges that network techs face in the workplace isn't strictly a technical challenge. At some point you, the learned network technician, will undoubtedly be called upon to explain to a non-learned non-technician the functions and goals of computer networking. This person may be your boss, your assistant, your client, or anyone else with a "need to know" interest in the goings-on of the computer network. Whatever the case may be, it's the hallmark of a true professional to be able to explain, in terms that the layman can understand, the benefits of computer networking and the basics of how a computer network functions.

Assume that you've been contracted by a large non-profit organization to evaluate and make recommendations for updating its computer network system. The Administrative Services Director, Liz Vallejo, is your point of contact. She has a background in mainframes and dumb terminals, and is completely new to PCs. She calls you in for a consultation, and asks you to explain some basic networking concepts so that she can knowledgably present her funding request.

Step 1   Your client is unclear on the benefits of networking her office computers. She asks you to explain what kind of things can be shared on a network. What do you tell her?

_____

_____

Step 2   Now that you've made your client understand the things that can be shared on a network, explain the benefit of sharing these resources.

_____

_____

Step 3   Your client then asks whether each workstation needs the appropriate software installed to access a document shared on a centralized server (such as Microsoft Word installed to open a remote Word document), or if the document can be run from the server. What do you tell her?

_____

_____

 25 MINUTES

Lab Exercise 2.03: Examining Servers and Clients

Back in the dinosaur days of mainframes and dumb terminals, it was easy to define the role that a computer fulfilled on the network. In fact, most of the time there was only *one* computer! Things are very different now, so it's much more important that you appreciate the roles that networked PCs fulfill.

Modern PCs aren't limited to one role or or another; in fact, a single system can act as both a client and a server. This ability comes from a number of small programs running in the background that enable your PC to do things like share files, printers, and other resources on the network; browse the network for resources shared on remote PCs; and access shared resources. These programs are called different things, depending on the operating system. Microsoft Windows and Novell NetWare, for example, call them *services*, while Linux calls them *daemons*. For the purposes of these exercises, I'm going to use the Windows terminology.

Windows XP Professional has services that enable the server function, appropriately called the *server service*, and the client function, called the *workstation service*. Let's examine the services that enable server and client functions on a PC.

Learning Objectives

In this lab, you will examine the services that enable a networked PC to act as a server, a client, or both. You will also look at the impact that turning these services off has on your ability to share resources and access shared resources on a network.

At the end of this lab, you will be able to:

- Describe the role of a network server and a network client
- Describe the function of the server service
- Describe the function of the workstation service
- Understand the impact that loss of services has on network access

Lab Materials and Setup

The materials you need for this lab are

- Two networked PCs running Windows 2000 Professional or Windows XP Home Edition or Professional

Getting Down to Business

Your client asks you to demonstrate the networking abilities of Microsoft Windows PCs. She is interested in seeing the networking in action, and also wants you to demonstrate the underlying services that support that ability. Assume that you've got two PCs available, connected via a network cable or hub, with networking hardware and software installed.

Step 1   Briefly define the terms *server* and *client*.

_____

_____

Step 2   Open the Services Microsoft Management Console (MMC) by clicking Start | Run and typing **SERVICES.MSC**. Then press the ENTER key (or click OK).

➜ Note

Windows Microsoft Management Consoles (MMCs) can be opened in a number of different ways. The most common way is to open the Control Panel, double-click the Administrative Tools icon, and then launch the appropriate MMC by double-clicking its icon. You can also select the Administrative Tools folder from the Start menu if you have this option enabled in the Taskbar and Start Menu properties. Finally, if you like to take the scenic route, you can open a blank MMC by clicking Start | Run and typing **MMC**. Afterward, select Console from the menu bar and choose Add/Remove Snap-in. In the resulting dialog box, click the Add button and select the Services console from the pop-up dialog box, then specify that the Snap-in will manage the local computer and click Finish. Click Close, and then OK to exit the open dialog boxes. Figure 2-1 shows the Windows Services MMC.

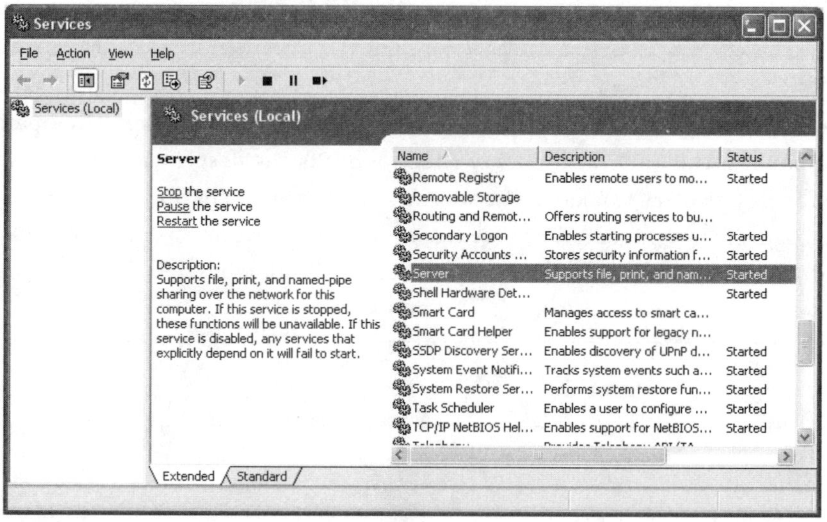

FIGURE 2-1 The Windows Services MMC

Scroll down the list of services until you see the Server service listing and double-click it to open the Server Properties dialog box, shown in Figure 2-2.

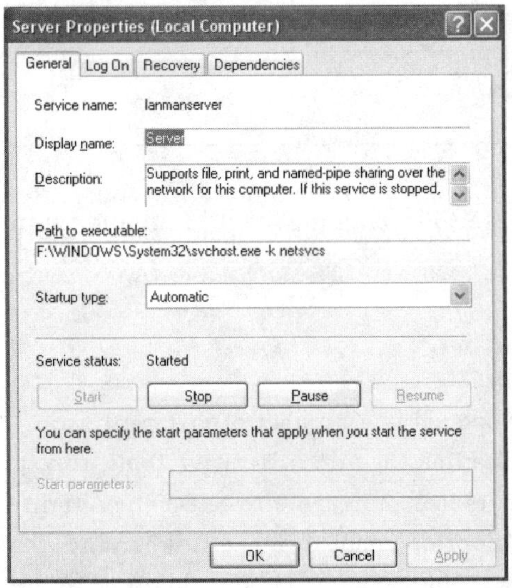

FIGURE 2-2 The Windows Server Properties dialog box

On the General property sheet, what is the description of the Server service? On the Dependencies property sheet, what services are listed as possibly affecting the Server service if they are paused or stopped? What services are dependent on the Server service? After you find this information, click the OK button to close the dialog box.

_____

_____

Step 3 Now scroll down the list, locate the Workstation service listing, and double-click it to open the Workstation service dialog box. On the General property sheet, what is the description of the Workstation service? On the Dependencies property sheet, what services are listed as possibly affecting the Workstation service if they are paused or stopped? What services are dependent on the Workstation service? After you find this information, click the OK button to close the dialog box.

_____

_____

Step 4   To see these services in action, you're going to share a resource—a folder—on your local PC and access a shared resource on a remote networked PC. Remember that Windows XP disables network access to the PC by default, so the steps listed here involve both turning on network sharing and then sharing a folder on the network. Note that network sharing only has to be turned on once. With network sharing turned on, it's a simple matter to configure sharing on any folder. I'll cover the manual steps for doing this in the next Lab Exercise, 2.04. For now, let's walk through the steps for setting up network sharing using the built-in wizard.

Open My Computer and alternate-click (CompTIA-speak for *right-click*) the Shared Documents folder. Select Sharing and Security from the pop-up menu. In the Shared Documents Properties dialog box, click the Sharing property sheet tab (if it's not already visible). Look in the section labeled Network Sharing and Security and make note of the default settings here:

_____

_____

Step 5   Click the link labeled Network Setup Wizard and follow the prompts of the wizard, accepting the default network sharing settings. Restart the system when the wizard finishes to complete network sharing configuration. After the system reboots, log in and open My Computer again. Alternate-click the Shared Documents folder. Note the new settings here:

_____

_____

Step 6   Confirm that the Shared Documents folder is shared on your network. Do this by navigating to your PC from another networked PC and attempting to open the Shared Documents folder. If you're working with a partner, have them perform this step. What are the results?

→ **Note**

Remember that the name given to a folder shared on a network does not necessarily have to match its name on the local system that shares it. By default, the Shared Documents folder is shared on the network under the name SharedDocs.

_____

_____

Step 7   Confirm that you are able to access shared resources on another networked PC from your local PC. Do this by opening My Network Places, navigating to another networked PC, and attempting to access its Shared Documents folder. What are the results?

_____

_____

Step 8   Now you'll examine the impact that stopping the Server service has on a remote PC's ability to access your shared resource. Bring up the Services MMC again and locate the Server service. Pause the service by double-clicking its icon and then clicking the Pause button on the General property sheet. Now attempt to access your local Shared Documents folder from a remote networked PC (or have your partner do this). What are the results?

_____

_____

Once you've completed this step, click the Resume button to start the service again.

Step 9   Now have a look at the impact that turning off the Workstation service has on your ability to access shared remote network resources from your local networked PC. Bring up the Services MMC again and scroll down to the Workstation service. Pause the service by double-clicking its icon and then clicking the Pause button on the General property sheet. Next, attempt to access a shared resource on a remote PC on your network. What are the results?

_____

_____

Once you've completed this step, click the Resume button to start the service again.

 30 MINUTES

Lab Exercise 2.04: Working with Network Resources

Resource sharing is where the line between mainframe computers and PCs is most sharply drawn. Unlike mainframe computers, PCs are built from the ground up to take advantage of resource sharing. Modern operating systems like Windows, Macintosh, and UNIX/Linux sport sophisticated networking capabilities that make resource sharing easier and more secure than ever.

Sharing resources is not the same thing as sharing the computer. When you share resources, you specify *what* resources a remote user can access on your PC, *who* can access those resources, and *how much* access those users have to the shared resource. By the same token, when you access a shared resource on another PC, you're subject to the same rules of *what* resources you can access and *how much* access you are granted.

Windows XP Professional, like Windows 2000 and NT before it, enables you to set two levels of access control—*share-level* and *resource-level* (sometimes called *local-level* or *NTFS-level*). I'm going to assume that you're comfortable with the concept of resource-level permissions from your A+ training, and instead focus on the network share-level permissions in this exercise.

Learning Objectives

In this lab, you will manually configure network access permissions on your shared resource. By lab's end, you will be able to:

- Configure permissions on a shared resource

Lab Materials and Setup

The materials you need for this lab are

- Two networked PCs running Windows 2000 Professional or Windows XP Home Edition or Professional

Getting Down to Business

In the last exercise, you demonstrated for your client how to configure basic network sharing. Now you'll demonstrate how you control specific levels of access to your shared resources.

Step 1 Take a moment to refer back to Step 5 of Lab Exercise 2.03. By default, the only network sharing configuration options are *Share this Folder on the Network* and *Allow Network Users to Change My Files*, and no security permission options are available. This is due to a feature called *simple file sharing*, which disables access to the full set of security configuration options. To turn this feature off, open My Computer, and click Tools on the menu bar. Then select Folder Options, and click the View tab. In the Advanced settings section, scroll down the list and clear the check box labeled *Use simple file sharing (recommended)*, then click the OK button. Now alternate-click the Shared Documents folder and select Sharing and Security from the pop-up menu. Make a note of the new sharing and security configuration options.

Step 2   On the Sharing property sheet, click the Permissions button and make a note of the default share-level permissions configured for the Shared Documents folder.

_____

_____

Step 3   Now put these security settings to the test. From your local PC, access the Shared Documents folder on a remote system on your network. Attempt to create a new text document by alternate-clicking inside the folder and selecting New | Text Document from the pop-up menu, giving it any name you choose. If working with a partner, have them access your local Shared Documents folder from their remote system to perform the same action. What are the results?

_____

_____

Step 4   Next, alter the default security permission settings on the Shared Documents folder. In the Shared Documents Properties dialog box, select the Sharing property sheet tab and click the Permissions button. In the Permissions for SharedDocs dialog box that pops up, clear the Allow check box for the Change security permission and click the Apply button. What is the result?

_____

_____

Step 5   Click OK to close the Permissions for SharedDocs dialog box, and then click the Apply button on the Shared Documents Properties dialog box. Now repeat the actions from Step 3 of this exercise. What is the result?

_____

_____

After you've completed the exercise, don't forget to restore the default security permissions to the Shared Documents folder.

Lab Analysis

1. What is the key difference between a mainframe with multiple terminals and a computer network with multiple servers and clients?

    _____

    _____

2. What network services were possible on the earliest networked mainframe computers?

    _____

3. What does computer networking accomplish?

    _____

    _____

4. What types of resources can be shared on a computer network?

    _____

    _____

5. How do you control access to resources shared on a computer?

    _____

    _____

Key Terms Quiz

Use the vocabulary terms from the list below to complete the sentences that follow. Not all of the terms will be used.

Client

Dumb terminal

File Transfer Protocol (FTP)

Local

Mainframe

Modem

Permissions

Remote

Resource

Server

Service

Sharing

Telnet

1. Multiple users are able to access data stored on mainframes through a _____.

2. A _____ is used to enable a remote terminal session to a mainframe.

3. A modern PC can act act as both a network _____ and a network _____.

4. Network sharing enables a local PC to use a _____ resource.

5. Resource access is controlled through _____.

Chapter 3

Building a Network with OSI

Lab Exercises

Delivering data across a network is a process both elegant in its simplicity and mind-boggling in its complexity. For one thing, data files don't move across the network intact. Instead, any kind of data transfer—whether you're browsing the Web, copying files to a co-worker's computer, or streaming music across the Internet (legally, of course)—is broken down into smaller chunks, which are packaged, addressed, moved, and then reassembled at the other end. This is true of any computer network, regardless of the operating system, protocols, or network media.

To appreciate the process, you have to understand a few important things. First, you should understand what kind of hardware and software a computer needs to connect to a network. You also need to understand how a computer sends and retrieves data using a network. Finally, you need to understand the rules that govern how Ethernet networks are structured and how data moves across these networks. In this lab, I'll talk about these concepts to help you develop a greater understanding of the big networking picture.

Let's get started.

 15 MINUTES

Lab Exercise 3.01: Using Network Hardware

Network connectivity starts with the network connection—the physical link between the PC and the network media. A good network tech can quickly locate and identify the network cabling and network interfacing hardware installed on a PC, and determine the PC's state of connectivity. The tech should also be able to identify the protocol(s) used by the PC to communicate on the network, as well as the PC's unique network identification and address. Let's look at the steps for doing all of this.

Learning Objectives

In this lab exercise, you'll examine a networked PC to locate the network interface card, determine the type of network cabling and connectors used, figure out the protocols used, and find out the PC's MAC and network address. At the end of this exercise, you'll be able to:

- Identify network hardware components

- Determine which protocols are configured for the PC

- Determine a PC's MAC and network addresses

Lab Materials and Setup

The materials you need for this lab are

- A Windows 2000 Professional or Windows XP Home Edition or Professional PC with a NIC installed

- A network cable

- A network hub (optional)

Getting Down to Business

Let's assume that you have been contracted as a network support specialist for 360 Art Services (360), a firm specializing in packaging, transporting, and installing artwork between museums, galleries, and private collections all over the United States. 360 has an office in each of the three major U.S. cultural centers, New York City, Los Angeles, and Houston. Your project is to network the computers in the Houston office together, and then configure networking between the Houston office and the New York and Los Angeles offices.

In speaking to the firm's owner, you determine that the Houston office space has several Windows XP Professional PCs in place, but that they are not currently networked together. The office may have network wiring installed, but nobody in the company knows enough about computers to confirm this for you. Your first task is to visit the location to determine the company's current network status.

Step 1   Locate the network interface card (NIC) installed on your computer system. How does the NIC attach to the PC?

_____

_____

Step 2   Identify the type of network cabling and network connector that plugs into the NIC.

_____

_____

Step 3   Identify the network protocols installed on the PC. Open your Local Area Connection Properties dialog box on a Windows 2000 Professional system by clicking Start | Settings | Networks and Dialup Connections | Local Area Connection, and clicking the Properties button. On a Windows XP Home or

Professional system, click Start | All Programs | Accessories | Communications | Network Connections. Then alternate-click the Local Area Connection icon and select Properties. What items are listed in the *This connection uses the following items* section on the General property sheet?

_____

_____

Step 4   Highlight the Internet Protocol (TCP/IP) item and click the Properties button. How is the protocol assigned to receive an address?

_____

_____

Step 5   Assuming that the PC is configured to obtain an IP address automatically, you now need to determine the IP address. Click Start | Run, and type **CMD** to bring up a command-line window. Then type **IPCONFIG /ALL**. Note the following: the Ethernet adapter Description, Physical Address (MAC address), and IP Address.

_____

_____

Step 6   Optionally, determine how the PCs on your network connect to each other.

_____

_____

 30 MINUTES

Lab Exercise 3.02: Understanding the Data Delivery Process

As I explained in Chapter 2, the network tech's role as installer and administrator sometimes takes a back seat to the tech's role as educator. Many clients, and certainly your bosses, want to know what you're doing when they see you stringing cables from hither to yon, or when you're gazing at some obscure-looking string of numbers in a command-line window. The good network tech is able to explain not just practical, nuts-and-bolts configuration tasks, but also the "fuzzier" conceptual topics that govern the functions of a network.

Learning Objectives

In this lab, you'll examine the process of data delivery on a network. You will also identify the components involved in transferring data between two computers on a network. At the end of this lab, you will be able to:

- Identify the parts of a frame

- Examine the process of packet delivery

Materials and Lab Setup

The only materials you'll need for this lab are a pen and some paper.

Getting Down to Business

You've examined your client's office and determined that the PCs and physical offices meet the necessary requirements to connect through a network. Each PC is equipped with a network-capable OS (Windows XP Professional) and networking hardware (NIC), and the office is pre-wired with industry-standard CAT 5 UTP. Before you proceed, however, the client wants you to give a detailed explanation of how data moves from one PC to another on the network.

Step 1   List and define the parts of a generic data frame.

_____

Step 2   Briefly describe the process of data delivery from one networked PC to another.

_____

_____

Step 3   Your client contact asks if they'll need to upgrade their current software to a "networked" version in order take advantage of network services. What do you tell him?

_____

_____

 20 MINUTES

Lab Exercise 3.03: Examining the Layers of the OSI Seven-Layer Model

Given that the Open System Interconnect (OSI) seven-layer model's functions are largely hidden from our eyes, it's sometimes difficult to appreciate how each discrete level performs a necessary step of the data delivery process. Nonetheless, it's important for you to understand just how the OSI seven-layer model operates. Every modern network technology conforms to the OSI seven-layer model, so understanding OSI is key to understanding modern networking technology.

Learning Objectives

In this lab, you'll examine the layers of the OSI seven-layer model. By its end, you will be able to:

- Identify and define the seven layers in the OSI seven-layer model

- Recognize the functions of each layer in the OSI seven-layer model

Lab Materials and Setup

The only materials you'll need for this lab are a pen and some paper.

Getting Down to Business

Using the OSI seven-layer model, explain to your client the details of network data delivery.

Step 1 Arrange the OSI network model layers listed here in their proper order from top to bottom:

Data Link   _____

Application   _____

Physical   _____

Session   _____

Presentation   _____

Network   _____

Transport   _____

✔ **Hint**

From the top down, *all people seem to need data processing.* From the bottom up, *please do not throw sausage pizza away.*

Step 2   Read the following descriptions and fill in the appropriate OSI network model layer:

Description	OSI Network Model Layer
The topmost layer; it is here that programs access network services.	_____
This layer enables computers to establish, use, and close connections.	_____
This layer breaks up data into small chunks and "packages" them into frames.	_____
This layer determines the data format used for computers to exchange data.	_____
This layer is divided into two sublayers: the Logical Link Control layer and the Media Access Control layer.	_____
This layer converts the digital signal into a form compatible with the network media and sends it out.	_____
This layer adds routable addresses to data packets.	_____

Lab Analysis

1. Describe the function of the NIC.

   _____

   _____

2. What are the basic components of a frame?

   _____

   _____

3. PC 1 on network segment A sends a frame to a PC 2 on network segment B. Which PC's NIC on network segment B reads the frame?

   _____

   _____

4.   How do different software vendors design their programs to take advantage of networks?

_____

_____

5.   What is the purpose of the CRC?

_____

_____

Key Terms Quiz

Use the vocabulary terms from the list below to complete the sentences that follow. Not all of the terms will be used.

Application Program Interface (API)

Broadcast address

Cyclical Redundancy Check (CRC)

Frame

IPCONFIG /ALL

MAC address

Network interface card (NIC)

Network protocol

Router

TCP/IP

WINIPCFG

1. A _____ is a container for data chunks moving across a network.

2. Running the command _____ on a Windows 2000 or XP Professional computer will display the MAC address of the computer's network interface card.

3. The _____ is the portion of a frame that a NIC uses to determine whether data in the received frame is valid.

4. A networked computer discovers another computer's MAC address by sending a request via the _____.

5. A physical address is another name for the _____ of a NIC.

Chapter 4
Hardware Concepts

Lab Exercises

Most PC users never give a moment's thought to the mechanics of how their particular workstation ties into their corporate network. They just want to know that their data gets where it's supposed to go when they click the *Send* button in their e-mail program or click the *Save* icon in their word processor application. As a network technician, you're the one who has to make sure that your network users' data can get from here to there, and vice versa. In the last couple of lessons, we talked about the concepts and models that serve as a basis for modern networks. Now it's time to look at the nitty-gritty hardware that makes a network a network.

The first thing I'm going to talk about is the network's physical and logical layout—the *topology*. Next, I'll talk about the different types of physical network media, or *cabling*. Last, I'll go into the IEEE specifications that define the different network *standards*. Let's get started.

 15 MINUTES

Lab Exercise 4.01: Identifying Network Topologies

A network's topology can describe two different things: its logical organization or its physical infrastructure. The logical topology is made up of things like the IP address ranges and subnets, domain boundaries, organizational unit hierarchy, and the like. The physical topology is the actual network cabling, hubs, switches, bridges, routers, patch panels, and other hardware that carries the network's data. A network's logical topology is relatively easy to alter, but its physical topology usually can't be changed without a great deal of effort and expense. In this lab, we'll concentrate on the physical network topology.

If you're setting up a network from scratch, start with your topology design. You won't always have this luxury, of course. If you're walking into a situation where a network is already in place, for example, evaluating the topology design is a top priority. Identifying the current network topology is the key to determining the type of network cabling and hardware that you'll be using.

Good network techs document everything about their network, listing the location of every network cable installation (usually called a cable *run* or *drop*), describing the type of cabling used, and giving details about the associated network hardware (brand and model of each network hub, switch, router, and so on). Unfortunately, not all network techs take the time to create this documentation or update it when they make changes, so you may wind up having to gather this information on your own.

This is where your knowledge of the different network topologies, network cabling, and network hardware pays off.

Learning Objectives

In this lab, you'll examine several network topologies. By its end, you will be able to:

- Identify and describe the different standard network physical topologies

- Identify the advantages and disadvantages of selected topologies

- Suggest an appropriate topology solution

Lab Materials and Setup

The only materials you'll need for this lab will be a pencil and some paper.

Getting Down to Business

Your client, 360 Art Services, has contracted you to configure networking in their new Houston offices. You have determined that they have the necessary hardware and software in place to network their Windows PCs together, so now you need to determine what kind of network infrastructure is currently installed in their location.

The 360 Art Services office space consists of a large warehouse area and an adjoining suite of offices. The warehouse is split into an open storage area, a climate-controlled, secure storage area, and a workroom. The office suite consists of a lobby area with an adjoining meeting room, four medium-sized offices, a restroom, and a kitchen/dining area.

After speaking with your client extensively, you determine the following goals:

- The client wants network connectivity in the open storage area and workroom area of the warehouse and in each of the offices, as well as the lobby area and meeting room. The client tells you that the location currently has "some kind of network-looking wires" installed, but can't give you any more information.

- The client wants a consistent network topology throughout the location.

- The client wants the network to be fault-tolerant.

- The client wants the network to be high-performance.

- The client is anticipating growth in the company, and wants to be able to add more computers and network hardware to the network without a great deal of effort.

- The client states that expense is an issue, so they would prefer to use the existing network infrastructure if it's suitable. They are willing to install new equipment if necessary.

Step 1   You examine the office space and discover that there is a single, thin coax cable running between each of the offices and the lobby area, but not to the meeting room. You note that numerous T-type BNC connectors are affixed along the cable, which is terminated at each end. You do not find any patch panels, hubs, or any other type of network hardware in the office space. What does this tell you?

_____

_____

Step 2   The warehouse space has a single thick coax cable, terminated at each end, running through the center of the room in the ceiling rafters, with several thinner coax cables attached at fixed points and hanging down to the warehouse floor. What does this tell you?

_____

_____

Step 3   The warehouse workroom has a single shielded twisted pair (STP) cable that runs along the baseboard of the room. T-type BNC connectors are attached at several points, and the ends are joined together by a barrel-type BNC connector. What does this tell you?

_____

_____

Step 4   Based on your findings, do you recommend that your client use the current network topology or install a new network infrastructure?

_____

_____

Step 5   Explain the reasons for your recommendation.

_____

_____

Step 6   Based on the client's stated goals, what network topology do you recommend? List your reasons.

_____

_____

 20 MINUTES

Lab Exercise 4.02: Identifying Network Cabling Types

You have two choices when it comes to network cabling: glass-cored fiber optics or good, old-fashioned copper wire. The latter is currently the reigning king of network media, used in most network installations from small to gigantic, and in every type of network topology. Even so, copper wire network cabling comes in a variety of sizes and configurations. To make informed decisions about what kind of network cabling best suits a given network installation, you have to understand the features, functions, and limitations of different network cabling media.

Learning Objectives

In this lab, you'll learn to recognize and compare network cables. By its end, you will be able to:

- Identify the various network cabling options
- Compare the function, speed, and maximum data transfer distance of each cable
- Suggest a cost-efficient cabling option for a medium-sized network

Materials and Lab Setup

The materials you'll need for this lab are

- Pencil and paper
- A sample of RG-8 (Thick Ethernet), RG-62, and RG-58 (Thin Ethernet) coaxial cable (optional)
- Samples of unshielded twisted pair and shielded twisted pair Ethernet cable (optional)
- A sample of fiber-optic cable (optional)

Getting Down to Business

Your client is satisfied with your recommendation to install a new hybrid network topology, but is unclear on the reasons why the old network cabling can't be reused. You need to explain the differences between the types of network cabling, make a recommendation for a network cabling solution, and explain the reasons for your recommendation.

Step 1   Identify and describe the cable in Figure 4-1.

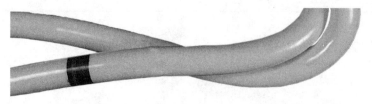

Figure 4-1 A network cable sample

_____

_____

Step 2   Identify and describe the cable in Figure 4-2.

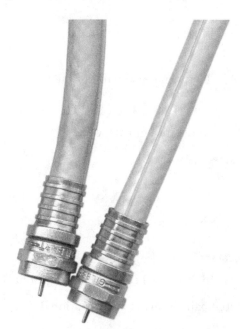

Figure 4-2 A network cable sample

_____

_____

Step 3   Identify and describe the cable in Figure 4-3.

Figure 4-3 A network cable sample

_____

_____

Step 4   Identify and describe the cable in Figure 4-4.

Figure 4-4 A network cable sample

_____

_____

Step 5   Identify and describe the cable in Figure 4-5.

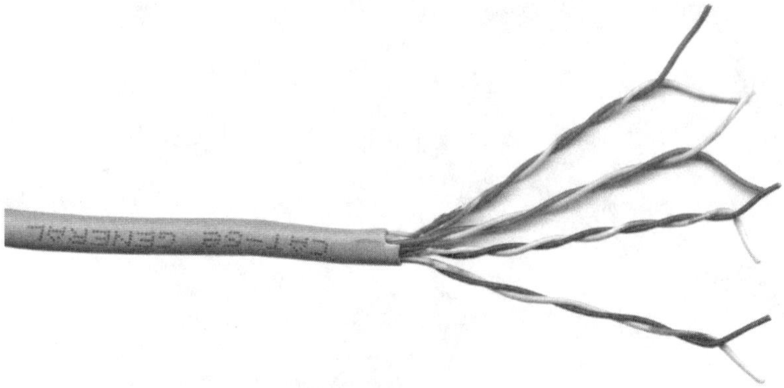

Figure 4-5 A network cable sample

_____

_____

Step 6   In this chart, fill in the correct data throughput speeds and usage for the UTP CAT types listed:

CAT Rating	Speed	Typical Use
CAT 1		
CAT 2		
CAT 3		
CAT 4		
CAT 5		
CAT 5e		
CAT 6		

Step 7   Identify and describe the cable in Figure 4-6.

_____

_____

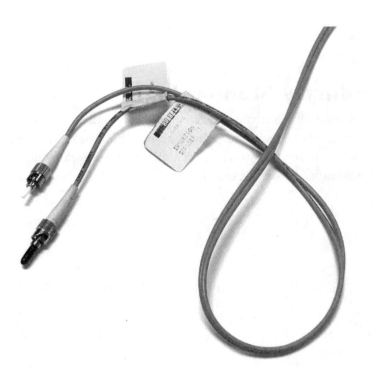

Figure 4-6 A network cable sample

Step 8   After explaining the differences between the common types of network cables, you need to decide on a type of cabling that suits the client's networking needs. Upon further discussion, you determine the following:

- The client will frequently transfer large graphics files between digital still cameras, workstations, and servers.

- They also need to transfer large video files from digital camcorders to workstations and servers.

Based on this information, what type of network cabling do you recommend for this network installation? List your reasons.

_____

_____

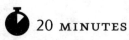 20 MINUTES

Lab Exercise 4.03: Industry Standards

The IEEE 802 committee sets the standards that all modern networking hardware must meet in order to function with other networking hardware. The 802 committee is divided into a number of subcommittees, each responsible for defining the standards and methods by which different networking devices are governed. Among these are the subcommittees that have established the 802.2, 802.3, 802.5, and 802.11 networking standards.

Before we wrap up this chapter, let's review these important IEEE standards and definitions.

Learning Objectives

In this lab, you'll identify the function of each of the important IEEE 802 subcommittees. By the end of this lab, you will be able to:

- Describe the IEEE subcommittee responsible for defining the standards of the most popular network technology implementations

Lab Materials and Setup

The only materials you'll need for this lab are a pencil and some paper.

Getting Down to Business

Your client is convinced that they must purchase new network cabling and hardware, but they're concerned that the equipment they purchase might not be compatible with the network equipment used in their New York and Los Angeles offices. You want to assure them that all modern networking equipment conforms to the same standards, and therefore compatibility is not an issue.

Step 1 In the following table, fill in the function of each of the most common IEEE 802 subcommittees listed.

Subcommittee Designation	Description
802.2	_____
802.3	_____
802.4	_____
802.5	_____
802.11	_____

Step 2   Explain why compliance with these IEEE standards is important.

_____

_____

Lab Analysis

1.   What happens to network communication when a single computer on a bus topology network fails?

_____

_____

2.   Explain the physical design of a star bus topology and the advantage of this topology.

_____

_____

3.   What is the difference between Thin Ethernet and Thick Ethernet?

_____

_____

4.   What are the most common grades and speeds of UTP cabling?

_____

_____

5.   Which IEEE 802 subcommittees represent the Ethernet and Token Ring standards?

_____

_____

Key Terms Quiz

Use the vocabulary terms from the list below to complete the sentences that follow. Not all of the terms will be used.

Bus topology

Coaxial

Ethernet

Fiber-optic

Mesh topology

Ring topology

Star topology

UTP (unshielded twisted pair)

1. The most common type of network cable used today is the _____ cable.

2. _____ describes a network in which all the computers connect to a central wiring point, or hub.

3. RG-8, often referred to as Thick Ethernet, is a _____ cable.

4. _____ cables transmit light for distances up to ten kilometers.

5. In a _____ network, each computer has a dedicated line connection to every other computer on the network.

Chapter 5

Ethernet Basics

Lab Exercises

Ethernet is, by far, the most widely used type of networking technology in the IT world today. For this reason, it's important for network techs to understand Ethernet's functions and features as defined by the IEEE 802.3 standard. These include such things as how Ethernet network nodes build data frames, how they access the network media, and how they send and receive data.

Beyond that, you need to appreciate that Ethernet isn't tied to one particular type of network hardware or media, but can be deployed across a variety of topologies. On the one hand, this is good because you have a number of solutions available to build an Ethernet network, but on the other hand, this means that you have to know the strengths and weaknesses of a bunch of different Ethernet cabling and hardware types. Further, you have to know how to overcome these limits when a network project requires that you do so.

In these labs, you'll review the bits and pieces of Ethernet data frame construction and media access methods; look at the physical characteristics of Ethernet networks using coax cable media; and talk about how you extend the limits of Ethernet.

Let's get started.

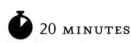 20 MINUTES

Lab Exercise 5.01: Understanding the Pieces of Ethernet Data Frames

The most basic unit of data transmission on an Ethernet network is the *frame*. Back in Chapter 3, I discussed how the NIC chops data files into small chunks called frames for easier transport on the network media. In a nutshell, the sending PC converts data into many small frames and taps them out on the network wire. The receiving PC pulls the frames off the network wire and reassembles the data into its original format. Sounds a bit like the transporter from "Star Trek," doesn't it?

Data frames vary in construction depending on the protocol used, but all frames have a few essential components in common. These include the *MAC address* of both the sending and receiving computer, an error-checking value called the *cyclical redundancy check* (CRC), and, of course, the data itself. Other values that may be included in the data frame are codes specifying the protocol type, service type, and so on.

Ethernet data frames range in size from 46 bytes at the minimum to 1500 bytes maximum. Data frames that are below the minimum size are padded with null data to bring them up to at least 46 bytes.

Because the data frame process is hidden from us, it's sometimes hard to get a real grasp of the mechanics involved. Luckily, network techs have tools available to help make these concepts a bit more tangible. The tool of choice for this purpose is the packet analyzer, usually called a *packet sniffer*. This isn't just a clever moniker; Sniffer Technologies is the real name of a company that makes packet analyzer devices, and somehow the name stuck for the whole category of tools. Packet sniffers are available as hardware-based devices and as software applications, but they all enable you to do the same thing: pull data frames off the network and cache them for offline analysis. Using a packet sniffer, you can view each of the components that make up the data packet.

Beyond the "because it's cool" factor, are there practical reasons for examining data frames? Plenty of them! Packet sniffers are some of the best tools for optimizing network performance. Using packet sniffers, you can determine the type of network traffic that is tying up a busy network. Lots of broadcast traffic, for example, might tell you that network nodes are having trouble resolving NetBIOS names. A malfunctioning NIC will send excessive (and usually incomplete) data frames—network techs call this *jabbering*. Either of these conditions (and others) can be detected using a packet analyzer.

In this lab, you'll use a packet sniffer application to capture data frames from your network and view the captured data.

✔ **Tech Tip**

The terms data *frame* and data *packet* are often used interchangeably.

Learning Objectives

In this lab, you'll install and run the *Ethereal* packet analyzer application, use it to capture data from your network, and examine the captured data. At the end of this lab, you will be able to:

- Perform a data frame capture from a network

- Examine the captured data to view each data frame's contents

Lab Materials and Setup

The materials you'll need for this lab are

- Setup file for the Ethereal packet analyzer application

- Setup file for the WinPcap driver file

- Two or more networked Windows PCs

Getting Down to Business

Assume that you've been contracted as a network specialist for Corona Booksellers, Inc. (CBI), a retailer specializing in technical books and training materials. CBI operates a profitable Internet presence, and maintains a small chain of brick-and-mortar storefronts throughout the Southwest region of the U.S. CBI is in the process of putting together a mobile division to sell materials at technical, industrial, and business trade shows and conventions throughout the country.

The mobile sales force will be split into two units. Each unit will use networked Windows PCs running specialized terminal emulation software to access a centralized database and process sales. Each unit travels with up to 15 PCs, depending on the size of the convention. For very large conventions, both units may be present, in which case up to 30 PCs will be networked together. Your task is to evaluate the current network configuration for the mobile sales units and make any recommendations for improving performance and reliability.

To make a detailed analysis of network traffic, you must install the software-based packet sniffer application called *Ethereal* on one of the networked PCs and confirm that it operates satisfactorily.

Step 1   The steps for this exercise and several exercises in subsequent chapters call for using a packet analyzer to capture data packets off your network. Ethereal is an excellent software-based packet analyzer that runs on just about any NOS platform. Ethereal has many compelling features that put it on par with other packet analyzer applications, and best of all, it's freeware. Follow these steps to download and install Ethereal:

1. Go to www.ethereal.com and click the Download link under the Resources menu.

2. On the Resources page, look under the section labeled *Windows 98/ME/2000/XP/2003 Installers*, and click the link for the HTTP or FTP server closest to you.

3. Download the Ethereal executable installation file (called ethereal-setup-0.10.5a.exe at the time of this writing) and the installation file for the packet capture driver (WinPcap_3_0.exe) to your Windows desktop.

4. Double-click the Ethereal installation file to start the Installation wizard, and follow the prompts to complete installation.

5. Double-click the WinPcap installation file to start the installation wizard, and follow the prompts to complete installation.

Step 2   Start the Ethereal packet sniffer, shown in Figure 5-1, by clicking Start | All Programs | Ethereal and selecting the Ethereal program icon.

The Ethereal display is divided into three panes: the top section is the Packet List pane, which lists a summary of each frame captured; the middle section is the Tree View pane, which displays details of each captured frame; and the bottom section is the Data View pane, which shows hexadecimal values of captured data. Also at the bottom of the display is a field that enables you to configure data frame filters.

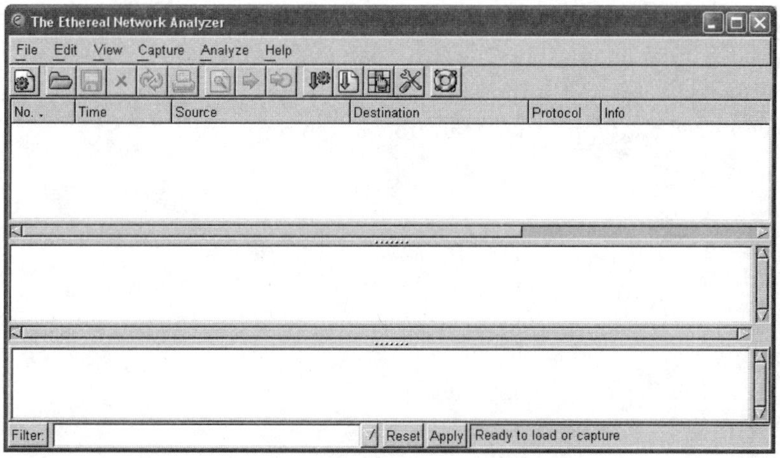

FIGURE 5-1 The Ethereal packet sniffer application

Step 3 Start a data frame capture by selecting Capture from the File menu and then selecting Start. This brings up the Ethereal: Capture Options dialog box, shown in Figure 5-2.

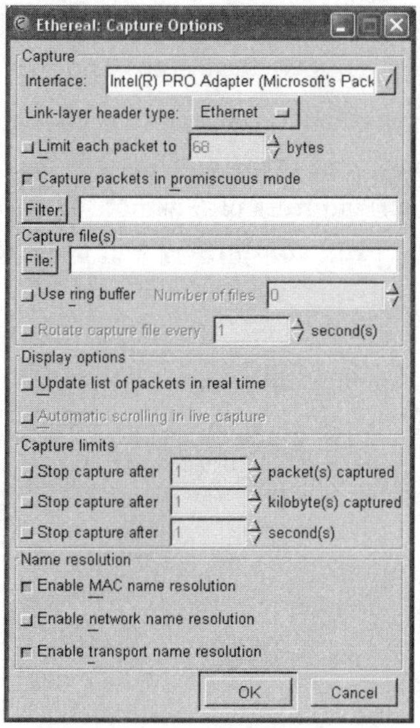

FIGURE 5-2 The Ethereal: Capture Options dialog box

List the default settings here:

Step 4   Start capturing data frames from your network by clicking the OK button (thus accepting the default capture settings). You'll see activity immediately. The Ethereal: Capture window, shown in Figure 5-3, shows the protocol types being captured, the number of frames per protocol type captured, and the percentage of the total frames captured that a particular protocol type represents.

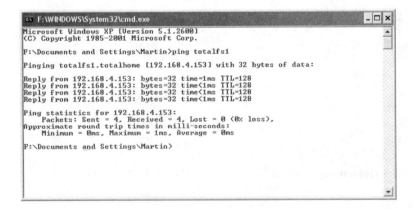

FIGURE 5-3 Ethereal: Capture in action

Step 5   Now, to see a concrete example of a data packet capture, run the PING command on your network. Open a command-line window by clicking Start | Run, typing **cmd**, and pressing the ENTER key. At the command prompt, type **ping**, followed by a space, and the name or IP address of a remote PC on your network. For example, to ping a remote PC called Computer2, type **ping computer2** and press the ENTER key. Figure 5-4 shows sample output from the PING command.

```
F:\WINDOWS\System32\cmd.exe

Microsoft Windows XP [Version 5.1.2600]
(C) Copyright 1985-2001 Microsoft Corp.

F:\Documents and Settings\Martin>ping totalfs1

Pinging totalfs1.totalhome [192.168.4.153] with 32 bytes of data:

Reply from 192.168.4.153: bytes=32 time=1ms TTL=128
Reply from 192.168.4.153: bytes=32 time<1ms TTL=128
Reply from 192.168.4.153: bytes=32 time<1ms TTL=128
Reply from 192.168.4.153: bytes=32 time<1ms TTL=128

Ping statistics for 192.168.4.153:
    Packets: Sent = 4, Received = 4, Lost = 0 (0% loss),
Approximate round trip times in milli-seconds:
    Minimum = 0ms, Maximum = 1ms, Average = 0ms

F:\Documents and Settings\Martin>
```

FIGURE 5-4 Pinging a remote PC on a network

What are the results of your PING operation?

_____

_____

_____

➔ **Note**

For those who don't remember this utility from your A+ experience, PING uses a built-in function of the TCP/IP protocol to send a series of small "echo" data packets (using TCP/IP's *Internet Control Message Protocol*, or ICMP) to a named network PC. When troubleshooting network connectivity issues, PING is a network tech's best friend!

Step 6   Close the command-line window by typing **exit** at the prompt. Let's look at the captured data for the PING operation you just ran. Note on the Ethereal: Capture window that the total number of ICMP frames captured shows eight frames. Now look at the data capture in detail. Click the Stop button to stop the data capture and load the captured data into the Ethereal viewer, as shown in Figure 5-5.

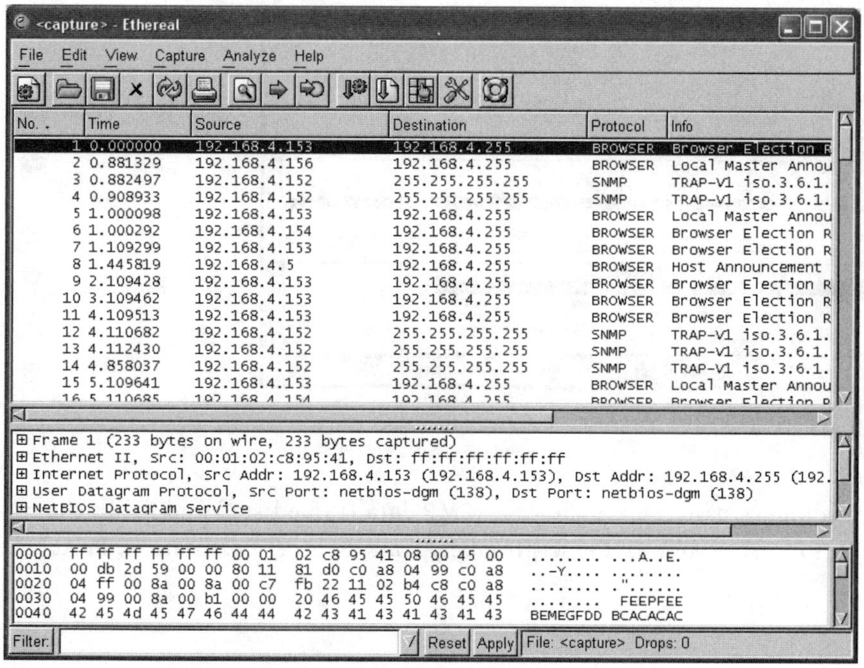

FIGURE 5-5 Captured data displayed in the Ethereal viewer

Step 7   Packet sniffers capture hundreds of data frames in just a matter of seconds, so you'll note that there's quite a bit of data to sift through. Use *filters* to make this information useful. A filter tells Ethereal to display only certain types of data frames. Applying an ICMP filter, for example, tells Ethereal to display only the data that pertains to the ICMP protocol. In this way, you can display only the results of the PING operation you just performed. To do this, place your cursor in the field at the very bottom of the Ethereal window next to the button labeled Filter. Type **icmp** in the field and click the Apply button (see Figure 5-6). What are the results?

_____

_____

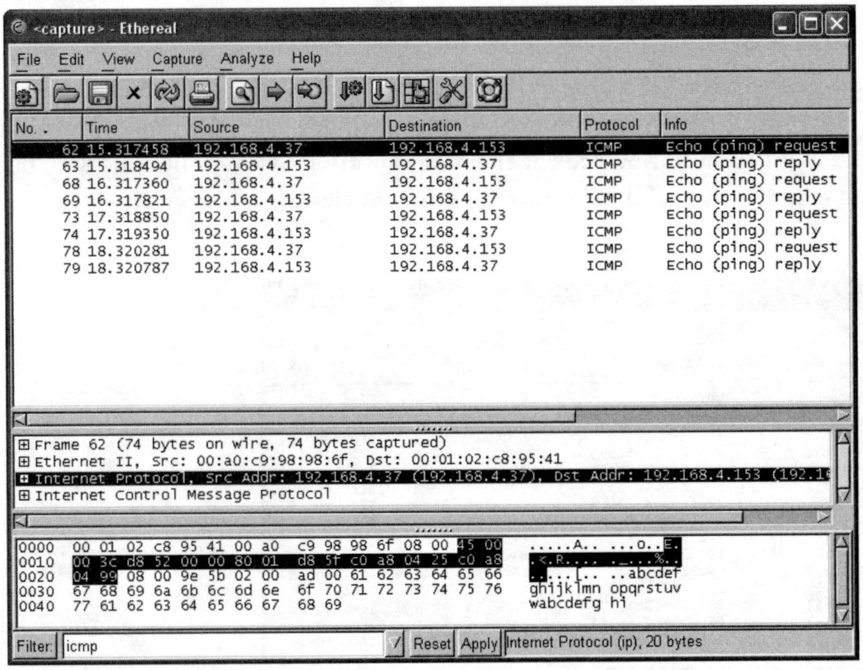

FIGURE 5-6 Captured ICMP data

Step 8   In the Packet List summary pane, select the first ICMP data frame listed and fill in the information displayed in the following column fields: Number, Time, Source, Destination, Protocol, and Info.

_____

_____

Step 9   In the Tree View pane, you'll see a wealth of information relating to the data frame, including frame information, Ethernet information, protocol information, and data payload information. Clicking the small plus sign (+) at the beginning of each line expands it into a tree view showing details. Expand the Frame, Ethernet, Internet Protocol, and Internet Control Message Protocol tree listings to determine the answers to the following questions:

- What is the total size in bytes of the data frame?

- What is the MAC address of the source and destination PCs?

- What is the IP header checksum?

- What is the size in bytes of the ICMP data?

_____

_____

Step 10   Before we wrap up this dissection of data frames, let's take a minute to examine the information displayed in the Data View pane of Ethereal. The pairs of alphanumeric characters you see listed in the Data View pane represent the hexadecimal values of each byte of the captured data frame. You may recall that the hexadecimal numbering system is a sort of shorthand way of representing binary. We get into details about this numbering system in Chapter 11, but for now concentrate on knowing how to find the hexadecimal value for each piece of the captured data frame information. Ethereal automatically highlights the hexadecimal portion shown in the Data View pane of any data selected in the Tree View pane. As an example, expand the Internet Protocol line in the Tree View pane and select the Source IP address. Note that the hexadecimal value of that IP address is now highlighted in the Data View pane.

What is the hexadecimal value for the selected IP address?

_____

_____

Ethereal is a fantastic tool for showing you the actual nuts-and-bolts data that we've talked about conceptually. You'll see more of this tool as we get into later chapters of this book. For now, let's move onto the methods that Ethernet devices use to gain access to the network.

➜ Note

Hexadecimal is a numbering system commonly used to represent binary values. Remember that everything is binary to a computer, so hexadecimal is simply a method for making binary a bit easier for people to understand.

 20 MINUTES

Lab Exercise 5.02: Accessing Ethernet Networks

Pop quiz! How many PCs can transmit data on a given network segment at the same time? Is it four? Eight? Sixty-four? Or is it one? As amazing as it seems, only a single PC can access any given network segment at a time. This is true no matter how many network nodes populate the network segment. When two PCs try to send data onto the network at the same time, the data frames *collide*, causing both frames to become corrupted.

Since it's only possible for one PC to tap out its data onto the wire at a time, the designers of Ethernet had to devise a method for the network nodes to access the network media without stepping on each other's frames. This network access method is called *Carrier Sense, Multiple Access/Collision Detection*, or CSMA/CD. The *CSMA* part of CSMA/CD defines the method by which network nodes monitor the network media to determine if any other nodes are currently transmitting data. The *CD* part defines how the network nodes deal with collisions when they occur. In this lab, we'll discuss how the CSMA/CD mechanism functions.

Learning Objectives

In this lab, you'll review the Carrier Sense, Multiple Access/Collision Detection function of Ethernet. At the end of this lab, you will be able to:

- Define the function of CSMA/CD

Lab Materials and Setup

The only materials you'll need for this lab exercise are a pencil and some paper.

Getting Down to Business

Your client has a distrust of networked computers because she doesn't understand how it's possible for multiple PCs to be on the same network at the same time without interrupting each other's network sessions or receiving data meant for another PC. You need to explain how CSMA/CD functions to enable the sharing of network media.

Step 1   In the following space, describe how the Ethernet Carrier Sense function enables network nodes to determine if the network media is in use.

_____

_____

Step 2   Your client wants to know if it's possible to configure the network so that the company president's PC always gets priority access to the network. Describe how the Ethernet Multiple Access rules govern which network node gets precedence with regard to network media access.

_____

_____

Step 3   Your client is concerned about data corruption due to multiple PCs accessing the network at the same time. Explain how Ethernet's Collision Detection function enables network nodes to recover from data collisions.

_____

_____

Step 4   Your client asks if there is a way to configure the network so that no data collisions occur. What do you tell her?

_____

_____

Step 5   If you have access to a network hub with a collision detection indicator, monitor and make note of the collision rate on your network for a short time period (ten minutes or so). What are your results?

_____

_____

 10 MINUTES

Lab Exercise 5.03: Ethernet Coaxial Cabling

In Chapter 4, you learned about the different types of network cabling that are commonly deployed as network media, including Ethernet, Token Ring, and fiber optic. Now let's concentrate on cabling specifications for Ethernet networks. In this lab, we review the type of coaxial (coax) cabling used on Ethernet networks—_10Base5_ and _10Base2_.

For the most part, 10Base5 coax cabling has gone the way of the coelacanth when it comes to networking solutions. Yes, you'll still see it deployed in older network installations, but these installations are rare. 10Base2 coax cabling, however, is still quite popular for setting up small networks, or networks that must be easily broken down and moved. This is due to the fact that this setup requires less cabling and fewer hardware components than Ethernet networks using STP or UTP cabling. It's up to you to understand when these types of Ethernet cabling are appropriate as a networking solution, or when they're inappropriate and should be replaced.

Learning Objectives

In this lab, you'll review the specifications for Ethernet coax cabling. By its end, you will be able to:

- Define the Ethernet 10Base2 and 10Base5 cabling standards

Lab Materials and Setup

The only materials you'll need for this lab are a pencil and some paper.

Getting Down to Business

Rather than invest funds for the new mobile sales division in new equipment purchases, your client recycled the equipment from a closed storefront location. As such, the PCs and network hardware are several years old.

You've examined the stock of PCs available, and have determined that they can be successfully redeployed for the mobile sales division. They are of fairly recent vintage, hardware-wise, and are supplied with a mixture of Windows 95/98 and 2000 Professional operating systems. Each PC is equipped with a NIC capable of connecting to a network via 15-pin AUI or BNC connectors. Your task now is to determine which type of coax cabling is preferable for your purpose.

Your client states the following goals:

- The cabling for both units of the mobile sales division network should be consistent.
- The cabling must be easily transported and installed.
- The cabling must be readily available.
- The cabling should be low-cost.
- The network cable should be capable of supporting a total network length of up to 150 meters.

Step 1   RG-8 coax cabling, when used for Ethernet networks, is referred to as *10Base5* cabling. What does this designation indicate?

Step 2   Explain how a PC connects to a 10Base5 Ethernet network cable.

_____

_____

Step 3   RG-58 coax cabling, when used for Ethernet networks, is referred to as _10Base2_ cabling. What does this designation indicate?

_____

_____

Step 4   Explain the difference between baseband and broadband signaling.

_____

_____

Step 5   Based on your client's requirements, which type of coax cabling do you recommend for their purposes?

_____

_____

 20 MINUTES

Lab Exercise 5.04: Terminating Ethernet Network Segments

Computer networks operate at extremely low voltages, but it's still important to appreciate the fact that wired Ethernet networks use electricity. As such, they must obey certain laws governing the way electricity conducts itself (so to speak) on the copper wire of the network media.

In order to maintain electrical integrity, network segments using coax cable must be closed, or _terminated_, and they must be terminated within the previously mentioned distance limits. Improper termination is a common cause of network failure for 10Base5 and 10Base2 networks. In this lab, you'll review why proper termination is important to your network, and you'll learn to troubleshoot errors related to improper termination.

Learning Objectives

In this lab, you'll work with termination on a 10Base2 network. By the end of this lab, you will be able to:

- Explain the need for proper network segment termination
- Troubleshoot improperly terminated network segments
- Properly install a BNC T-connector and terminating resistor (optional)

Lab Materials and Setup

The materials you'll need for this lab are

- Pencil and paper
- BNC T-connector and terminating resistor (optional)

Getting Down to Business

You are setting up one of the CBI mobile sales unit's networks for testing purposes. While connecting the PCs to the 10Base2 network cable bus, you note the following:

- The network cabling is longer than 185 meters.
- There are no terminating resistors fitted onto the BNC T-connectors at the ends of the cable bus.

You explain your findings to the project supervisor. She suggests that you either install the cabling without terminators or simply plug the ends of the network cable directly into the PC's NICs. Now it appears you need to explain the importance of proper termination to her.

Step 1   The reason that Ethernet coax cable is terminated is to prevent *reflection*. Describe what reflection is, its common causes, and why it must be prevented.

_____

_____

Step 2   Each type of Ethernet network cabling is rated to work within certain distance limitations. Extending the network segment beyond those distance limits causes *attenuation*. Describe what attenuation is, its common causes, and why it must be prevented.

_____

_____

Step 3   What is the proper way to terminate 10Base2 Thinnet coax cables using a BNC T-connector and terminating resistor?

_____

_____

Step 4   Optionally, practice installing a piece of 10Base2 Thinnet cable and a terminating resistor on a BNC T-connector, and then plug the T-connector onto a NIC's BNC connector.

Step 5   If you have access to two or more PCs networked together via 10Base2 coax cabling, remove the terminating resistor from one BNC T-connector and then attempt to access the network. What are the results?

_____

_____

 20 MINUTES

Lab Exercise 5.05: Extending Ethernet Networks

The specifications for Ethernet, such as the number of supported network nodes and the length of network cable runs, impose some serious limitations for network designers. How can you stretch the network cabling beyond the stated distance limits? How do you configure a network to support more network nodes?

To achieve these purposes and more, we use specialized network hardware devices. Two such devices are _bridges_ and _repeaters_. In this lab, we'll discuss the functions of bridges and repeaters, and learn how to use bridges and repeaters to extend the capabilities of Ethernet networks.

Learning Objectives

In this lab, you'll discuss the function of bridges and repeaters. By its end, you will be able to:

- Define and compare bridges and repeaters

- Recommend a hardware solution for a company network

Lab Materials and Setup

The only materials you'll need for this lab exercise are a pencil and some paper.

Getting Down to Business

Your client has contracted you to set up two small 10Base2 networks (maximum of 30 network nodes each) in adjoining rooms at a convention center. They will use a centralized database stored on a server attached to one network. The two networks need to be joined together so that computers on both network segments can use this database.

Step 1   In the following space, describe the function of a bridge.

_____

_____

Step 2   In the space that follows, describe the function of a repeater.

_____

_____

Step 3   You need to join the two network segments together using a hardware device. Because of the heavy demands that the database operations place on the network, it's important that you minimize excessive network traffic. Which hardware device is best suited for your purposes?

_____

_____

Step 4   While setting up a 10Base2 network segment for your client, you discover that the total length of the network cable bus must be 250 meters. What recommendation do you make?

_____

_____

Lab Analysis

1. How does a bridge device improve performance on an Ethernet network?

    _____

    _____

2. How can a repeater limit the effect of a broken network cable on a 10Base2 Ethernet network?

    _____

    _____

3. What is the purpose of the black bands marking 10Base5 Ethernet cabling every 2.5 meters?

    _____

    _____

4. What network devices currently use broadband signaling?

    _____

    _____

5. What is the main feature that a bridge offers an Ethernet network that a repeater does not provide?

    _____

    _____

Key Terms Quiz

Use the vocabulary terms from the list below to complete the sentences that follow. Not all of the terms will be used.

Attenuation

Baseband

Binary

BNC connector

Bridge

Broadband

CSMA/CD

DIX connector

Frame

Hexadecimal

Packet

Packet sniffer

Reflection

Repeater

Transceivers

T-connector

Vampire tap

1. A _____ takes packets from one segment and retransmits them onto another Ethernet segment.

2. Excessive network cable length increases _____, which results in data corruption and collisions.

3. _____ values, such as C0 A8 04 25, are a type of "shorthand" used to represent binary values.

4. A 10Base2 NIC connects to the bus cable using a _____.

5. A system called _____ determines which computers can use a shared cable at any given time to send data.

Chapter 6

Modern Ethernet

Lab Exercises

Ethernet has gone through a number of evolutionary changes to bring us to where we are today. Modern Ethernet networks are based on the same technologies and standards that power 10Base2 and 10Base5 networks—they use the same frame types, access methods, and so on—but they also address many of the weaknesses inherent in those older technologies. Modern Ethernet enables network techs to build large, fault-tolerant, scalable, fast networks at lower costs and with less effort than earlier Ethernet networks.

In this lab, you'll examine the specifications and hardware that make up *10BaseT* Ethernet, look at the design aspects (such as the 5-4-3 rule) to keep in mind when planning a modern Ethernet network, and then talk about the Ethernet developments that take us beyond 10BaseT. Let's get started.

 20 MINUTES

Lab Exercise 6.01: Modern Ethernet: 10BaseT and 10BaseFL

Although 10Base2 and 10Base5 Ethernet networks had their time and place, modern Ethernet networking really began with the development of 10BaseT. The 10, as you know, represents the total throughput speed of 10 megabits per second (Mbps), and Base means baseband. What, then, does the T stand for? Unlike 10Base2 and 10Base5, the T in 10BaseT doesn't represent the total rated distance of the network segment. Instead, the T represents the type of network cabling used, *twisted pair* cabling. Likewise, 10BaseFL indicates Ethernet using *fiber-optic* cabling.

Modern Ethernet solutions offer many advantages over earlier Ethernet implementations. Let's spend some time exploring these advantages.

Learning Objectives

In this lab, you'll examine the standards and technology of 10BaseT Ethernet. By its end, you will be able to:

- Define the 10BaseT Ethernet specifications, requirements, and limitations

Lab Materials and Setup

The materials you'll need for this lab are

- Pencil and paper

- CAT 5 UTP Ethernet cabling

- Fiber-optic Ethernet cabling (optional)

Getting Down to Business

Your client, 360 Art Services, has contracted you to design and install a PC network in its new office facility. The 360 Art Services office space consists of a large warehouse area and an adjoining suite of offices. The warehouse is split into an open storage area, a climate-controlled, secure storage area, and a workroom. The office suite consists of a lobby area with an adjoining meeting room, four medium-sized offices, a restroom, and a kitchen/dining area. You have previously surveyed the site and recommended that they implement an Ethernet star bus topology using CAT 5 UTP. They have accepted your recommendation, and are ready to enter the planning stage of network deployment.

Recall from Chapter 4 that your client's goals include the following:

- The client wants network connectivity in the open storage area and workroom area of the warehouse, and in each of the offices, as well as the lobby area and meeting room.

- The client wants a consistent network topology throughout the location.

- The client wants the network to be high-performance.

- The client is anticipating growth in the company, and wants to be able to add more computers to the network without a great deal of effort or expense.

- The client states that although expense *is* an issue, they are willing to install new equipment if necessary.

Step 1   Take a short length of CAT 5 UTP and strip off the cladding. In the following space, describe the cable.

_____

_____

Step 2   What is the purpose of the EIA/TIA 568A and 568B standards?

_____

_____

Step 3   Ethernet networks using 10BaseFL fiber-optic hardware and cabling share most of the qualities of 10BaseT networks, but are considerably more expensive and offer no performance advantages. What are the circumstances under which 10BaseFL is preferable to 10BaseT?

_____

_____

 30 MINUTES

Lab Exercise 6.02: Ethernet Network Design: The 5-4-3 Rule

Experienced network techs often call Ethernet networks _collision domains_ to reflect the Ethernet network media access method—Carrier Sense Multiple Access/Collision Detection (CSMA/CD). Ethernet networks are built around the assumption that collisions occur, and that they must be detected. The total size of an Ethernet network cannot exceed any connected network node's ability to detect data frame collisions. These requirements mean that Ethernet networks should conform to a set of limitations called the 5-4-3 rule. The 5-4-3 rule governs how large an Ethernet network can be while still being able to service all network nodes.

Learning Objectives

In this lab, you'll review the definition of the 5-4-3 rule and examine how this rule impacts your network design, including your use of network repeaters and hubs to interconnect network nodes and segments.

By the end of this lab, you will be able to:

- Define the 5-4-3 rule for Ethernet networks
- Design an Ethernet network that conforms to the 5-4-3 rule

Lab Materials and Setup

The only materials you'll need for this lab are a pencil and some paper.

Getting Down to Business

You are ready to present your preliminary network design to your client. Recall from Chapter 4 that your client's goals include the following:

- The client wants network connectivity in the open storage area and workroom area of the warehouse, and in each of the offices, as well as the lobby area and meeting room.

- The client wants a fault-tolerant network.

- The client is anticipating growth in the company, and wants to be able to add more computers to the network without a great deal of effort or expense.

- The client states that although expense *is* an issue, they are willing to install new equipment if necessary.

Figure 6-1 shows your initial design for your client's Ethernet network. The open storage area's network nodes are attached to hub A, the workroom's network nodes are attached to hub B, the administrative offices network nodes are attached to network hub C, and the lobby and meeting room area's network nodes are attached to hub D. Each hub is connected to the next via unpopulated link segments LS1, LS2, and LS3.

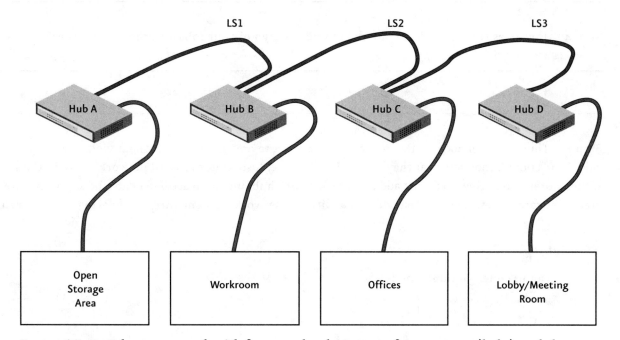

FIGURE 6-1 An Ethernet network with four populated segments, four repeaters (hubs), and three unpopulated link segments

Step 1 Explain the function of an Ethernet network hub.

_____

_____

Step 2 One of your client's concerns is the ability for the network to stay up and running if one or more of the PCs becomes unplugged. Describe how 10BaseT networks achieve fault tolerance.

_____

_____

Step 3 In the following space, explain how Ethernet hubs affect your calculation of the 5-4-3 rule.

_____

_____

Step 4 How does the 5-4-3 rule dictate the physical design of your 10BaseT Ethernet network?

_____

_____

Step 5 Thus far, each node on the network can connect to any other node without violating the 5-4-3 rule. Your client announces that they've decided that they also want to install network nodes in their secure storage area. Now you must add another network hub, hub E, to accommodate the secure storage area's network nodes. How can you add this additional network segment without violating the 5-4-3 rule?

✔ Hint

You can use one additional hub.

_____

_____

 20 MINUTES

Lab Exercise 6.03: Beyond 10BaseT: High-Speed Ethernet

Modern Ethernet networks began with 10BaseT, but they certainly haven't stopped there. Driven by network-intensive applications and services, Ethernet developers have found ways to ramp up Ethernet data throughput speeds so they are as much as 100 times faster than the original Ethernet specifications.

High-speed Ethernet comes in several flavors—some that use many of the same hardware components as 10BaseT Ethernet, and some that require specialized hardware and software components. These high-speed Ethernet solutions include the aptly named *Fast Ethernet, Gigabit Ethernet, switched Ethernet*, and *full-duplex Ethernet*. In this lab, you'll examine the specifications and requirements of high-speed Ethernet.

Learning Objectives

In this lab, you will examine high-speed Ethernet options for modern network environments. By its end, you will be able to:

- Define the specifications, requirements, and limitations of the various high-speed Ethernet solutions

Lab Materials and Setup

The only materials you'll need for this lab are a pencil and some paper.

Getting Down to Business

Your client contact informs you that the company has secured a contract to store and ship a number of valuable artworks. This contract stipulates that the company must upgrade the security on its premises. For this purpose, they've hired a security specialist who has designed a PC-based video surveillance system. The security solution incorporates several remote video cameras connected to a PC with special controller hardware and server software. The security controller PC is then connected to the network, providing live video feed to any networked PC running the security application software. This solution is also capable of supplying a live video feed to remote PCs.

To support the live security video feed, the client's network must provide faster data throughput than is possible with 10BaseT Ethernet. Your client wants your recommendations for a high-speed Ethernet solution.

Recall from Chapter 4 that your client's goals include the following:

- The client wants a consistent network topology throughout the location.

- The client wants the network to be high-performance.

- The client states that although expense *is* an issue, they are willing to install new equipment if necessary.

Step 1   Your security system vendor recommends that your organization use network equipment capable of 100-Mbps throughput to ensure that video traffic doesn't bog down the network. Which of the following high-speed Ethernet solutions is the most suitable: 100BaseTX, 100BaseT4, 100BaseFX, or 1000BaseT?

_____

_____

Step 2   Upon surveying your client's office site, you discover that the secure storage area is beyond 100 meters from the nearest network hub location. To get around this, your client's security specialist suggests installing a 100BaseFX link segment to connect the secure storage area's computers to the rest of the network. What are the benefits and drawbacks of this solution? What can you suggest as an alternate solution?

_____

_____

Step 3   What is the result of mixing 10BaseT Ethernet network hubs with 10/100BaseT NICs?

_____

_____

Step 4   What is necessary to upgrade your client's described network to Gigabit Ethernet?

_____

_____

Step 5   Describe how using Ethernet switches instead of hubs improves performance on the network without requiring all new network cabling and NICs.

_____

_____

Step 6 Describe the advantages and requirements of using full-duplex Ethernet over half-duplex Ethernet.

_____

_____

Lab Analysis

1. What are the results of breaking the 5-4-3 rule on an Ethernet network?

_____

_____

2. What is required to implement full-duplex Ethernet?

_____

_____

3. What kind of network cabling is necessary to implement Gigabit Ethernet?

_____

_____

4. You are servicing a client's network and need to connect (cascade) two eight-port Ethernet hubs together. Neither hub has an uplink port. You have a length of CAT 5 UTP, a crimping tool, and a pair of RJ-45 connectors. How can you link the hubs together?

_____

_____

5. High data throughput speeds and longer throughput distances are two advantages of fiber-optic cabling over copper cabling. Describe two other advantages that fiber-optic cabling offers over copper wire.

_____

_____

Key Terms Quiz

Use the vocabulary terms from the list below to complete the sentences that follow. Not all of the terms will be used.

10BaseFL

10BaseT

100BaseT

1000BaseT

5-4-3 rule

CAT 3, CAT 5, CAT 5e

Crossover cable

Fast Ethernet

Full-duplex

Gigabit Ethernet

Half-duplex

Hub

Link segment

Repeater

RJ-45

Star bus topology

STP

Switched Ethernet

UTP

1. A _____ is a special twisted pair cable that can connect hubs together.

2. UTP network cabling uses an eight-pin _____ connector.

3. A _____ device is one that can send and receive data simultaneously.

4. _____ refers to several Ethernet technologies that operate at 100 Mbps or faster.

5. A _____ retransmits data frames over multiple ports at the same time.

Chapter 7

Non-Ethernet Networks

Lab Exercises

The CompTIA Network+ certification exam expects you to display a jack-of-all-trades level of network knowledge. As such, it's important for you to recognize that Ethernet, although it dominates the PC networking world, is by no means the only available networking solution.

At one time, Ethernet had serious competition from another widely implemented networking technology: Token Ring. In recent years, Token Ring has been reduced to a niche market, but that market is very much alive and kicking. CompTIA expects you to be able to switch gears between Ethernet and Token Ring with ease.

Other once-popular networking technologies that have largely fallen by the wayside include ARCnet and LocalTalk. These specialized technologies never saw a high degree of adoption in the networking industry, but they're still considered relevant enough to merit attention on the CompTIA Network+ exam.

Finally, you'll need to understand the technologies that network techs employ to tie the scattered local area networks (LANs) of the world together. These so-called backbone network technologies include Fiber Distributed Data Interface (FDDI) and Asynchronous Transfer Mode (ATM).

 30 MINUTES

Lab Exercise 7.01: Alternative to Ethernet: Token Ring Networks

In today's networking world, Token Ring is the only serious alternative to Ethernet networking. Originally developed by IBM as a proprietary networking solution, Token Ring has since been ratified by the IEEE organization under the 802.5 standard designation.

Token Ring's data throughput speeds are on par with those of Ethernet, and modern Token Ring uses the same type of network cabling as Ethernet, but that's where the similarities end. The media access method and the network topology configuration both differ from Ethernet, as does the network hardware.

Learning Objectives

In this lab, you'll examine the important specifications of Token Ring networks. By its end, you will be able to:

- Define Token Ring's specifications as defined by the IEEE 802.5 standard

- Understand how Token Ring network technology accesses shared network media

- Describe the network topology and network cabling that Token Ring uses

- Identify Token Ring connection hardware

- Describe how Token Ring network hubs interconnect

Lab Materials and Setup

The only materials you'll need for this lab are a pencil and some paper.

Getting Down to Business

Your client, Dr. Peter Simione, is moving his psychiatry practice into a suite of offices in a professional building. The previous tenant had installed network cabling and networking hardware (Token Ring hubs, called *Multistation Access Units* and abbreviated as MAU or MSAU) to accommodate a Token Ring network. Your client wants to determine whether it would be worthwhile to equip his office PCs with Token Ring NICs and software in order to utilize the existing network cabling and hardware, or if he should invest in Ethernet network hardware.

Your client's goals are as follows:

- The network should provide adequate performance for document sharing, Internet e-mail, and web browsing.

- The network should be fault-tolerant.

- The network should be easy to set up and maintain.

- The client is willing to purchase new equipment if the current equipment doesn't meet the goals.

Step 1   Token Ring's network media access method is considered by many network techs to be more elegant than Ethernet's CSMA/CD method. Describe Token Ring's media access method, and list at least two qualities of the Token Ring media access method that are superior to Ethernet.

_____

_____

_____

Step 2   The original Token Ring networking technology used a ring network topology consisting of a length of coax cabling connecting all network nodes in a circle. Modern Token Ring uses the star ring network topology. Describe the star ring network topology, and list at least two advantages of this topology over the older ring network topology.

_____

_____

Step 3 Describe the data throughput speeds of Token Ring.

_____

_____

Step 4 Modern Token Ring uses twisted-pair cabling. Fill in the following chart with the appropriate specification for the cabling type:

Twisted-Pair Cabling Type	Maximum Distance	Maximum Number of Network Nodes	Connector Type	Usage
Shielded twisted pair (STP)				
Unshielded twisted pair (UTP)				

Step 5 Identify the connector in Figure 7-1.

FIGURE 7-1 A network connector

Step 6 To support all the network nodes that your client wants to install on the network, you would need to increase the number of ports available. To increase the number of ports available to network nodes, Ethernet hubs are interconnected (cascaded) via uplink ports or crossover cables. What is the proper way to increase the number of ports available to network nodes on Token Ring MAUs?

_____

_____

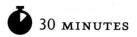 30 MINUTES

Lab Exercise 7.02: Legacy Networks: ARCnet and LocalTalk

Let's break out the time machine and jump back to the late 1970s. The PC industry as we know it is still a few years down the road, and both Ethernet and Token Ring technologies are still just twinkles in network developers' eyes. What are our networking options?

First and foremost is Attached Resource Computer network (ARCnet). ARCnet held a large part of the networking market for a number of years, and in fact still resonates today, mainly in the specialized embedded-computing market. ARCnet's low cost and adaptability are among the strong points that keep it relevant in the networking world.

Now jump ahead to the mid-1980s—yes, the era of big hair and power ties—and you'll see another networking technology take hold. This is LocalTalk, Apple Computer's unique networking solution. LocalTalk functionality was built into Apple Macintosh computers, and like most things Mac, was extremely simple to configure and use. Unfortunately, LocalTalk had some pretty serious limitations in terms of performance and scalability. These limitations ultimately relegated it to a very limited role in the business networking world. Nonetheless, it's still important for you to understand LocalTalk's capabilities and implementation.

Learning Objectives

In this lab, you'll examine the specifications and implementation of ARCnet and LocalTalk. By the end of the lab, you will be able to:

- Define the specifications and implementations of ARCnet and LocalTalk

- Understand how ARCnet and LocalTalk network technologies access shared network media

- Describe the network topologies and network cabling requirements for ARCnet and LocalTalk

Lab Materials and Setup

The materials you'll need for this lab are

- Pencil and paper

- PC with Internet access

Getting Down to Business

Your client, ConHugeCo Ltd., has contracted you to perform a site survey on a newly acquired property. The building formerly housed a small manufacturing operation that used computer-controlled manufacturing devices. Your task is to evaluate the equipment to determine if it should be scrapped or redeployed in the ConHugeCo organization.

You discover that the manufacturing equipment uses ARCnet networking technology, while the office suites are equipped to use LocalTalk. Your client wants you to explain how these technologies function, and asks if the equipment is still viable.

Step 1   Describe the method that ARCnet network nodes use to access the network media.

_____

_____

Step 2   Describe the ARCnet network topology structure.

_____

_____

Step 3   One of ARCnet's limiting factors is its speed. List the low and high data throughput specifications of ARCnet.

_____

_____

Step 4   Your client's office site has an RG-62 coaxial cable installed, spanning a total length of 575 meters from network node to network hub. Can this network cabling be used to implement an ARCnet network connection?

_____

_____

Step 5   Although ARCnet is not currently widespread in the mainstream networking market, it is very successful in specialized networking markets. The ARCnet industry group's web address is www.arcnet.com. Visit the web site and spend a few minutes researching the areas where ARCnet is currently deployed. List at least three specialized networking functions that ARCnet fulfills.

_____

_____

_____

Step 6 Where are you most likely to find LocalTalk networks implemented? What software is needed to utilize LocalTalk?

_____

_____

Step 7 What type of network topology does Apple LocalTalk use?

_____

_____

Step 8 Identify the network connector shown in Figure 7-2.

FIGURE 7-2 A network connector

Step 9 What type of network cabling can you use to deploy a LocalTalk network?

_____

_____

Step 10 List at least three reasons why LocalTalk is still relevant in today's networking world.

_____

_____

_____

 30 MINUTES

Lab Exercise 7.03: LAN to WAN Technologies: FDDI and ATM

No local area network (LAN) is an island unto itself. To be truly useful, networks need a way to reach out and connect to other networks. To this end, network designers have developed technologies that enable us to interconnect LANs across great distances to form so-called wide area networks (WANs). In this way, we build networks that cross cities, regions, countries, and even the globe.

LAN to WAN technologies come in many flavors with such exotic-sounding designations as X.25, Frame Relay, and Synchronous Optical Network (SONET). The two main WAN technologies covered in the CompTIA Network+ exam are Fiber Distributed Data Interface (FDDI) and Asynchronous Transfer Mode (ATM).

FDDI is a highly specialized, high-speed networking technology used mainly to supply backbone support for large networks. ATM also offers high data throughput, but it's used for a wider variety of purposes, including voice, fax, and multimedia communications.

Learning Objectives

In this lab, you'll examine the important aspects of these technologies. By its end, you'll be able to:

- Describe the network media access methods used by FDDI
- Understand the implementations of FDDI and ATM networking technologies

Lab Materials and Setup

The materials you'll need for this lab are

- Pencil and paper
- PC with Internet access

Getting Down to Business

Your client, Corona Booksellers, is evaluating several high-speed networking solutions to provide connectivity among their various regional store locations. You've been contracted to provide information on two technologies: Fiber Distributed Data Interface (FDDI) and Asynchronous Transfer Mode (ATM).

Step 1 FDDI uses a token-passing network media access method similar to Token Ring, but with one key difference. Describe the difference between the network media access methods of Token Ring and FDDI.

Step 2   Metropolitan area networks (MANs) are a type of network implementation used to cover large physical areas, such as college campuses or business complexes. MANs differ from WANs in that the network segments are typically not connected together via routers or bridges, but instead are directly connected via fiber-optic network cabling. Describe why FDDI is a good match for MAN technology.

_____

_____

Step 3   The ATM industry group's web address is www.atmforum.com. Visit the web site and find the answers to the following questions:

- What is another name for ATM?

- What other LAN and WAN technologies are interoperable with ATM?

_____

_____

Lab Analysis

1.   Define the difference between contention-based and deterministic network media access methods.

_____

_____

2.   List at least three reasons that Token Ring networks are not implemented as often as Ethernet networks.

_____

_____

_____

3.   Explain the difference between the ring and star ring network topologies.

_____

_____

4. List at least three reasons that the venerable ARCnet persists as a relevant networking technology.

_____

_____

_____

5. What are the typical functions of high-speed networking technologies such as ATM and FDDI?

_____

_____

Key Terms Quiz

Use the vocabulary terms from the list below to complete the sentences that follow. Not all of the terms will be used.

IEEE 802.5

ARCnet

ATM

Deterministic

FDDI

LocalTalk

Logical ring

Multistation Access Unit (MAU or MSAU)

Passive hubs

Token passing

Token Ring

1. ARCnet network nodes are connected by hardware devices called _____.

2. _____ was originally developed for Apple Macintosh computer networks.

3. A Token Ring hub is called a _____.

4. _____ is widely deployed in the computer-controlled robotics industry, and for communication with automated teller machines (ATMs).

5. The token passing media access method is described as _____.

Chapter 8

Installing a Physical Network

Lab Exercises

Now that you're familiar with the major network types, topologies, and technologies that network techs have at their disposal, it's time to dive into the physical aspects of network implementation. These include installing the network media and network hardware that ties your network together; installing the network adapters that connect your network nodes (PC workstations, servers, printers, and so on) to the network; testing network connections; and troubleshooting any ensuing network errors. These tasks are meat and potatoes for network techs, and you'll perform them many times, so this is a good place to start practicing.

 30 MINUTES

Lab Exercise 8.01: Examining Structured Network Cabling

Installing the cabling that carries data frames from one network node to another (affectionately called "pulling cable") is the most physically demanding task in a network installation, and thus requires the most preparation. Believe me, once you've got your network cabling installed, you *don't* want to have to go back in the walls and pull it out again! Issues include planning the installation, pulling the cabling, connecting network access jacks, and finally testing the connections to ensure that your installation is successful.

Learning Objectives

In this lab, you will examine the principles that lead to a successful structured network cabling installation. By the lab's end, you will be able to:

- Understand the proper planning issues that go into a network deployment
- Make informed recommendations for a network installation

Lab Materials and Setup

The materials you'll need for this lab are

- Pencil and paper
- Access to a network equipment room (optional)

Getting Down to Business

Installing structured network cabling begins with planning. You should physically survey the site and examine the site's floor plan for any hazards that you may not be able to spot visually. Then you can examine the logistics of your planned installation, such as the methods that you will use to deploy and install the horizontal cabling, network outlet drop locations, and so on. You also need to select the most appropriate type of cabling for the job, making sure to comply with any applicable codes and regulations. Then you should document your plans and note any discrepancies during installation (remember to label your runs and outlets while you're at it). Finally, you need to test your network cabling for continuity and troubleshoot any problems that arise. These are the basic steps that apply to any network cabling installation, from the small office/home office (SOHO) environment with only a few workstations to the large enterprise with thousands of clients.

Step 1   Your client, Mullens Community College (MCC), is in the process of expanding its campus network facilities. You are examining a network cabling installation proposal that was submitted by a previous network consultant. The proposal calls for installing the following network cable runs:

Location	Distance
Equipment Room Hub to Network Node A	48 meters (157 feet)
Equipment Room Hub to Network Node B	55 meters (180 feet)
Equipment Room Hub to Network Node C	60 meters (197 feet)
Equipment Room Hub to Network Node D	68 meters (223 feet)
Equipment Room Hub to Network Node E	75 meters (246 feet)
Equipment Room Hub to Network Node F	84 meters (275 feet)
Equipment Room Hub to Network Node G	91 meters (300 feet)
Equipment Room Hub to Network Node H	102 meters (334 feet)
Equipment Room Hub to Network Node I	113 meters (371 feet)
Equipment Room Hub to Network Node J	122 meters (400 feet)
Equipment Room Hub to Network Node K	125 meters (410 feet)

The proposal calls for using CAT 5e UTP network cabling. Which, if any, of the network cabling runs are outside the limits for that type of cabling? What solutions can you offer to overcome any limit violations?

Step 2   MCC's proposed expansion plans include extending the network into a basement area that is being renovated into offices. The walls of this area are concrete. What is the best way to install the network cable drops in this area?

_____

_____

Step 3   The current proposal specifies plain PVC UTP horizontal cabling for the network expansion. The cabling will be installed in the space above a suspended ceiling. Is this a suitable solution? Can you provide and justify an alternative horizontal cabling solution?

_____

_____

Step 4   List at least four requirements for a network equipment room that will house a rack-mounted patch panel, a stack of hubs or switches, and at least one file server.

_____

_____

Step 5   After you examine the expansion proposal and floor plans for MCC, you ask for access to the site itself so that you can perform your own site survey. The administrator at the site doesn't understand why you need this access. What explanation can you provide?

_____

_____

Step 6   Visit a network equipment room and make note of the following:

- Does the condition of the room meet the requirements listed in Step 4?

_____

- What is the size of the network equipment rack?

_____

- Is the network cabling installed in accordance with EIA/TIA standards for horizontal cabling?

- Is the proper type and fire rating of cabling installed?

- Is the network equipment clearly and accurately labeled?

 30 MINUTES

Lab Exercise 8.02: Installing Network Adapters

Your PC's physical link to the network is the network adapter. You're probably used to hearing this piece of equipment referred to simply as a network interface card (NIC), because traditionally they take the form of an internal ISA or PCI add-on peripheral card. Modern PCs aren't limited to this type of hardware, however, and you'll see network adapters implemented as external devices that connect via a USB port or PC Card (PCMCIA) slot, or as internal devices built into the motherboard.

→ **Note**

You'll rarely find ISA cards of any sort on any Pentium-class or later PC, but the Network+ exam still considers ISA prevalent enough to test you on it.

Installing and configuring network adapters is a task that many network techs do so often it becomes second nature. Let's spend some time reviewing the proper procedure for setting up a network adapter on a Windows PC.

Learning Objectives

In this lab, you will install a network adapter, such as an internal NIC or USB network adapter, on your PC. You will then install the OS drivers and confirm that installation was successful. By the end of this lab, you will be able to:

- Properly install a network adapter, as well as operating system drivers

Lab Materials and Setup

The materials you'll need for this lab are

- Windows 2000 Professional or Windows XP Home Edition or Professional PC

- An internal PCI NIC with driver media

- A USB network adapter with driver media

- A Phillips-head screwdriver

- An anti-static wrist strap and anti-static mat (optional, but preferable)

Getting Down to Business

Your client, 360 Art Services, has purchased a number of PCs for its office network. The PCs are equipped with network-compatible operating systems (Windows XP Professional), and all but three have available PCI slots. Of the three that lack available slots, two have available USB ports, while one, an older laptop, has only PC Card slots available. In the steps that follow, you will go through the steps to install a network adapter properly on a PC.

Generally speaking, it's best to read and follow the hardware manufacturer's instructions for installing a network adapter. The following steps list the most common methods for installing network adapters. First, you'll go through the steps for installing an internal PCI NIC; then you'll walk through installing an external USB network adapter.

All modern internal NICs are Plug-and-Play–compliant, making installation as simple as plugging the component in and following the prompts of the Windows hardware wizard. When installing external USB network adapters, you are usually required to install the drivers *before* plugging the component into an available USB port. Again, refer to the maker's instructions for particulars.

Step 1   Choose Start | Shut Down, and then select Shut Down and click the OK button to turn the PC off. Once the PC is completely powered down, unplug all cables, including the power cable from the power supply.

Step 2   Place the PC case on an anti-static mat and attach your anti-static wrist strap (a.k.a. *nerd bracelet*), then remove the PC case cover to expose the interior.

→ Note

Be sure to follow all proper anti-static procedures when working inside your PC case. Use an anti-static mat and anti-static wrist strap if you have them. If you lack these components, the next best thing is to discharge any static electricity in your body by touching a grounded metal component on the PC case (such as the power supply casing). Before you start poking around inside the PC case, remove any rings, bracelets, watches, or any other items that may snag on exposed components.

Step 3   Locate an available PCI expansion bus slot. Remove the slot cover, and then insert the PCI NIC into the slot. Be sure to handle the NIC only by its edges, and firmly press the card straight down into the slot, as shown in Figure 8-1. Once the NIC is properly seated in the slot, secure it in place with a screw.

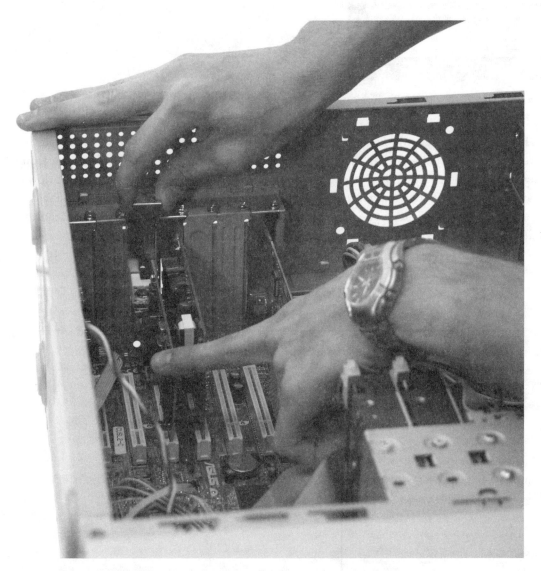

Figure 8-1 Inserting a NIC into an open PCI slot

Step 4   Replace the PC case cover and reattach all cables to the PC, including the power cable, then start the PC and log on when the desktop appears. Windows XP has built-in support for almost every NIC on the market, so assuming your PC has Windows XP installed, Plug-and-Play kicks in, detects the card, installs Windows' built-in drivers, and alerts you that the NIC is ready to use, as shown in

Figure 8-2. In most cases, the Windows NIC driver works fine, but it's usually a good idea to use the latest driver provided by the NIC manufacturer. You'll walk through the steps for updating a NIC driver in the next exercise. For now, move on to the next step to confirm NIC installation.

FIGURE 8-2 The Windows XP Professional *New network device installed* alert

Step 5   When the Found New Hardware Wizard completes, open the Windows Device Manager by choosing Start | Control Panel and then selecting the Performance and Maintenance category icon (if you're using Category View). Click the System icon to bring up the System Properties applet. Now click the Hardware property sheet tab, and click the Device Manager button. Locate the the icon labeled *Network adapters* and double-click it to expand the list of installed NICs. Double-click the NIC's icon to open its Properties dialog box, as shown in Figure 8-3. Is the NIC functional? What are the NIC's resource settings?

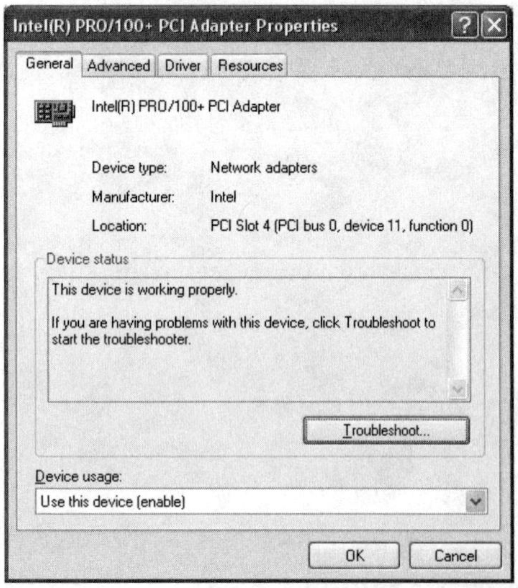

FIGURE 8-3 The NIC Properties dialog box

Step 6 USB network adapters have the advantage of being "hot-pluggable," meaning that you don't need to shut down the PC to install them. To ensure proper functionality, however, install the hardware driver *before* plugging the network adapter into a USB port. Insert your driver media into the appropriate drive on the PC and launch the setup program (if it doesn't start automatically), then follow the prompts to install the hardware drivers. Once you've done this, plug your USB network adapter into an available USB port. What are the results?

_____

_____

 30 MINUTES

Lab Exercise 8.03: Diagnostics and Troubleshooting

Network connectivity issues come in many shapes and sizes. Just like networks themselves, these can range from the simple to the complex. In this exercise, you'll walk through some simple diagnostic and troubleshooting steps.

Network adapter hardware is fairly foolproof, assuming that it's been installed and configured correctly. A couple of quick tests confirm whether a lack of network connectivity lies with the network adapter hardware or somewhere else.

Generally speaking, network cabling doesn't suffer from a lot of wear and tear—after all, there are no moving parts and the voltage carried is very low. Nonetheless, network cabling is subject to physical damage and interference, so it's important for you to be able to diagnose and repair this type of failure. To do this, you'll need a couple of tools of the trade, as described in the upcoming sections.

Learning Objectives

In this lab, you will go through some basic network connectivity troubleshooting scenarios, so by lab's end you'll be able to:

- Troubleshoot simple network connectivity issues

Lab Materials and Setup

The materials you'll need for this lab are

- Two networked Windows PCs

- A network patch cable

- A network hub

- A cable tester
- A toner unit
- Access to an equipment room and patch panel (optional)

Getting Down to Business

The first symptom of a network connectivity issue usually manifests as a loud screeching noise coming not from the PC, but from the PC user. Typically, this noise will be accompanied by a vocal error message, such as "I can't get on the Internet!" or "I can't get my e-mail!" "I can't get my files!" is also pretty common. In most cases, network connectivity problems are simple in nature. Accordingly, you should begin your diagnosis and troubleshooting with simple solutions.

Assume for a moment that one of your network users is unable to access network resources. In the following steps, you'll go through a simple diagnostic and troubleshooting scenario.

Step 1   Your first step is to determine whether or not the PC has a network connection, and then determine the state of the connection. Windows provides a couple of methods to determine the network connection state quickly. First, look in the System Tray area of the taskbar. Is there a Local Area Connection status icon? If so, click the icon to bring up the Local Area Connection Status dialog box and fill in the following information:

Status   _____

Duration   _____

Speed   _____

If no icon is visible, skip to Step 2.

Step 2   Choose Start | Control Panel, select the Network and Internet Connections category icon (if you're in the Category View), and then click the Network Connections icon. Alternate-click the Local Area Connection icon and select Status from the pop-up menu to bring up the network connection's status dialog box. What is the status of the network connection?

_____

_____

Step 3   For the command-line inclined, you can determine the network connection status by opening a command-line window (choose Start | Run, type **cmd**, and press the ENTER key), and typing **ipconfig /all**. What are the results of this command?

_____

_____

Step 4 Next, locate the PC's network adapter and check the status lights. What is the result?

_____

_____

Step 5 Disconnect the PC's network cable from the network adapter. What are the results?

_____

_____

Step 6 Unplug the network cable from the network hub or wall outlet and connect it to your cable tester. Press the Test button. What are the results?

_____

_____

Step 7 Optionally, if you have access to a network equipment room with a wired patch panel, attach the tone generator unit from a network toner to an active network drop wall outlet. Then go to the patch panel and use the tone probe unit to locate the patch panel connector that corresponds to the network outlet. What are the results?

_____

_____

Lab Analysis

1. A user complains that he cannot get on your corporate network. You discover that the user moved his desk and PC to another part of his office, and in doing so forcibly pulled the CAT 5 network cable out of its wall outlet. A quick visual inspection doesn't reveal any obvious damage to the patch cable. How do you determine if the patch cable is damaged?

_____

_____

2. What specialized equipment is used to connect the endpoint of a cable run to a patch panel?

_____

_____

3. How tall is a network cabling rack mount with a designation of "44U"?

_____

_____

4. Name the three most common expansion buses used to connect network interface hardware to a PC.

_____

_____

5. The terms _DIX connector_ and _AUI transceiver_ are often incorrectly used interchangeably. Explain the difference between a DIX connector and an AUI transceiver.

_____

_____

Key Terms Quiz

Use the vocabulary terms from the list below to complete the sentences that follow. Not all of the terms will be used.

110-punchdown

Activity light

AUI (attachment user interface)

Autosensing

Building entrance

Cable drop

Cable tester (media tester)

Collision light

Direct cable connection

DIX (Digital-Intel-Xerox) connector

EIA/TIA

Equipment room

Fire rating

Horizontal cabling

Link light

Mounting rack

Multispeed

Network backbone

Network interface card (NIC)

Null modem cable

Patch cable

Patch panel

Plenum

Punchdown tool

PVC (polyvinyl chloride)

Run

Solid core

Stranded core

Structured cable

Tone generator

Tone probe

Units (U)

Wire crimper (crimper)

Work area

1. Building codes specify that network cabling installed in air circulation spaces (such as the space between a suspended ceiling and structural ceiling) must be _____ grade.

2. Use a(n) _____ and _____ to trace network cabling between a wall outlet and a patch panel.

3. To establish a direct connection between two PCs that lack NICs, use a _____ cable.

4. Practically all modern Ethernet NICs are _____ and _____.

5. The simplest test of network connectivity is to check the NIC's _____.

Chapter 9
Wireless Networking

Lab Exercises

Wireless networking is the solution to, and the cause of, many network technicians' headaches. Wireless networking is being adopted at a phenomenal rate in all areas of the IT industry, from small home and office networks to large corporate enterprises, school campuses, industrial complexes, and trendy coffee shops. As a networking solution, wireless is an exciting evolution that provides flexibility, scalability, and decent data throughput speeds. On the down side, wireless networks can be difficult to configure, prone to interference, and insecure.

I say "can be" because there are a number of things you, the network tech, can do to overcome the weaknesses of wireless networking to make it a robust, secure, and available solution. The CompTIA Network+ exam expects you to be able to implement wireless solutions of all types, so you're going to cover not just the ubiquitous Ethernet Wi-Fi wireless technology, but also the more obscure HomeRF and Bluetooth technologies. You need to understand the basic facts and figures of each wireless technology, the accepted industry standards that apply to them, and how to implement and troubleshoot these technologies. Let's get started.

 40 MINUTES

Lab Exercise 9.01: Wireless Networking Basics

Many wireless networking solutions have come and gone, but the three most popular are those based on the IEEE 802.11 standard and those that use Bluetooth technology. Of those solutions, 802.11-based Wi-Fi Ethernet is by far the most prevalent, but you should not limit your wireless networking knowledge exclusively to one technology.

Wireless networking is becoming increasingly important to businesses of all sizes, and provides the solution to many network connectivity barriers. Plus, it's *cool!*

Learning Objectives

In this lab, you will review the basic information of how wireless networks function. By its end, you'll be able to:

- Explain the basic functions of a wireless Ethernet network

Lab Materials and Setup

The only materials required for this lab are a pencil and some paper.

Getting Down to Business

Your client, Red Blazer Realty, is moving into office space in a building designated as a historic land-mark. There are restrictions against modifying the building structure, so the client cannot install net-work cabling within the structure of the the building. They'd also prefer not to use external network cabling raceways, so they want you to explain their wireless networking options. The client's goals are as follows:

- The network should be able to support up to 40 PCs.

- The network must be secure against unauthorized wireless access, but allow authorized visi-tors to join with minimal configuration.

- The network should use industry-standard technology that is widely available.

Step 1   Explain the basic hardware and software required to implement wireless networking.

_____

_____

Step 2   Explain the differences between ad-hoc and infrastructure modes.

_____

_____

Step 3   Describe at least three methods that enable you to increase security on wireless networks.

_____

_____

Step 4   Your client is concerned that a single wireless access point won't provide enough range to cover their office space. How can you increase the wireless coverage area?

_____

_____

Step 5   Your client is concerned about wireless network nodes interfering with each other's broadcasts and corrupting data. Describe how wireless Ethernet's CSMA/CA network media access scheme functions.

_____

_____

Step 6   Given your client's stated goals, which wireless networking solution do you suggest?

_____

_____

 45 MINUTES

Lab Exercise 9.02: Wireless Networking Standards

While it's true that the world of wireless networking is dominated by 802.11-based Wi-Fi Ethernet, that's not your only option, and it's not the perfect solution to every wireless problem. Understanding the various operating ranges, speeds, compatibility issues, and so on enables you to make informed decisions while planning a wireless network rollout.

Learning Objectives

In this lab, you will review the important specifications of the most popular wireless networking technologies. By its end, you will be able to:

- Define the important specifications of wireless networking technologies

Lab Materials and Setup

The only materials required for this lab are a pencil and some paper.

Getting Down to Business

Your client, 360 Art Services, frequently needs to exchange data with visiting clients who use wireless-enabled laptop computers. Now the company wants to integrate wireless networking into its existing 100BaseT Ethernet network, and provide wireless access for the lobby area and meeting room of its warehouse office space. You've been asked to explain the company's wireless options.

Step 1 Your client has done a bit of preliminary research online and has visited a couple of large PC retailers, which has made him more confused than ever. He knows that his choices consist of Wi-Fi, HomeRF, and Bluetooth wireless networking, but is unclear on important details. Your client is leaning towards HomeRF because a salesman stressed the ease of setup and low cost of HomeRF equipment. In the following space, explain the key differences between these wireless networking technologies.

_____

_____

Step 2 Use the following 802.11 specification values to fill in the following table. Some values may be used more than once.

2.4 GHz   5 GHz   2 Mbps   11 Mbps   54 Mbps   150 feet   300 feet   802.11
802.11a   802.11b   802.11g

Standard	Frequency	Maximum Speed	Maximum Range	Compatibility
802.11	_____	_____	_____	_____
802.11a	_____	_____	_____	_____
802.11b	_____	_____	_____	_____
802.11g	_____	_____	_____	_____

Step 3 One of your client's employees uses a PDA that is equipped for Bluetooth wireless technology, but she admits to having no idea what that means. How can she use the PDA's Bluetooth functionality?

_____

_____

Step 4 Provide an appropriate description for the following Bluetooth services (profiles):

Bluetooth Service	Description
Generic Access Profile	_____
Service Discovery Profile	_____
Cordless Telephony Profile	_____
Intercom Profile	_____
Serial Port Profile	_____

Bluetooth Service	Description
Headset Profile	_____
Dial-up Networking Profile	_____
Fax Profile	_____
LAN Access Profile	_____
Generic Object Exchange Profile	_____
Object Push Profile	_____
File Transfer Profile	_____
Synchronization Profile	_____

Step 5   Explain how you will connect the wireless network nodes in the lobby/meeting room area of your client's location to the existing 100BaseT network.

_____

_____

 45 MINUTES

Lab Exercise 9.03: Configuring Wireless Networking

With only slight variations, installing and configuring wireless network equipment is much like doing so for a wired network. Since you already know how to install network adapters and network hubs, I'll forego a detailed discussion of those procedures here and concentrate on steps for configuring your wireless network nodes to talk to each other in ad-hoc and infrastructure mode.

Learning Objectives

In this lab, you will configure PCs for wireless networking. By its end, you will be able to:

- Configure PCs for Wi-Fi wireless networking in ad-hoc mode and infrastructure mode

- Configure a wireless access point for wireless networking in infrastructure mode

- Configure a PC for Bluetooth wireless networking in ad-hoc mode

Lab Materials and Setup

The materials you will need for this lab are

- Two Windows XP Home or Professional Edition PCs equipped with Wi-Fi network adapters

- Two Windows XP Home or Professional Edition PCs equipped with Bluetooth network adapters

- Wireless access point

Getting Down to Business

You have acquired a wireless access point for your client, 360 Art Services, and now need to integrate it into the existing network infrastructure. Your client also wants you to demonstrate how to enable a visiting client to connect wirelessly to another PC, and to the company's wired network.

Step 1 If you have not already done so, install a wireless network adapter into an available slot on your PC, following the manufacturer's instructions. If you're using a PCI or PCMCIA wireless network adapter, this should be a simple matter of inserting the hardware and then, once PnP detects the device, following the prompts to install the hardware drivers. If you're using a USB device, install the hardware drivers *before* connecting the device to the PC. Once you've successfully installed the device and device drivers, you should see an icon for the wireless configuration utility in your PC's system tray. Double-clicking the icon brings up the utility's dialog box. Windows XP's Wireless LAN Configuration Utility is shown in Figure 9-1. The appearance of your wireless configuration utility may vary somewhat, but they all function in practically the same manner. Double-click the icon to bring up your wireless configuration utility.

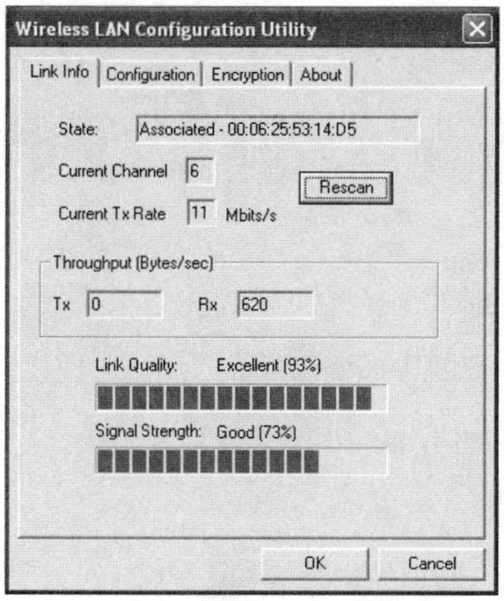

Figure 9-1 Windows XP's Wireless LAN Configuration Utility

Step 2   On each PC that you want to operate in ad-hoc mode, change the following settings:

- Set the network adapter to operate in ad-hoc mode.

- Configure a unique (non-default) SSID name, such as NETPLUSLAB.

- Configure a common broadcasting channel.

What are the results?

_____

_____

Step 3   Configuring your wireless network to operate in infrastructure mode requires a couple of extra steps when compared to ad-hoc mode. First, you must physically install your wireless access point onto your wired network segment; then you need to configure the access point to pass network traffic from wireless nodes to other wireless nodes, and from wireless nodes to the wired network segment. Installation is a simple matter of plugging the access point into a power source and then connecting it to a network outlet, hub, or patch panel via a patch cable. Configuration is done using—you guessed it—a configuration utility supplied by the wireless access point's maker. In some cases, the utility is browser-based, and you simply open your web browser, point to a special local IP address (such as 192.168.1.1), and enter a password when prompted to access the utility. Other access points require that you install a dedicated configuration utility program. After you launch this program, you can reach the access point via a direct USB connection to the access point, or through your wired LAN. Figure 9-2 shows the configuration utility for a Linksys wireless access point.

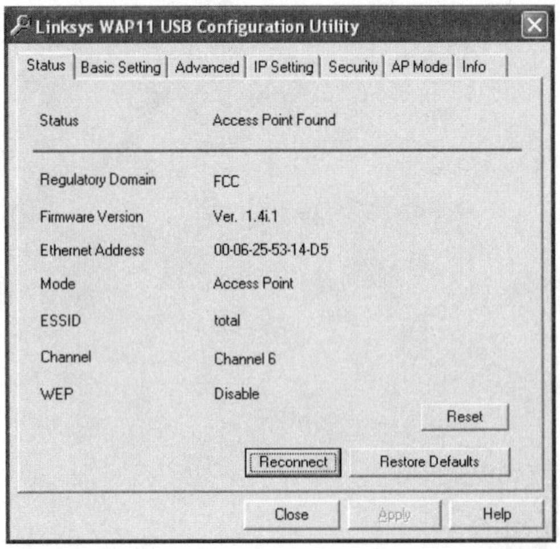

FIGURE 9-2 The Linksys WAP11 USB Configuration Utility

As with the wireless network adapter configuration utility, the wireless access point configuration utility may vary in appearance, depending on the maker, but the functions should be practically identical. Launch your access point configuration utility and do the following:

- Configure a unique (non-default) SSID name, such as NET+LAB.

- Change from the default broadcasting channel to a different channel.

- Change the default access point name.

- Disable SSID broadcasting.

- If the access point is configured as a DHCP server (the default setting on many brands), disable this setting.

Save the new configuration settings on the access point. What are the results? Are wireless network nodes able to communicate with the access point? Are wireless network nodes able to communicate with each other?

_____

_____

Step 4   Now configure your wireless network nodes with settings that match the new configuration of your wireless access point (SSID, broadcast channel). What are the results? Are wireless network nodes able to communicate with the access point? Are wireless network nodes able to communicate with each other?

_____

_____

Step 5   To beef up security, locate and configure the following settings on your wireless access point:

- Change the default password for the configuration utility to a unique password.

- Enable 128-bit WEP encryption on the wireless access point, and configure each wireless network node with the appropriate WEP key.

- Enable MAC filtering (if supported on your access point). Run the IPCONFIG command from the command line on a wireless network node to determine its MAC address, then enter this address into the MAC table on the wireless access point. What are the results?

_____

_____

Step 6 Install your Bluetooth wireless device's configuration software and drivers according to the manufacturer's instructions, inserting the Bluetooth wireless adapter when prompted. Note that you may have to reboot your computer to complete the installation of the device. Follow the prompts to complete the installation of Bluetooth services support. Once you've completed installation of Bluetooth, search for other Bluetooth wireless devices by opening My Bluetooth Places (Start | All Programs | My Bluetooth Places) and click the *Search for devices in range* link under Bluetooth Tasks. What are the results?

Step 7 Double-click the icon for another wireless Bluetooth device to discover the services (profiles) that the device supports. What are the results?

Step 8 To configure your Bluetooth device for non-discovery mode, alternate-click the Bluetooth device's configuration utility icon in the System Tray, and then select Advanced Configuration. Your Bluetooth device's configuration utility may vary. Figure 9-3 shows the Accessibility tab for a Belkin Bluetooth wireless adapter with the *Let other Bluetooth devices discover this computer* option checked. To set the device to non-discovery mode, uncheck this option. What are the results?

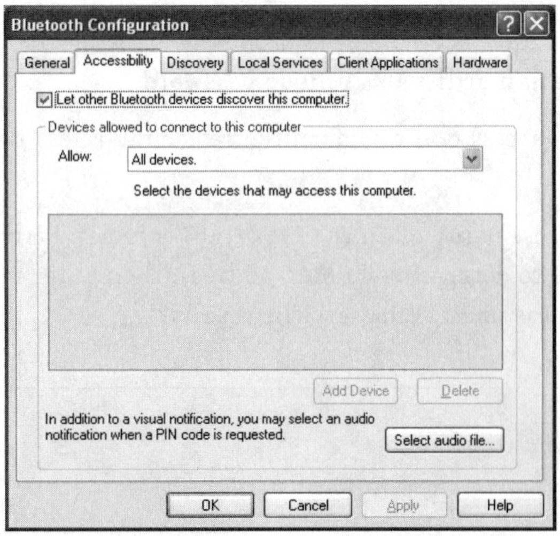

Figure 9-3 The Accessibility tab for a Belkin Bluetooth wireless adapter with the *Let other Bluetooth devices discover this computer* option checked

 30 MINUTES

Lab Exercise 9.04: Troubleshooting Wireless Networks

As famous sci-fi writer Arthur C. Clarke once said, a sufficiently advanced technology is indistinguishable from magic. Wireless networking isn't *quite* that advanced, but the results are nonetheless quite impressive—when they work correctly. When they don't work correctly, wireless networks afford network techs some unique opportunities to display their troubleshooting acumen.

Learning Objectives

In this lab, you will troubleshoot some common wireless networking issues. By its end, you will be able to diagnose and troubleshoot common wireless networking problems.

Lab Materials and Setup

The materials you'll need for this lab are

- Two Windows XP Home or Professional Edition PCs equipped with Wi-Fi network adapters

- Two Windows XP Home or Professional Edition PCs equipped with Bluetooth network adapters

- Wireless access point

Getting Down to Business

You have successfully installed and configured a wireless network for your client, 360 Art Services, and have been asked to demonstrate steps for troubleshooting simple problems before you leave.

Step 1   List at least three steps you should take to determine if a loss of wireless connectivity is due to your wireless network adapter's hardware or software configuration.

_____

_____

Step 2   After determining that your wireless network adapter is functioning correctly, how can you find out whether your network node has proper connectivity and signal strength to the wireless network?

_____

_____

Step 3   Name at least three factors that could cause poor signal strength between wireless network nodes.

_____

_____

Step 4   Assuming that a loss of wireless connectivity is not caused by improper hardware or software configuration, excessive distance between wireless network nodes, or environmental factors, what should you check next?

_____

_____

Step 5   One of your client's employees has a Bluetooth wireless adapter installed on her desktop PC, but her desktop doesn't see her new Bluetooth-equipped PDA. What should she check?

_____

_____

Lab Analysis

1. Explain the types of wireless consumer electronics that may cause interference with an 802.11g wireless network.

_____

_____

2. Explain the different broadcast methods used by Direct Sequence Spread Spectrum (DSSS) and Frequency Hopping Spread Spectrum (FHSS) devices.

_____

_____

3. Both 802.11a and 802.11g wireless devices operate at a maximum of 54 megabits per second. Why is 802.11g the more popular standard?

_____

_____

4. Bluetooth wireless technology is not a direct competitor to 802.11-based wireless technology. What uses are most appropriate for Bluetooth technology?

_____

_____

5. How many active devices can participate in a Bluetooth piconet? How many inactive (parked) devices can participate?

_____

_____

Key Terms Quiz

Use the vocabulary terms from the list below to complete the sentences that follow. Not all of the terms will be used.

Ad-hoc mode

Association

Bluetooth

HomeRF

Basic Service Set (BSS)

Direct Sequence Spread Spectrum (DSSS)

Extended Basic Service Set (EBSS)

Frequency Hopping Spread Spectrum (FHSS)

Infrastructure mode

Non-discovery mode

Profiles

Service Set Identifier (SSID)

Wi-Fi

Wireless access point

1. The process of Bluetooth wireless devices announcing their presence and the services (or pro-files) that they support is called _____.

2. A study group at your school consisting of 7–10 students meets regularly to exchange notes and research. The group members all have Wi-Fi–equipped laptop computers. The meetings take place at different locations on and off the school campus. The group members should configure their laptops to use _____ when they meet.

3. The biggest difference between 802.11-based wireless networking and HomeRF wireless network-ing is that 802.11-based technology uses the _____ broadcasting method, while HomeRF uses the _____ broadcasting method.

4. To keep your Bluetooth wireless device from announcing its presence to other devices, set it to _____ mode.

5. Wireless access points enable network techs to connect wireless network nodes to a wired net-work segment in _____ mode.

Chapter 10
Protocols

Lab Exercises

Every computer on a network must have an installed, functioning protocol in order to communicate with other computers on a network. Not only must a system have a protocol, but also all of the systems on the network must have the same protocol installed in order to communicate.

The following exercises build on some practical aspects of dealing with the installation and troubleshooting of protocols on Windows systems.

 30 MINUTES

Lab Exercise 10.01: The NET Command

Every accomplished network technician intimately knows the command line tools that Microsoft includes in Windows. Relying solely on graphical tools can backfire in a big way on a PC that's acting up, plus the command line tools enable you to accomplish necessary tasks quickly and efficiently. This book has already shown you a few such tools (IPCONFIG and ARP), but one of the most fascinating and handy tools is one that's been around since the DOS days and is still available in the latest versions of Windows—the NET command.

> **→ Note**
>
> The NET command that comes with Windows 9x systems is very different from the one that comes with Windows 2000/XP/2003. You'll be warned when these variances affect the lab steps.

Learning Objectives

This lab introduces you to the Windows NET command, showing you some of its capabilities and some practical uses for the command in a Windows network. By the end of the lab, you'll be able to:

- Describe how to run the NET command and how to access help for the different NET command features
- Use the NET command to test network connectivity in Windows 9x
- Use the NET command to view systems on the network
- Use the NET command to stop and start network services in Windows 2000/XP

Lab Materials and Setup

For this lab, you will need

- A PC running Windows 98 or Me

- A PC running Windows 2000 or XP

Getting Down to Business

You've got a problem with your video in Windows, preventing you from starting Windows in any way other than Safe Mode with network support. What can you do to verify that the network is up without resorting to graphical tools?

Your goals are as follows:

- You need to see if you have network connectivity with other Windows computers.

- You want to view all of the other computers on the network.

- You want to send messages to others on the network from a command prompt.

Step 1   Using a Windows 9x, 2000, or XP system, get to a command prompt. Run the NET command and see the results. Running the NET command alone only gives you the options you can run with the command. Try running the NET command with one of the options, followed by a **/?**. For example, try typing **net start /?**. Note how this gives you more detailed help. (This help function works with almost every command-line utility.)

Step 2   This step is only valid for Windows 98 systems! The NET command that comes with Windows 98 has a very handy function called NET DIAG. NET DIAG enables you to verify that you can connect to a DIAG server. Type **net diag** at a command prompt (you do not have to be in Safe Mode to make this work). After a moment, the program will say

```
No diagnostic servers were detected on the network.

Is Microsoft Network Diagnostics currently running on any other computers on the
network ? (Y/N)
```

At this point, press the N key. This will make your system the diagnostic server. Go to another system and run NET DIAG again. In a moment, assuming you have a good network connection, a working NIC, and a protocol installed, the second system will report connecting to the first system. What do you see on both systems? Disconnect the cable and report what you see.

If possible, run one system as the diagnostic and have multiple systems connect to the diagnostic server. Can you tell which systems are connecting to the server? Report your results.

_____

_____

Step 3   Try running the NET VIEW command on any computer. What do you see? What are those names? Compare what you see using the NET VIEW command to Network Neighborhood/My Network Places. Try some of the optional switches like **net view *computername*** and report the results.

_____

_____

Step 4   This step is only valid for Windows 2000/XP systems! Use the NET VIEW command to gather the names of a few computers on your network. Use the help functions to discover how to use the NET SEND command. Send a message to another computer and note how it displays. Figure out how to send a message to all of the computers on your network. What command enables you to send to all computers?

_____

_____

These exercises only begin to show the power of the NET command. Later chapters will show even more features.

🕐 30 MINUTES

Lab Exercise 10.02: Interconnecting Protocols

Even though TCP/IP is the dominant protocol, other protocols, in particular IPX/SPX and NetBEUI, are still found on plenty of systems. Using multiple protocols has a number of benefits as well as disadvantages, as you'll see in this lab exercise.

Learning Objectives

In this lab, you'll install and uninstall different protocols on a Windows system to see the effect of multiple protocol networks. By the end of the lab, you'll be able to:

- Install and uninstall protocols in Windows 9x and Windows 2000/XP systems

- Understand the effect of multiple protocols in a Windows network

- Describe practical situations where multiple protocols might make sense in a network

Lab Materials and Setup

The materials you'll need for this lab are

- Pencil and paper

- Multiple networked Windows PCs (any version of Windows is fine; a mix of versions is preferable). Be sure to have the Windows installation discs handy for all systems.

Getting Down to Business

Your client, ConNotSoHugeCo Ltd., has contracted you to check out their small network, which uses one one Windows 2000 server. The boss needs a few specific systems to have Internet access, but he does not want the other systems to access the Internet. He's already tried deleting the web browsers as well as some other tricks, but wants your opinion on how to prevent employees from accessing the Internet.

Step 1   Install NetBEUI on every system on the network. Document the steps needed to do this, keeping in mind that different versions of Windows involve different steps.

It takes some extra work to install NetBEUI on Windows XP. For help, refer to Microsoft Knowledge Base article 301041.

✔ **Hint**

The Microsoft Knowledge Base (MSKB) is an online depository of support documents relating to all versions of Windows. To search the MSKB, go to http://support.microsoft.com and enter either a search term or MSKB article ID number.

_____

_____

_____

_____

Step 2   Remove the TCP/IP protocol from two systems, documenting your steps along the way. Be careful when removing any protocol from a Windows 9x system! If you remove all of the network protocols, you'll remove networking completely—so make sure NetBEUI is installed on Windows 9x systems before removing TCP/IP. The Network Properties dialog box in Windows 2000 and XP has checkboxes next to the different protocols—what do they enable you to do?

_____

_____

_____

_____

Step 3 Explain how this configuration would allow some systems Internet access while denying others access. Include a diagram of each system on your network, showing the two "Internet" systems as well as the "Server."

_____

_____

_____

_____

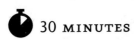 30 MINUTES

Lab Exercise 10.03: NetBIOS Naming

NetBIOS names are subject to strict naming conventions. NetBIOS's need for unique names often creates rather interesting conflict scenarios when two or more systems accidentally share the same name—an all-too-common occurrence in the real world.

Learning Objectives

In this lab, you'll see the effect on Windows when NetBIOS names are created and when systems on the same network share the same name. By lab's end, you should be able to:

- Describe the proper formatting of NetBIOS names

- Recognize and correct name conflicts in a Windows network

Lab Materials and Setup

The materials you'll need for this lab are

- Pencil and paper

- Multiple networked Windows PCs (any version of Windows is fine; a mix of versions is preferable). Be sure to have the Windows installation discs handy for all systems.

Getting Down to Business

You take on a new client the popular pet shop "I Can't Believe It's A Gerbil!" The shop has an old Windows 98 network in its corporate office. Of late, they've been getting errors that say "Duplicate Name found on Network," and the machines showing these errors are having trouble getting on the network. You need to fix this issue and to make sure the customer understands enough about NetBIOS names not to repeat this error.

Step 1 NetBIOS names can be up to 15 characters in length. Go into the Network Neighborhood Properties and try creating a NetBIOS name in Windows 98 with more than 15 alphabetic characters. What happens?

_____

_____

Step 2 Try Step 1 on a Windows 2000 or XP machine. What message does the computer give you? Using what you know about NetBIOS, Windows 98, Windows XP, and other naming options, describe why this happens.

_____

_____

_____

Step 3 Repeat the process using an alphabetic name that includes one of the following characters: a space, a comma, the number 3, or a hyphen. Describe the results when using these characters in both Windows 98 and Windows XP.

_____

_____

Lab Analysis

1. Why do you think the NET command continues to survive in every version of Windows?

   _____

   _____

2. Why do you think the NET commands in Windows 98 are so much simpler than the ones in Windows XP?

   _____

   _____

3. Describe the three most popular proprietary network protocols and name the company that developed each of them. Given that TCP/IP was based on industry standards and freely available, why didn't they use TCP/IP?

   _____

   _____

4. Windows 2000 and XP no longer use NetBIOS and instead use DNS for their naming tool. What are some of the shortcomings of NetBIOS that might have motivated Microsoft to make this change?

   _____

   _____

Key Terms Quiz

Use the vocabulary terms from the list below to complete the sentences that follow. Not all of the terms will be used.

AppleTalk

Connection-oriented

DLC

IP

IPX

NetBEUI

NetBIOS

NetBT

Network layer

Session layer

TCP

Transport layer

1. Before Macintosh computers adopted TCP/IP, they used the _____ protocol.

2. A _____ name is limited to 15 characters.

3. Microsoft's method of implementing NetBIOS names over a TCP/IP network is called _____.

4. NetWare's _____ protocol runs at the Network layer of the OSI seven-layer model.

5. The ancient _____ protocol is still supported by Windows, mainly for older network printers.

Chapter 11

TCP/IP

Lab Exercises

Prior to the mass availability of the Internet, network techs considered TCP/IP to be "just another protocol." In fact, many techs preferred to use protocols such as NetBEUI and IPX/SPX because they are simpler to configure than TCP/IP.

Obviously, that's changed. Why? Because the Internet runs on TCP/IP. The incredible growth of the Internet in the last decade has caused TCP/IP to move to the top of the heap of network protocols. Practically all modern networks are TCP/IP networks, regardless of whether they're Ethernet or Token Ring, wired or wireless, Windows, Linux, UNIX, or Macintosh. No matter which type of network you work on, chances are that you'll be working extensively with TCP/IP.

In this chapter, you'll examine the basics of IP addressing and the configuration of subnet masks; examine how a network node—or, as they're usually called when discussing TCP/IP, a network *host*—determines whether an IP address is local or remote; look at the important network services that operate with TCP/IP; and then discuss the important TCP/IP port associations. Let's go!

 45 MINUTES

Lab Exercise 11.01: IP Addressing Basics

There are several key concepts to IP addressing that all good network techs understand. The first of these is that all IP host addresses follow defined rules that specify whether or not they're considered valid for the TCP/IP network. You should appreciate that a network host's IP address is simply a numeric representation of a binary value. It's this binary value that identifies each node on the TCP/IP network. Finally, you should recognize that there are defined IP address classes, and that each of those classes comes with its own default subnet mask.

IP addresses must follow a specific format in order to be valid. Knowing the rules for valid IP addresses is particularly important when you must manually configure a network node's IP address. Configuring an IP address in the wrong format means that your PC won't communicate on the network.

There's a T-shirt available from thinkgeek.com that reads, "There are only 10 types of people in the world: Those who understand binary, and those who don't." It's good for a laugh to anyone who understands the basics of IP addressing. You don't have to speak binary as fluently as Data from "Star Trek: the Next Generation" to be a good network tech, but you should be able to perform simple IP address-to-binary conversions without much trouble.

You also need to understand the default IP address class ranges specified by the Internet Assigned Numbers Authority (IANA), and what it means to define a *classful* versus a *classless* IP address. Let's go over these IP addressing basics.

Learning Objectives

In this lab, you will review the basic rules of IP addressing. By its end, you will be able to:

- Recognize valid IP addresses

- Convert IP addresses from numeric to binary values

- Identify IP address class ranges

Lab Materials and Setup

The materials you will need for this lab are

- Pencil and paper

- Calculator with scientific view (the Windows calculator will do just fine!)

Getting Down to Business

Your client, Mullens Community College, has asked you to work with its IT department to review a proposal for configuring a new TCP/IP network segment submitted by another consultant. The project manager wants you to explain many of the terms and choices that he doesn't understand.

Step 1 Your client's previous consultant left notes with IP configurations for network hosts that look questionable. Identify whether the following IP host addresses are valid or invalid. Give the reasons that the invalid IP host addresses are invalid.

IP Address	Valid/Invalid
131.107.2.224	_____
255.268.3.98	_____
169.253.78.23	_____
1.3.6.10	_____
254.224.204	_____
127.0.0.1	_____
255.255.255.255	_____
0.0.0.0	_____

IP Address	Valid/Invalid
189.34.127.255	_____
168.254.6.8.10	_____

Step 2 Your client asks you to explain how the computer knows how to use IP addresses to send and receive data on the network. You need to demonstrate how the PC sees IP addresses as binary values instead of decimals. The built-in Windows calculator is an invaluable tool for configuring and converting IP addresses into their rudimentary binary format. Start the calculator by choosing Start | Run and typing **calc**. Then select View from the menu bar and click Scientific to change the view to scientific mode, as shown in Figure 11-1.

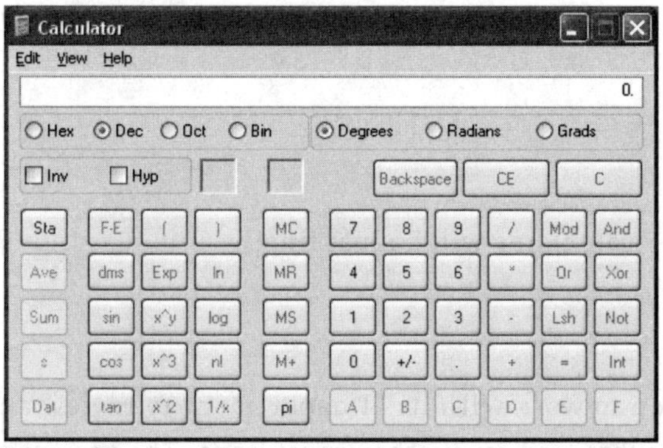

FIGURE 11-1 The Windows calculator in scientific view mode

Note the radio buttons that enable you to convert between hexadecimal, decimal, octal, and binary values. By default, the decimal number system is selected. To convert a value from decimal to binary, simply enter the value and then select the binary (Bin) radio button. For example, the decimal value for the IP address of the Microsoft web site, 207.46.245.156, converts to 11001111 00101110 11110101 10011100 in binary. Use the Windows calculator to convert the following IP addresses into their binary values.

✔ **Hint**

For accurate results, convert each decimal value one at a time rather than entering the entire string of IP address digits all at once. Note also that smaller decimal values will generate fewer than eight digits when converted to binary. This is simply the Windows calculator leaving off the leading zeroes of the binary octet. When this happens, simply "pad" the binary value with enough leading zeroes to bring the total number of digits to eight. For example, the decimal value 46, converted to binary in the Windows calculator, displays a six-digit binary value of 101110. To bring this value "up to code," add two zeroes at the beginning for a result of 00101110.

IP Address	Binary Format
a) 134.105.23.5	_____
b) 185.34.67.223	_____
c) 34.68.13.216	_____
d) 235.236.12.24	_____
e) 253.17.88.33	_____

Step 3   Now close the Windows calculator and use the chart below to convert the following IP addresses into binary values the "old-fashioned" way.

128	64	32	16	8	4	2	1
___	___	___	___	___	___	___	___

✔ **Hint**

Each digit in the table represents a value of 1 (or "on") in a binary octet. To convert a decimal value to binary using this table, start with 128 and work your way to the right, marking a 1 in each position where your decimal value "fits," and subtracting that value from the decimal total, then move to the next, and the next until you arrive at 0. For example, take the decimal value 155 and match it to the chart. Can 128 fit into 155? Yes, so mark a 1 in that position. That leaves 27. Can 64 fit into 27? It can't, so mark a 0 in that position. Same for 32. 16 fits into 27, so mark a 1 in that position. This leaves 11. 8 fits into 11, so mark a 1 in that position. You now have 3 left. The 4 position gets a 0 since it's too large to fit into 3. Now you see that it's a simple matter to distribute the remaining 3 between the final positions, 2 and 1.

128	64	32	16	8	4	2	1
1	0	0	1	1	0	1	1

IP Address	Binary Format
a) 207.198.48.6	_____
b) 18.247.78.156	_____
c) 245.217.9.109	_____
d) 110.190.200.254	_____
e) 63.251.83.54	_____

Step 4 Your client wants you to explain the different IP address classes. In the following table, fill in the appropriate IP address ranges for each IP address class.

IP Address Class	Beginning IP Address	Ending IP Address	Private IP Address
Class A	_____	_____	_____
Class B	_____	_____	_____
Class C	_____	_____	_____
Class D	_____	_____	_____
Class E	_____	_____	_____

Step 5 The IP address classes skip the entire 127.x.x.x range. Open a command-line window and type **ping 127.0.0.1**. What are the results?

_____

_____

Step 6 Before closing the command-line window, type **ipconfig**. What is your PC's IP address? What IP address class is it?

_____

Step 7 The previous consultant's notes include references to IPv6. How does IPv6 differ from IPv4? Give an example of an IPv6 IP address.

_____

_____

Step 8 What is the motivation behind the development of IPv6?

_____

_____

 45 MINUTES

Lab Exercise 11.02: Configuring Subnet Masks

When it comes to IP addressing, the IP address is only half the story. The other component is the subnet mask. Network hosts need both an IP address and a matching subnet mask in order to communicate on a network.

Subnet masks conform to standard configurations for each IP address class, but network techs can also use custom configurations that bend (or even break) the rules. Depending on your particular TCP/IP network needs, subnet mask configuration can be simplicity itself or a headache-inducing chore. Whatever the case, the more you know about subnet masks, the easier your task will be. Let's look at how to configure subnet masks.

Learning Objectives

In this lab, you will configure subnet masks for IP addresses. By its end, you will be able to:

- Recognize default IP address class subnet masks
- Identify network and host IDs
- Define a custom subnet mask

Lab Materials and Setup

The materials you need for this lab are

- Pencil and paper
- Calculator with scientific view

Getting Down to Business

Your client now wants you to explain whether or not it's possible to divide the company's TCP/IP network into several administrative units.

Step 1 Define the function of an IP address's subnet mask.

_____

_____

Step 2 In the following table, fill in the appropriate default subnet mask for each IP address class:

IP Address Class	Default Subnet Mask
Class A	_____
Class B	_____
Class C	_____

Step 3 Based on the default subnet masks for the preceding classes, identify the network and host IDs for the following IP address examples:

IP Address	Network ID	Host ID
131.194.192.3	_____	_____
45.200.49.201	_____	_____
194.39.110.183	_____	_____
208.154.191.9	_____	_____
126.9.54.172	_____	_____

Step 4 Explain what is meant by using a slash notation (for example, /24) following an IP address. For example, what does the value 201.23.45.123/24 represent?

_____

_____

Step 5 What is the motivation behind using a custom subnet mask versus a default subnet mask?

_____

_____

Step 6 Your client acquires a class B static IP address of 165.1.0.0. How many hosts can your TCP/IP network support using the default subnet mask?

_____

_____

✔ **Hint**

To determine the number of subnets that an IP address can be chopped up into, first convert the subnet mask into binary. Then separate the network portion from the host portion. Count the number of bits in the network portion of the address that are set to the 1 ("on") position. Finally, use the formula $2^x - 2$ to determine the number of subnets supported. A class C network using the default subnet mask of 255.255.255.000, for example, converts to 11111111 11111111 11111111 00000000 in binary. Separate the network portion (11111111 11111111 11111111) from the host portion (00000000). Note that there are no bits set to 1 in the host portion of the address, so using the formula $2^0 - 2$, you get −1, thus the network cannot be subdivided into more subnets using the default subnet mask. To determine the number of hosts supported by a subnet, convert the 32-bit subnet value to binary, and separate the network portion from the host portion. Count the number of bits in the 0 ("off") position in the host portion of the subnet mask. Then use the formula $2^x - 2$, with x being the number of bits. Using the default class C subnet mask example previously shown, note that there are 8 bits in the 0 position in the host portion, so $2^8 - 2 = 254$ possible hosts.

Step 7   Your client company wants to subdivide the network into at least four subnets to accommodate the different departments that will share the network. Now you need to configure the subnet mask to accommodate the request. How many bits of the host portion of the subnet mask do you need to "borrow"? What will the resultant subnet mask be in decimal value? How many hosts will each subnet support?

✔ **Hint**

To determine the decimal value of the subnet mask, add together the numeric value of each borrowed binary bit. For example, assume you're using a class C IP address with a default subnet mask of 255.255.255.0. If the first four bits of the host portion of the subnet mask are borrowed to create more network subnets, add 128 + 64 + 32 + 16 for a decimal value of 240. Append the default subnet mask with this value (that is, 255.255.255.240).

Step 8   Fill in the following chart with appropriate values for each subnet mask:

Decimal Value of Subnet Mask Host Portion with:	# Subnets	# Class A Hosts	# Class B Hosts	# Class C Hosts
No bits borrowed	_____	_____	_____	_____
One bit borrowed	_____	_____	_____	_____
Two bits borrowed	_____	_____	_____	_____
Three bits borrowed	_____	_____	_____	_____
Four bits borrowed	_____	_____	_____	_____
Five bits borrowed	_____	_____	_____	_____
Six bits borrowed	_____	_____	_____	_____
Seven bits borrowed	_____	_____	_____	_____
Eight bits borrowed	_____	_____	_____	_____

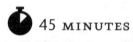 45 MINUTES

Lab Exercise 11.03: Local vs. Remote TCP/IP Addresses: The Function of the Default Gateway

Wise network techs, after plowing through the bits and pieces of configuring subnet masks, inevitably ask themselves, "Why am I doing this again?" It's a valid question, because when your brain is over-heating from thinking in terms of *some number to the power of some other number minus yet another number*, it's easy to lose sight of the real purpose behind all of these mathematical gymnastics. The answer is deceptively simple: to distinguish between local and remote network addresses!

That's right. The whole point of all the previous ciphering and decimal-to-binary flip-flopping is to tell the network host how to distinguish between data packets meant for the LAN and those meant to go beyond the LAN. In the following exercises, you'll review how a network host uses the IP address and subnet mask to determine if a data packet is meant for the local or remote network, and how data packets that are meant for remote networks get there.

Learning Objectives

In this lab, you will review how network hosts distinguish between local and remote addresses, and the function of the default gateway. By the end of this lab, you will be able to:

- Describe how a network host distinguishes between local and remote addresses

- Describe the function of a default gateway

Lab Materials and Setup

The materials you will need for this lab are

- Pencil and paper

- Calculator with scientific view

Getting Down to Business

Your client contact asks you to explain how computers on one network segment know whether data is for them or for a different network segment. He also wants to know how computers on different networks send data to each other.

Step 1 Describe the process that a network host uses to determine whether a data packet is local or remote. Provide an example using the following IP addresses:

- Host IP address 188.254.200.13, subnet mask 255.255.240.0

- Data packet destination IP address 188.254.157.9

✔ **Hint**

You must first convert the IP addresses and subnet mask to their binary values. 1 AND 1 = 1. Any other ANDed binary combinations = 0.

_____

_____

Step 2 Compare the following IP addresses and determine whether they are local or remote:

Host IP Address	Host Subnet Mask	Destination IP Address	Local or Remote?
a) 210.145.149.123	255.255.255.0	210.145.253.199	_____
b) 192.168.4.189	255.255.255.224	192.168.1.107	_____

Host IP Address	Host Subnet Mask	Destination IP Address	Local or Remote?
c) 10.154.187.89	255.192.0.0	10.152.179.88	_____
d) 132.100.45.5	255.255.252.0	132.100.45.45	_____
e) 151.251.100.101	255.255.0.0	166.200.110.10	_____

✔ Hint

A good online subnet calculator is available at www.subnetonline.com/subcalc/subnet1.html.

Step 3 When a network host determines that a data packet is intended for a remote network, what does it do with the packet?

_____

_____

Step 4 Name two ways that a network host determines the IP address of its default gateway.

_____

_____

Step 5 What is the function of the default gateway?

_____

_____

Step 6 Open a command-line window by choosing Start | Run and typing **cmd**. At the command prompt, type **ipconfig**. What is the IP address of your PC's default gateway?

_____

_____

 30 MINUTES

Lab Exercise 11.04: TCP/IP Advanced Network Service Settings: DNS, WINS, DHCP

One of the reasons that TCP/IP is so widely adopted is that it's extremely flexible. Not only does the TCP/IP protocol suite work on any number of computer platforms and applications, it also interfaces with a variety of advanced network services. These include naming services like the Domain Name Service (DNS), Windows Internet Naming Service (WINS), and the Dynamic Host Configuration Protocol (DHCP) IP addressing service.

Each of these services provides valuable functions that make your job as a network tech easier. Let's look at what these services do, and how you configure your TCP/IP network host to use them.

Learning Objectives

In this lab, you will define the DNS, WINS, and DHCP network services and review how to configure a TCP/IP host to use them. By the end of this lab, you will be able to:

- Describe the functions of the DNS, WINS, and DHCP advanced network services

- Configure a PC to use DNS, WINS, and DHCP

Lab Materials and Setup

The materials you will need for this lab are

- Pencil and paper

- PC running Windows XP Home or Professional Edition

Getting Down to Business

Your client's previous network consultant left a proposal that calls for configuring each networked PC's network configuration manually. Your client contact wants you to explain the function of the different services listed in the PC's configuration specifications. He's also concerned that this manual configuration will take up too much effort, and wants you to provide options for making configuration changes automatically.

Step 1   Describe the function of the DNS service on a TCP/IP network.

Step 2   Local PCs cache any addresses resolved by DNS on the hard disk. To view a display of resolved addresses cached on your PC, open a command-line window by choosing Start | Run and typing **cmd.** Then type **ipconfig /displaydns.** What are the results?

_____

_____

Step 3   Describe the function of the WINS service on a TCP/IP network.

_____

_____

Step 4   Local PCs cache any addresses resolved by WINS on the hard disk. To view a display of resolved addresses cached on your PC, type **nbtstat –c** at the command-line window. What are the results?

_____

_____

Step 5   Describe the function of the DHCP service on a TCP/IP network.

_____

_____

Step 6   To view your PC's TCP/IP configuration, including advanced settings such as the DNS, WINS, or DHCP servers, type **ipconfig /all** at the command-line window. What are the results?

_____

_____

Step 7   Network techs sometimes must manually refresh a network host's DHCP lease, such as when a major change has been made to the network's configuration. To release and renew a network host's DHCP lease manually, you must execute two commands. First, type **ipconfig /release** at the command prompt. What are the results?

_____

_____

Step 8 Now type **ipconfig /renew** at the command prompt. What are the results?

_____

_____

Step 9 To change your PC's TCP/IP configuration, click the Start button and select My Network Places. Then click the View Network Connection link. Double-click the Local Area Connection icon that you want to configure to open its Status dialog box. Then, on the General property sheet tab, click the Properties button. Highlight Internet Protocol (TCP/IP), and click the Properties button. This opens the Internet Protocol (TCP/IP) Properties dialog box shown in Figure 11-2.

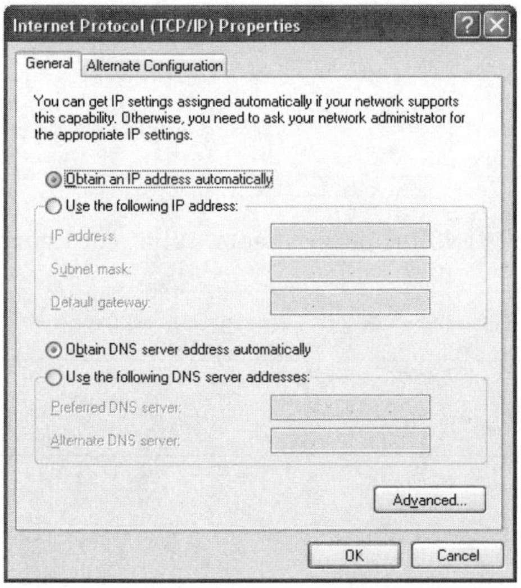

FIGURE 11-2 The TCP/IP Properties dialog box

Describe your current TCP/IP configuration settings and options.

_____

_____

Step 10 In the Internet Protocol (TCP/IP) Properties dialog box, click the Advanced button to open the Advanced TCP/IP Settings dialog box, as shown in Figure 11-3.

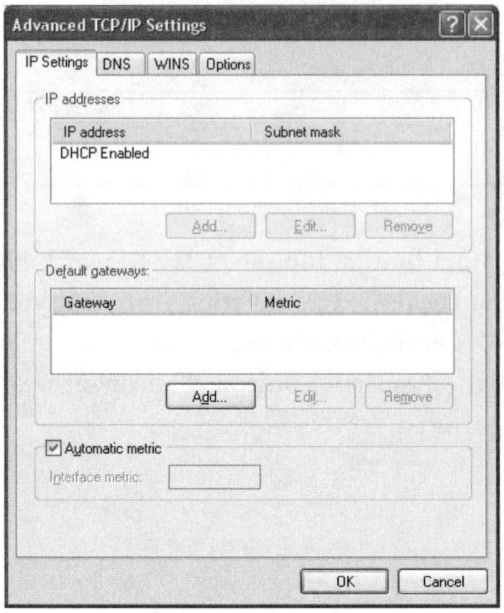

FIGURE 11-3 The Advanced TCP/IP Settings dialog box

Take a few minutes to examine the IP Settings, DNS, and WINS property sheets. What configuration options do they offer?

_____

_____

⏱ 20 MINUTES

Lab Exercise 11.05: TCP/IP Port Associations

By this point, you should appreciate the complexity of TCP/IP's many network functions. To the unini-tiated, it might seem like these many capabilities could spill over into one another, but TCP/IP does a great job of keeping its different functions separate. It does this by using port associations.

Learning Objectives

In this lab, you will define the function of TCP/IP port associations and review the common port num-ber assignments. You'll also download and use Microsoft's PORTQRY command-line utility to determine your PC's current port status. By the end of this lab, you will be able to:

• Define the function of TCP/IP port associations

- Describe common port number assignments

- Scan your PC to determine its current port status

Lab Materials and Setup

The materials you will need for this lab are

- Pencil and paper

- PC running Windows XP Home or Professional Edition

- Internet access

Getting Down to Business

Your client has read a bit about different ports being used on networked computers, and wants you to explain what these ports are and how they work.

Step 1   Describe the function of a TCP/IP port.

_____

_____

Step 2   Match the following port numbers to the appropriate protocols.

Port 20	Port 21	Port 23	Port 25	Port 69	Port 80
Port 110	Port 137	Port 138	Port 139	Port 161	

→ Note

Some protocols use more than one port number.

Protocol	Port
SMTP	_____
TFTP	_____
FTP	_____
HTTP	_____
POP3	_____
NNTP	_____
HTTPS	_____
NetBIOS	_____

✔ **Hint**

Windows lists all of the well-known protocol services and ports that are associated with them in a document called SERVICES. Access this list in Windows XP by opening Notepad (Start | All Programs | Accessories | Notepad) and navigating to \WINDOWS\SYSTEM32\DRIVERS\ETC. Other network operating systems maintain an equivalent document of port-to-service mappings. Linux, for example, also uses a file called SERVICES located in the /etc directory.

Step 3 The SERVICES file is a static list of well-known ports on a Windows PC. To determine active port status, Microsoft provides the PORTQRY command-line port scanner utility to help you troubleshoot TCP/IP port issues on local and remote PCs. Visit Microsoft's download center web site at http://www.microsoft.com/downloads/details.aspx?familyid=89811747-C74B-4638-A2D5-AC828BDC6983&display-lang=en, and then download and install the utility. PORTQRY has many functions and can display detailed port status information, but just to get a feel for the function of the utility, select Start | Run and then type **portqry –local**. What are the results?

→ **Note**

Companies change their web sites periodically, and Microsoft is no exception. If the link above does not work, simply go to www.microsoft.com and search for PORTQRY. You should have no trouble finding the correct download.

Lab Analysis

1. Explain the main operational difference between TCP and UDP. How does this difference affect which services use TCP or UDP?

---

2. Describe the function of private IP addresses, and list the private IP address ranges for Class A, B, and C TCP/IP networks.

_____

_____

3. Explain how using DHCP simplifies client administration for network techs.

_____

_____

4. For what purpose is the 127.x.x.x IP address range reserved?

_____

_____

5. What is the purpose of a subnet mask?

_____

_____

Key Terms Quiz

Use the vocabulary terms from the list below to complete the sentences that follow. Not all of the terms will be used.

Address Resolution Protocol (ARP)

Classful subnet

CIDR

Default gateway

Domain Name Service (DNS)

Dynamic Host Configuration Protocol (DHCP)

File Transfer Protocol (FTP)

Fully Qualified Domain Name (FQDN)

Host ID

HyperText Transport Protocol (HTTP)

Internet Assigned Numbers Authority (IANA)

Internet Protocol version 4 (IPv4)

Internet Protocol version 6 (IPv6)

IPCONFIG

Name resolution

NetBIOS

Network ID

Post Office Protocol v3 (POP3)

Simple Mail Transfer Protocol (SMTP)

Simple Network Management Protocol (SNMP)

Subnet mask

Telnet

Transmission Control Protocol (TCP)

Trivial File Transfer Protocol (TFTP)

User Datagram Protocol (UDP)

Windows Internet Naming Service (WINS)

WINIPCFG

1. Many network hardware devices such as routers are managed via a network connection using
   _____.

2. _____ resolves NetBIOS names into IP addresses.

3. To determine the IP address, subnet mask, and default gateway on a Windows NT/2000/XP
   PC, type _____ at a command prompt; on a Windows 9x PC, type
   _____.

4. The _____ is the IP address of a router that passes data packets outside of
   your LAN.

5. FEDC:BA98:7654:3210:0800:200C:00CF:1234 is an example of an _____
   address.

Chapter 12
Network Operating Systems

Lab Exercises

You're familiar with the computer operating system (OS), and have a good grasp of what the OS does on your PC. The OS is what makes a personal computer personal. It gives you an interface to the various PC functions and applications that make the business world go around. Any modern OS has networking functionality built in, and can act as a network server (a system that shares its own network resources) as well as a network client (a system that uses resources shared on another system). You've also had exposure to special versions of the OS that are designed to run network services—the appropriately named network operating system (NOS).

Network operating systems come in a number of different flavors and pack different features, but they all perform the same tasks for any network. That is, they enable users to access shared resources—files and folders, printers, Internet connections, and so on—while enabling network techs to control levels of access to these resources, and even control access to the network itself.

In this chapter, you'll explore the key differences between a run-of-the-mill desktop OS and the more muscular and feature-packed NOS. First, we'll take an overview of the basics of NOS functions and models, then we'll look at major network operating systems that are available. Finally, we'll finish with a discussion of network configuration essentials. Let's get started.

 30 MINUTES

Lab Exercise 12.01: Defining the Role of the Network Operating System

In the modern networking world, all operating systems can be considered network operating systems. That is, the essential components for networking functionality—the client services, protocols, hardware driver support, and so on—are all built right into the NOS. At the same time, a good network tech must appreciate a number of differences between the client-class and server-class network operating systems.

In this exercise, you'll explore the special qualities that distinguish the different versions of network operating systems. You'll review the functions—called *roles* or *models*—that network servers fulfill on a network. You'll also review the types of network organizational structures and compare the advantages of each. Finally, you'll define the all-important service that enables large networks to operate efficiently—the *directory service*.

Learning Objectives

In this lab, you will examine the basic characteristics of network operating systems and network organizational structures. By its end, you will be able to:

- Define characteristics of the major network operating systems

- Define resource-based, server-based, and organization-based network models

- Define a directory service

Lab Materials and Setup

The only materials you'll need for this lab are a pencil and some paper.

Getting Down to Business

Your client, Dr. Peter Simione, has formed a partnership with a medical practice in an adjoining office suite. The two practices are planning on merging their respective networks into a single organizational unit. Dr. Simione's practice uses Apple Macintosh computer systems in a peer-to-peer network. The Macs run OS X 10.2 and use TCP/IP. The adjoining practice, Howard, Fine, & Howard Psychiatric Services, uses Windows 9x, 2000, and XP client PCs connected to two file servers running version 3.12 of Novell NetWare. This version of NetWare only supports the IPX/SPX protocol, not TCP/IP. The PCs use IPX/SPX and the Microsoft Client Services for NetWare to communicate with the NetWare servers, and TCP/IP to connect to the Internet.

Your client is willing to invest in new computer equipment if necessary. Considering this, his goals are as follows:

- Integrate all PCs into a single network structure using the TCP/IP protocol.

- Be able to support Windows and Macintosh network clients.

- Enable centralized administrative control over shared resources.

- The new network structure must be secure, reliable, easily expandable, and easy for the doctors to manage by themselves given their limited experience with the Windows, Macintosh, and NetWare network operating systems.

- Network users should only have to remember one password to access resources anywhere on the network.

Given these goals, your client wants you to explain how the various network operating systems work, and the different network structure options that are available.

Step 1   Describe how a server-class network operating system differs from a client-class NOS. Describe how these types of operating systems differ in hardware support. Which vendors offer both client and server versions of their network operating systems, and which ones are server-class only?

_____

_____

Step 2   Describe a resource-based, peer-to-peer network, listing at least two advantages and disadvantages to this type of network model.

_____

_____

Step 3   Describe a server-based, client/server network, listing at least two advantages and disadvantages to this type of network model.

_____

_____

Step 4   Describe an organization-based, directory service network, listing at least two advantages and disadvantages to this type of network model.

_____

_____

Step 5   In an organization-based network, how do all of the servers maintain consistent copies of user and computer accounts, as well as their resource data?

_____

_____

Step 6   Which NOS and network structure options can you recommend for your client?

_____

_____

 60 MINUTES

Lab Exercise 12.02: Recognizing the Major Network Operating Systems

The desktop OS market is undoubtedly dominated by Microsoft Windows, but the NOS market is a far different story. While it's true that Microsoft Windows Server edition is one of the major players in the field, it has yet to dominate other established products such as Novell NetWare, UNIX/Linux, and even Apple's Macintosh OS X Server.

As a network tech, you'll be expected to switch gears among the various NOS incarnations with relative ease. Let's take a quick review of the main selling points of these network operating systems.

Learning Objectives

In this lab, you will explain the specifications of the major network operating systems. By its end, you will be able to:

- Describe the main features of the Microsoft Windows NOS
- Describe the main features of the Novell NetWare NOS
- Describe the main features of the UNIX/Linux NOS
- Describe the main features of the Apple Macintosh OS X NOS
- Describe typical roles of each main NOS

Lab Materials and Setup

The materials you will need for this lab are

- Pencil and paper
- PC with Internet connectivity

Getting Down to Business

Your client now wants to discuss specifics concerning the major network operating systems so that he can make an informed decision on a server software purchase.

Step 1 Describe the major differences between the current client-class and server-class versions of Windows.

Step 2   Your client is considering purchasing one of the many Server editions of Microsoft Windows, but is unclear on how their features compare. Fill in the following chart with appropriate specifications for these server-class editions of Windows:

Version	Maximum CPUs	Maximum RAM	Clustering	Compatibility	Directory Service	Network Services*
Windows 2000 Server						
Windows 2000 Advanced Server						
Windows 2000 Datacenter Server						
Windows Server 2003 Standard						
Windows Server 2003 Enterprise Edition						
Windows Server 2003 Datacenter Edition						

*For example, DNS, DHCP, RAS, Terminal Services, Web services, VPN

✔ Hint

To compare the features of Windows 2000 Server, go to http://www.microsoft.com/windows2000/serverfamily/default.asp. To compare the features of Windows Server 2003, go to http://www.microsoft.com/windowsserver2003/evaluation/features/compareeditions.mspx.

Step 3   Describe at least three typical roles for Windows Server systems on a network.

_____

_____

Step 4   Your client is somewhat familiar with Novell NetWare, having used that NOS at a previous office site. He would like you to explain how the current version of NetWare compares to current versions of Microsoft Windows Server. Fill in the following chart with the appropriate specifications for Novell NetWare 6.5.

Version	Maximum CPUs	Maximum RAM	Clustering	Compatibility	Directory Service	Network Services*
Novell NetWare 6.5						

*For example, DNS, DHCP, RAS, Terminal Services, Web services, VPN

✔ **Hint**

To discover the features of Novell NetWare 6.5, go to http://www.novell.com/products/netware/whitepapers.html and click the link called NetWare 6.5 vs. Win2003.

Step 5   Describe at least three typical roles for NetWare server systems on a network.

_____

_____

Step 6   Your client has heard about UNIX and Linux, and would like information concerning these network operating systems. Because there are so many versions of UNIX and Linux on the market, you decide to use the popular IBM AIX UNIX and SuSE Linux as examples. Fill in the following chart with the appropriate specifications for IBM AIX UNIX:

Version	Maximum CPUs	Maximum RAM	Clustering	Compatibility	Directory Service	Network Services*
IBM AIX UNIX 5L						

*For example, DNS, DHCP, RAS, Terminal Services, Web services, VPN

✔ **Hint**

To discover common hardware features of IBM AIX UNIX, go to http://www.ibm.com/servers/eserver/pseries.

Fill in the following chart with the appropriate specifications for SuSE Linux:

Version	Maximum CPUs	Maximum RAM	Clustering	Compatibility	Directory Service	Network Services*
SuSE Linux Standard Server 8						
SuSE Linux Enterprise Server 8						

*For example, DNS, DHCP, RAS, Terminal Services, Web services, VPN

✔ **Hint**

To compare common features of the popular SuSE Linux versions, go to http://www.suse.com/
en/business/products/server/which_version/index.html.

Step 7   Describe at least three typical roles of UNIX and Linux servers on a network.

_____

_____

Step 8   Fill in the following chart with the appropriate specifications for Apple Macintosh OS X Server
running on the Apple Xserve G5 hardware platform:

Version	Maximum CPUs	Maximum RAM	Clustering	Compatibility	Directory Service	Network Services*
OS X Server (on Xserve G5 hardware platform)						

*For example, DNS, DHCP, RAS, Terminal Services, Web services, VPN

✔ **Hint**

To discover common features of the Apple Macintosh OS X Server, go to http://www.apple.com/
server/macosx/specs.html.

Step 9   Describe at least three typical roles of Apple Macintosh OS X Server.

_____

_____

Step 10   Given your client's networking goals, what server-class NOS implementation options are the
most suitable?

_____

_____

 30 MINUTES

Lab Exercise 12.03: Examining Common Network Operating System Functions

Despite their differing heritages, all network operating systems provide similar services. Different network operating systems also have similar requirements and planning considerations when it comes to successfully connecting network clients to those network services. These include network client and protocol requirements, naming contexts, organizational structures, and security considerations.

Learning Objectives

In this lab, you will review common network functions, such as authentication and naming requirements. By the end of the lab, you will be able to:

- Describe network client authentication and protocol requirements

- Describe network naming contexts and organizational structures

- Describe security considerations, such as password requirements and proper security of the Administrator account

Lab Materials and Setup

The only materials you'll need for this lab are a pencil and some paper.

Getting Down to Business

Your client wants you to make recommendations concerning security requirements and his network's organization.

Step 1   Client Services for NetWare (CSNW) and Gateway Services for NetWare (GSNW) are two different approaches to achieving interoperability between Microsoft Windows network clients and Novell NetWare servers using IPX/SPX. Explain how the two approaches differ.

_____

_____

Step 2   To locate resources on a network, network hosts must use a common naming scheme, called a *context*. Explain the differences between the NetBIOS and DNS naming contexts.

_____

_____

Step 3   Explain the difference between logging onto a client workstation with a local user account and logging onto a client workstation with a domain user account. Where is user authentication taking place?

_____

_____

Step 4   Local workstations and domains both have user accounts designated as the administrator. Explain the function of the Administrator account. Who should have access to this account? How should you secure the Administrator account?

_____

_____

Step 5   Regardless of which NOS the network uses, all user accounts should be configured with strong passwords. Examine the following user account passwords and determine whether they can be considered strong or weak passwords. Provide reasons why they are strong or weak.

Username	Account Name	Password	Strong or Weak?	Explanation
Connor Simione	Csimione	connor	_____	_____
Julia Corbett Simione	JuliaCS	JCorbettS1531	_____	_____
Anne Acuña	Aacuna	Acuña6063	_____	_____
Isabella Acuña	IsabellaA	swordprincess	_____	_____
Robin McElfresh	RobinMcE	Rockin'Robin123	_____	_____
Bob Lange	DrBob	IwishIwasaCam-u-el	_____	_____
Jennifer DeBerry	Jenny	867-5309	_____	_____
Sandra Santos	Ssantos	sandysaint	_____	_____
Tomas Esquivel	TomasE	BtB!Cwfi?	_____	_____
Elissa Robinson	Elissa	ERobinson	_____	_____

✔ **Hint**

For the purposes of this exercise, strong passwords are those that have at least three of the following qualities: a mixture of uppercase and lowercase characters, the inclusion of nonstandard characters, a mixture of letters and numbers, a length of at least eight characters, and avoidance of items that are easy to guess based on the user or user account name (for example, the user's name, initials, or birth date).

Step 6   What is the difference between a local user profile and a roaming, server-based user profile? What is the advantage of using server-based user profiles?

_____

_____

Lab Analysis

1. Describe the function of a directory service, such as Novell NDS or Microsoft AD.

    _____

    _____

2. Linux has a reputation for being powerful, stable, and secure. What is another motivation for adopting Linux server technology? Conversely, what is a major argument against adopting Linux on the server side?

    _____

    _____

3. Explain the difference between a Windows NT 4.0 domain's primary domain controller (PDC) and backup domain controller (BDC). How do their respective copies of the Security Account Manager (SAM) database differ? What happens if the domain's PDC fails?

    _____

    _____

4. How should you instruct your network users to respond to someone who might request their user account password?

    _____

    _____

5. What is the most significant way that the Novell NetWare OS differs from either Microsoft Windows or Linux server-class versions?

    _____

    _____

Key Terms Quiz

Use the vocabulary terms from the list below to complete the sentences that follow. Not all of the terms will be used.

Administrator	Password
Client/server	Peer-to-peer
Domain users and groups	Protocol
Groups	Replication
Linux	Resource-based network operating system
Local users and groups	Security
Mac OS	Server-based network operating system
Models	Super user account
Network interface	UNIX
Network operating system (NOS)	User account
Network-based network operating system	User profile
Novell NetWare	Workstation

1. Microsoft Windows domains using Active Directory use a process called _____ to ensure the synchronization of account and resource data between domain controllers.

2. A _____ is a collection of settings linked to a particular user account. These settings include the Windows desktop configuration, Internet Explorer favorites, home folders, and so on.

3. The two main network and NOS categories are _____ and _____.

4. Although not popular in the desktop OS market, the open-source _____ NOS is very popular in the server market due to its stability, security, and low cost.

5. Every NOS has a built-in user account that has full control over every aspect of the OS. The default name for this account in Microsoft Windows is _____.

Chapter 13

Managing Network Resources

Lab Exercises

Sharing resources and accessing those shared resources pretty much defines the reason for the existence of networks. What's a resource in this context? Network-accessible resources in the most basic sense are folders and printers. John shares his c:\workfiles folder on the network so his coworkers can access the contents of that folder. That's great, right? Here's the part that matters. *Managing* shared resources—setting up servers and clients, and controlling access to shared resources—provides network techs with a paycheck.

In this chapter, you'll go over the steps for naming shared resources and securing resources with NTFS permissions. You'll also review how to share resources on a network, and access shared resources, using the Windows graphical user interface and the command line. Let's get started.

 30 MINUTES

Lab Exercise 13.01: Resource Naming Conventions

Like network hosts—workstation PCs and servers—shared resources have to have a unique name to identify them on the network. Not surprisingly, these network names must follow certain rules, or *conventions*, to be usable. Modern network operating systems are very flexible when it comes to naming conventions and can use one or more conventions, often at the same time. Most PCs use NetBIOS, the naming convention employed by all versions of Windows, and DNS, the naming convention used for the Internet. This lab looks at how naming works using NetBIOS, network share, and DNS naming conventions, and discusses the usage of the Universal Naming Convention (UNC) and Universal Resource Locater (URL) naming conventions.

Learning Objectives

In this lab, you will demonstrate proper NetBIOS, network share, and DNS naming conventions, UNC network paths, and URL Internet/intranet addresses. By its end, you'll be able to:

- Explain and demonstrate NetBIOS, network share, and DNS naming conventions
- Explain and demonstrate UNC and URL paths

Lab Materials and Setup

The only materials needed for this lab are a pencil and some paper.

Getting Down to Business

Your client wants to expand her network of Windows 98 SE and Windows 2000 PCs to include several Windows XP PCs. The project manager also insists that the network shares should use a consistent naming scheme throughout the organization. The project manager has some ideas for a naming scheme, listed in the following table. It's up to you to apply the proper network share naming rules to determine which naming scheme will work.

Step 1   The project manager has designated two of the Windows XP computers as graphics workstations, and wants to name one "Photoshop Workstation" and the other "Illustrator Workstation." Both will have folders filled with images that must be accessible over the network to all the other PCs. What would you suggest as far as the NetBIOS names go to ensure interoperability with the other PCs?

_____

_____

Step 2   The following table lists a number of folders to be shared on your client's network, along with the names the project manager wants to use as their network share names. Which share names are valid, and which are invalid? How can you change the invalid names to make them valid so that you and the project manager can work for a standardized naming scheme throughout the client's network?

Resource Name	Proposed Share Name	Valid or Invalid?	Explanation
Cindy's Pics	CindyPics	_____	_____
Development Database	Development_Database	_____	_____
Shared Documents	Shared Docs	_____	_____
Music on Richelieu	Richelieu-sic	_____	_____
Hunter and Gatherer Database	h/g_dbase	_____	_____

Step 3   Explain the DNS naming guidelines. How many characters are allowed? Which characters are permitted? How should you name systems and shared resources on the network to ensure compatibility among all versions of Windows?

_____

_____

Step 4 Your organization is planning the naming structure for its shared network resources. To demonstrate proper UNC formatting, write out the UNC path for each of the following network resources:

- Server Name = FileServer1, Share Name = Dev, Resource Name = Project1Schedule.mdb

  UNC Path = _____

- Server Name = MikesPC, Share Name = Pics, Resource Name = RenFest2004.ppt

  UNC Path = _____

- Server Name = Richelieu, Share Name = Shared Docs, Resource Name = OMH Template.dot

  UNC Path = _____

- Server Name = AnneMac, Share Name = AnneDocs, Resource Name = Isabella Pics

  UNC Path = _____

- Server Name = SquidDC1, Share Name = Logon, Resource Name = Desktop.bat

  UNC Path = _____

Step 5 Your organization is planning the naming structure for its corporate intranet web site. To demonstrate proper URL formatting, write out the URL path for each of the following network resources:

- Domain Name = GiantSquidOnline.com, Protocol = FTP, Share Name = Transfer, Resource Name = JuneSchd.xls

  URL Path = _____

- Domain Name = RobotMonkeyButler.net, Protocol = HTTP, Share Name = Recipes, Resource Name = Banana-ritas.htm

  URL Path = _____

- Domain Name = 360artservices.com, Protocol = HTTP, Share Name = Documents, Resource Name = Ratesheet.doc

  URL Path = _____

- Domain Name = JohnLeePhotos.com, Protocol = FTP, Share Name = Dropbox, Resource Name = 13-07.tif

  URL Path = _____

- Domain Name = LearnEsperanto.org, Protocol = HTTP, Share Name = Downloads, Resource Name = Lessons_Update.exe

  URL Path = _____

 40 MINUTES

Lab Exercise 13.02: Network Resource Security Permissions

In the networking world, there's a fine line between sharing and over-sharing. Yes, you want your users to be able to access the resources they need, but at the same time, you want to be able to keep them out of resources they don't. It's up to you, as the network tech, to be able to lock down access to resources on your network.

In this exercise, you'll review the network share and local resource (NTFS) permission levels, and go through the steps for configuring security at both the network share level and the local level.

Learning Objectives

In this lab, you will review and demonstrate network share and NTFS permission levels. By its end, you should be able to:

- Explain and demonstrate the configuration and function of security permissions at the network share level

- Explain and demonstrate the configuration and function of security permissions at the local resource (NTFS) level

Lab Materials and Setup

The materials you'll need for this lab are

- Pencil and paper

- Two networked PCs running Windows 2000 Professional or Windows XP Professional

Getting Down to Business

Your clients store sensitive data on their network, and are concerned about network security. They want you to explain and demonstrate how they can secure files and folders against both external and internal unauthorized access.

Step 1   In Windows XP Professional, *simple file sharing* is turned on by default. If you have not already done so, follow these steps to disable simple file sharing:

1. Open My Computer by choosing Start | My Computer.

2. On the menu bar, select Tools, and select Folder Options.

3. In the Folder Options dialog box, click the View property sheet tab.

4. In the Advanced settings section, scroll down until you see the *Use simple file sharing (Recommended)* option.

5. Clear the checkbox and click the OK button. What are the results?

✔ **Hint**

> If you followed the instructions from Chapter 2, Lab Exercise 2.04, your system should already be configured with simple file sharing disabled.

_____

_____

Step 2 Describe how network share-level and local resource-level permissions differ.

_____

_____

Step 3 In the following chart, list the actions permitted with each network share security level:

Action	Full Control (Y/N?)	Change (Y/N?)	Read (Y/N?)
Viewing file names and subfolder names	_____	_____	_____
Traverse to subfolders	_____	_____	_____
Viewing data in files and running programs	_____	_____	_____
Adding files and subfolders to the shared folder	_____	_____	_____
Changing data in files	_____	_____	_____
Deleting subfolders and files	_____	_____	_____
Changing share permissions	_____	_____	_____

Step 4 To view and configure a network resource's share permissions, open My Computer and locate the folder called Shared Documents. To view the configured network share settings and permissions on the resource, alternate-click the folder icon and select Properties from the pop-up menu. In the Shared

Documents Properties dialog box, click the Sharing tab. Is the resource currently shared on the network? What are the configured network share settings?

_____

_____

Step 5 In the following chart, list the actions permitted with each NTFS security level:

Action	Full Control (Y/N?)	Modify (Y/N?)	Read & Execute (Y/N?)	List Folder Contents (Y/N?)	Read (Y/N?)	Write (Y/N?)
Traverse to subfolders	_____	_____	_____	_____	_____	_____
List folder/ read data	_____	_____	_____	_____	_____	_____
Execute files	_____	_____	_____	_____	_____	_____
Read attributes	_____	_____	_____	_____	_____	_____
Create files/ write data	_____	_____	_____	_____	_____	_____
Create folders/ append data	_____	_____	_____	_____	_____	_____
Delete subfolders and files	_____	_____	_____	_____	_____	_____
Delete	_____	_____	_____	_____	_____	_____
Read permissions	_____	_____	_____	_____	_____	_____
Change permissions	_____	_____	_____	_____	_____	_____
Take ownership	_____	_____	_____	_____	_____	_____

Step 6 Now let's take a look at the local resource security settings configured for the Shared Documents folder. Alternate-click the folder and select Properties, then click the Security property sheet tab to view the NTFS settings, shown in Figure 13-1. List the groups and users that have access to the Shared Documents folder, along with their respective access permissions, in the following space.

_____

_____

FIGURE 13-1 Shared Documents folder NTFS settings

Step 7   Change the network share permissions for the Shared Documents folder so that the Everyone group is allowed the Read permission, and then click OK. To test this setting, perform these steps:

1.   Create a text document called TEST.TXT in the Shared Documents folder.

2.   Then you or your partner should navigate to the Shared Documents folder from a remote PC on the network. When asked for a user name and password, supply the name of a local user account (not the Administrator account).

3.   Access the folder and open the TEST.TXT text document. Enter a string of text into the document (any text will do), and attempt to save the changes. What are the results?

_____

_____

Step 8   Provide an explanation for the results of Step 7.

_____

_____

Step 9   Note that network share permissions are applied only when you access a folder or file through the network. At the local resource level, NTFS permissions are the only way to enforce security. To view local NTFS security restrictions in action, do the following:

1.   Return to the Properties dialog box for the Shared Documents folder and click the Security property sheet tab. In the *Group or user names* section, highlight the Everyone group and click the Remove button, then click the OK button to close the dialog box.

2.   Create a new user account by opening Control Panel and clicking the *Create a new account* link. Follow the prompts to create a new limited user (non-computer administrator) account.

3.   Now log off from your current Windows session and log on with the new user account. Open My Computer and navigate to the Shared Documents folder, then open the TEST.TXT document. Enter a string of text and attempt to save the document. What are the results?

_____

_____

Step 10   Provide an explanation for the results of Step 9.

_____

_____

 45 MINUTES

Lab Exercise 13.03: Sharing Resources on a Network

The actual process of sharing a folder, printer, or other resource on a network can require that you enter a string of convoluted text at the command prompt window, or it could be a simple matter of making a few well-aimed mouse clicks. As a Network+ certified network tech, you'll need to know both methods.

You'll also need to be able to determine quickly what resources a particular PC is sharing on the network, and which shares are currently in use. In this exercise, you'll look at how to make a local resource a shared resource, manage the level of sharing, and monitor access to the share.

Learning Objectives

In this lab, you will demonstrate how to share local resources on a network. By its end, you'll be able to:

- Explain and demonstrate the various methods that enable network techs to configure sharing of local resources on a Windows network

- Monitor remote network sessions to your shared local resources

Lab Materials and Setup

The only materials you'll need for this lab are two networked PCs running Windows 2000 Professional or Windows XP Professional.

Getting Down to Business

Now that you've explained how to name and secure network resources, your client wants you to demonstrate the network sharing process.

Step 1   You've already walked through the steps to make a local resource folder shared on the network, but did you know that you can share the same folder multiple times under different names, with different security permissions? Follow these steps to configure additional network shares on the Shared Documents folder:

1. Open the properties dialog box for the Shared Documents folder and click the Sharing property sheet tab.

2. Click the New Share button and enter a new network share name for the Shared Documents folder, such as Share and Enjoy, and then click the OK button.

3. Click the OK button to close the Shared Documents properties dialog box.

4. From a remote PC, use Windows Explorer to navigate to the local PC and view the list of shared resources. What are the results?

_____

_____

Step 2   As with most things in the Windows administrator's world, there's more than one way to share a resource. The text-based NET utility provides all of the functionality you need to create and configure network shares from a command-line window. Follow these steps to create a new network share for the Shared Documents folder from the command line:

1. Choose Start | Run and then type **cmd**.

2. Type **net share** to view the current network shares configured on the PC. What are the results?

_____

_____

Step 3 To create a new network share for the Shared Documents folder from the command line, type **net share "Share and Share Alike"="c:\documents and settings\all users\documents"**. What are the results?

✔ **Hint**

Don't forget to type the quotes!

_____

_____

➜ **Note**

To view the valid parameters for the NET SHARE command, type **net share ?**.

Step 4 The NET command provides a number of additional functions, including the ability to view current sessions established with network shares on the PC, disconnect sessions, and stop sharing of a network resource. To see these functions in action, you or your partner should access the local Shared Documents folder from a remote network PC to establish a session. Then type **net session** at the command prompt of the local PC. What are the results?

_____

_____

Step 5 Disconnect an established session by typing **net session \\computername /delete**. For example, to disconnect a session established by a computer named Martin, type **net session \\martin /delete**. If the specified PC has files open, you are asked whether or not you wish to continue the disconnect operation. Type **y** for yes and press ENTER. What are the results?

_____

_____

Step 6   The syntax to use the NET command to stop sharing a network resource is *net share sharename :*
drive:path /delete. For example, to stop sharing the Share and Share Alike network share for the Shared
Documents folder, type **net share "Share and Share Alike" : "c:\documents and settings\all**
users\documents" /delete. If users currently have open sessions with the network share, you are
informed that the operation will force the files to be closed, and asked whether you want to continue.
Type **y** for yes and press ENTER. What are the results?

Step 7   Back on the GUI side of things, the Windows Computer Management MMC enables network
techs to view, configure, and manage network shares in one fell swoop (and with a minimum of typing). Click the Start button and then alternate-click the My Computer icon and select Manage to open
the Computer Management console. Under System Tools, expand the Shared Folders icon and click the
Shares icon, as you can see in Figure 13-2. What are the results?

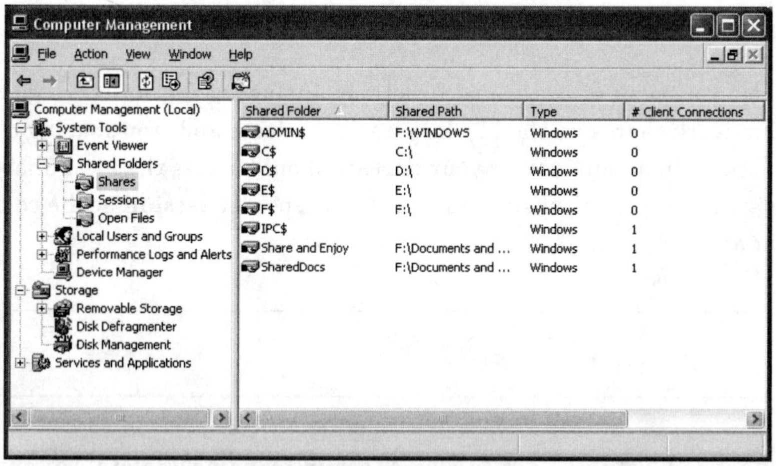

FIGURE 13-2 Computer Management MMC, Shared Folders node view

Step 8   To use the Computer Management MMC to create a new network share on the PC, alternate-
click the Shares icon and select New File Share from the pop-up menu. In the Create Shared Folder dialog box, shown in Figure 13-3, click the Browse button to navigate to the Shared Documents folder, and

then enter a new network share name (such as Share This!) and click the Next button. At the next screen, set the network share permission level and click Finish. What are the results?

_____

_____

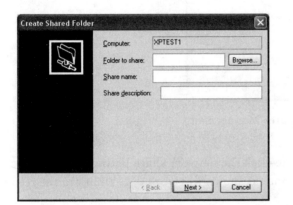

FIGURE 13-3 The Create Shared Folder dialog box

Step 9   To use Computer Management to view current network sessions on your PC, click the Sessions icon. What are the results? What files are currently being used in these sessions?

_____

_____

Step 10   To view the individual files being accessed in the network session, click the Open Files icon. What are the results?

_____

_____

Step 11   To use Computer Management to close a network session, alternate-click an established session and select Close Session from the pop-up menu, as shown in Figure 13-4. When asked to confirm the action, click the Yes button. What are the results?

_____

_____

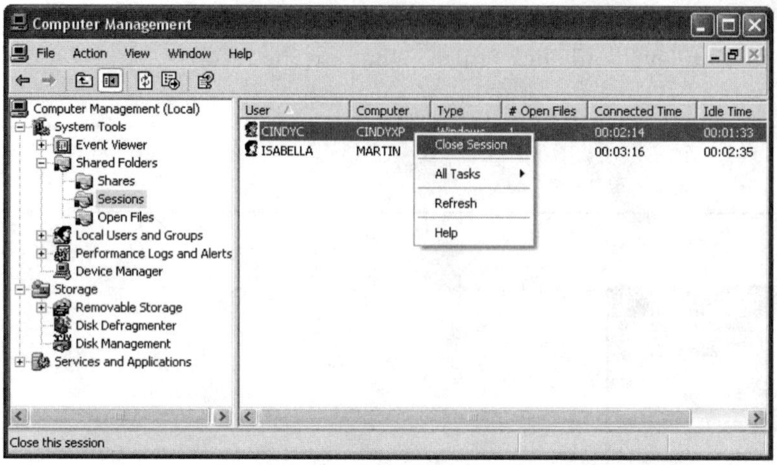

FIGURE 13-4 The Close Session command in Computer Management

Step 12   To stop sharing a network resource, alternate-click the network share listing in the Shares view and then select Stop Sharing from the pop-up menu, as shown in Figure 13-5. What are the results?

_____

_____

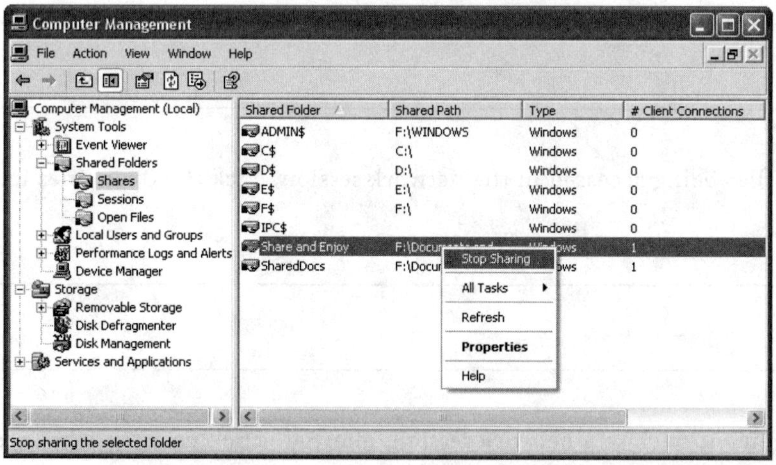

FIGURE 13-5 The Stop Sharing command in Computer Management

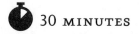 30 MINUTES

Lab Exercise 13.04: Accessing Shared Resources on a Network

Just as there's more than one way to share a resource, there are also myriad ways to access those shared resources over the network. The CompTIA Network+ exam expects you to be able to toggle between browsing to network shares via the Windows GUI and navigating to them through the command line. In this exercise, you'll look at the steps for getting from "here" to "there," regardless of the interface.

Learning Objectives

In this lab, you will demonstrate how to access network resources from the local PC. By its end, you'll be able to:

- Explain and demonstrate the various methods that enable network techs to view and access resources shared on a Windows network from a local PC

Lab Materials and Setup

The only materials you'll need for this lab are two networked PCs running Windows 2000 Professional or Windows XP Professional.

Getting Down to Business

Your client now wants you to demonstrate how to view and access shared resources on a network.

Step 1   The most user-friendly means of mapping network drives is using the Add Network Place wizard. To get to this tool, open My Computer and click the My Network Places link. At the next screen, under the Network Tasks menu, click the *Add a network place* link to start the Add Network Place Wizard, shown in Figure 13-6.

Follow these steps to map a network drive using this tool:

1. Click the Next button, and then select *Choose another network location* and click Next again.

2. At the next screen, either type in the URL of the network share you want to map to (for example, to map to the SharedDocs network share on the computer XPtest1, type **\\xptest1\shareddocs**), or click the Browse button and navigate to the shared folder; then click Next.

3. At the next screen, you can type a name for the new network mapping, or simply accept the default name.

FIGURE 13-6 The Add Network Place Wizard

4. Click Next again to review your settings, and then click Finish. What are the results?

_____

_____

Step 2 Windows also has a built-in tool that's a bit more businesslike for mapping network drives. To get to this tool, simply open either My Computer or My Network Places, click the Tools menu, and select Map Network Drive.

Follow these steps to create a new network mapping:

1. Select the local network drive letter you want to associate with the network resource mapping. By default, Windows XP automatically selects the last available drive letter (such as Z:) and works its way backwards for each additional mapping (in other words, drive Y: comes next, then X:, and so on).

2. Type in the UNC path to the network share, or click the Browse button and navigate to it that way.

3. To make this network mapping *persistent* so it's available every time you log on, make sure the *Reconnect at logon* checkbox is selected.

4. Optionally, to supply alternate credentials for this mapping, such as when mapping to a network drive that requires elevated security permissions, click the link labeled *Connect using a different user name* and enter the appropriate user name and password in the Connect As dialog box.

5. Click the Finish button. What are the results?

_____

_____

Step 3 The NET utility enables you to view shared network resources and configure network mappings the old-fashioned way. Open a command-line window and type **net view** at the prompt. What are the results?

_____

_____

➜ **Note**

To view the valid parameters for the NET VIEW command, type **net view ?**.

Step 4 To view a list of network resources available on a specific system, type **net view ***computername* at the command prompt. For example, to view a list of resources shared on a PC named XPtest1, type **net view \\xptest1**. What are the results?

_____

_____

Step 5 Now use the NET USE command to make a new local network mapping to an available network resource. First, open a command-line window and type **net use** at the prompt to view a list of network mappings configured on the PC. What are the results?

_____

_____

Step 6 Using the list of available network resources displayed from the NET VIEW command earlier, create a network mapping via NET USE by typing **net use** *devicename* *****computername******resourcename*. For example, to make a network mapping that uses the local drive X: to map to the shared resource Shared-Docs on a computer called XPtest1, type **net use x: \\xptest1\shareddocs**. Optionally, add the **/persist-**

ent:yes parameter to make the network mapping available every time you log on. Confirm that the network mapping was successful by typing **net use** without any parameters. What are the results?

_____

_____

_____

> → **Note**
>
> To view the valid parameters for the NET USE command, type **net use ?**.

Lab Analysis

1. An employee has left your company unexpectedly, and you have been asked to secure his Windows XP Professional computer system. You know that he had numerous shares created on his system, but you don't know specifically which folders are being shared. What are two ways to determine quickly what is being shared on the system?

    _____

    _____

2. Sheena is a temporary worker who has just been hired as a full-time employee at your company. Her user account has been made a member of the Clerks group, but it's also still a member of the Temps group. Each group has the following NTFS permissions assigned to the Database folder:

Permission	Full Control	Modify	Read & Execute	List Folder Contents	Read	Write
Clerks	—	Allow	Allow	Allow	Allow	Allow
Temps	—	Deny	Allow	Allow	Allow	Deny

    What are Sheena's effective NTFS permissions for the folder? Provide an explanation.

    _____

    _____

3. Simon, one of the users on your network, has a computer system formatted with FAT32 and configured to dual boot between Windows 98 and Windows 2000. He shares a folder named "HR" with

everyone on the network, but there are some sensitive documents for which he wants to control access. He creates a subfolder in the "HR" share, and moves the sensitive files into it. He configures the permissions on the subfolder to enable access only for users with the proper password. What is the biggest security flaw in this plan?

_____

_____

4. What is the minimal standard permission necessary to be able to share a printer on a Windows 2000/XP Professional workstation?

_____

_____

5. A user on your network, Angelina, is a member of the three groups—Writers, Artists, and Directors—which share a common printing device. Printing permissions are configured as follows:

Permission	Print	Manage Printers	Manage Documents
Artists	Allow	Allow	Deny
Writers	Allow	Allow	—
Directors	Allow	Allow	Allow

What are Angelina's effective permissions for the printer? Provide an explanation.

_____

_____

Key Terms Quiz

Use the vocabulary terms from the list below to complete the sentences that follow. Not all of the terms will be used.

Bindery

Capturing

File and Print Sharing Service

Full control

Line Printer Daemon (LPD)

Line Printer Remote (LPR)

Mapped drive

Mapping

NetWare Directory Services (NDS, now called eDirectory)

Network File System (NFS)

Network share

Novell Storage Services (NSS)

NTFS permissions

Permissions

Persistent connection

Power users

Rights

Share permissions

Trustee rights

Universal Naming Convention (UNC)

Universal Resource Locator (URL)

UNIX/Linux

SYSCON

1. The format \\\<servername\>\\<sharename\> is an example of a _____ path.

2. Prior to NDS/eDirectory, Novell NetWare servers used the _____ to store user rights data.

3. _____ runs on a UNIX/Linux system acting as a print server; _____ runs on a client system, and enables the system to process print jobs on UNIX/Linux servers.

4. On Windows 9x systems, _____ permissions include Full, Read-Only, and Depends on Password.

5. When mapping a network resource to a local drive, you must specify that the mapping use a _____ in order to preserve the mapping after a reboot.

Chapter 14

Going Large with TCP/IP

Lab Exercises

You can create a very basic TCP/IP network using little more than manually configured IP addresses, a common subnet mask, and a default gateway setting on every system. While this TCP/IP network will run, you'll miss much of the functionality of a proper TCP/IP network. First of all, you'll be stuck using IP addresses for everything. Instead of typing in something like www.totalsem.com into your web browser, you'll need to enter the IP address of the totalsem.com web server. If you ever need to make changes to your network's IP addressing, you'll need to walk from system to system making those changes. Last—and certainly the least of your issues in more modern Windows networks—you may not be able to get NetBIOS names from some of your older Windows systems running Windows 9x or NT. The answers to resolving these three issues lie in three different TCP/IP applications: DNS, DHCP, and WINS. DNS resolves fully qualified domain names to IP addresses; DHCP enables you to configure the IP settings dynamically; and WINS resolves NetBIOS names to IP addresses.

The following labs deal with real-world situations that involve DNS, WINS, and DHCP. You will diagnose and repair typical problems relating to these applications, using the utilities described in Chapter 14 of the textbook.

🕐 30 MINUTES

Lab Exercise 14.01: DNS Troubleshooting

The hierarchal structure of DNS makes it a robust, tolerant, and fast way to resolve fully qualified domain names (FQDNs) to IP addresses. When DNS problems take place, however, the number of potential areas that may be the cause of the problem maddens even the most seasoned network technician. The secret to solving DNS issues is twofold. First, remember that DNS is robust and not prone to error. Many errors that might point to DNS issues are actually something else. Second, remember how DNS works. Many times the best way to diagnose and fix a DNS issue is to think through the process of DNS resolution and then test potential problem areas. Knowing how DNS works will also give you the ability to get around problems you can't fix—like a downed DNS server.

Learning Objectives

In this lab, you will review the DNS name resolution process. By its end, you'll be able to:

- Recognize some typical DHCP problems and know how to deal with them

- Use command line tools to test DNS settings and servers

Lab Materials and Setup

The materials you'll need for this lab are

- Pencil and paper

- Windows 2000 or XP system connected to the Internet

Getting Down to Business

You just received a series of calls from users all over the network. Some complain that they cannot access certain web sites, and others report problems with e-mail. You need to get some answers to this riddle and get the network running! You have a single in-house Windows DNS server that supports all of your Windows 2000 and XP systems (there are no systems running earlier versions of Windows).

→ **Note**

If you can re-create this scenario in class—great! If not, still go through the exercise. Use the differences between your classroom setup and the one described here to compare and contrast results!

Step 1 You look at the system of one user who has complained that she cannot access any web sites in her web browser, even though she can access other computers on the local network. What test could you run to determine whether this is a DNS problem?

_____

Step 2 You now are certain enough you have a DNS problem that you want to check the DNS server from the client system. What command could you run from a command prompt to confirm that the DNS server is working? Why is PING a less than optimal choice?

_____

_____

Step 3   If your NSLOOKUP command was successful, what two items would you want to check on the client system to make sure the client itself wasn't giving incorrect DNS data?

_____

_____

Step 4   Run the Ethereal program on your client system and start to capture packets. Open your web browser and access a URL for a web site you've never visited—for example, go to the www.cheese.com web site. After the web page appears, stop the capture. Look for two lines in the capture file (they should look similar to Figure 14-1). The first line is the initial query from your system, while the second line is the response. You'll have plenty of other lines in your capture file—look for the ones labeled DNS under the Protocol column.

Destination	Protocol	Info
216.109.127.16	TCP	1379 > http [SYN] Seq=0 Ack=0 Win=65535 Len=0 MSS
192.168.4.155	DNS	Standard query A www.cheese.com
192.168.4.27	TCP	http > 1360 [FIN, ACK] Seq=0 Ack=0 Win=28944 Len=0
66.235.245.150	TCP	1360 > http [ACK] Seq=0 Ack=1 Win=65535 Len=0
192.168.4.27	TCP	http > 1379 [SYN, ACK] Seq=0 Ack=1 Win=65535 Len=0
216.109.127.16	TCP	1379 > http [ACK] Seq=1 Ack=1 Win=65535 Len=0
66.235.245.150	TCP	[TCP ZeroWindow] 1360 > http [RST] Seq=0 Ack=2114
192.168.4.27	DNS	Standard query response A 66.228.210.68
66.228.210.68	TCP	1381 > http [SYN] Seq=0 Ack=0 Win=65535 Len=0 MSS
216.109.127.16	HTTP	GET /hpt4/hp=1/ct=1an/sh=768/sw=1024/ch=451/cw=928
192.168.4.27	HTTP	HTTP/1.1 200 OK
216.109.127.16	TCP	1379 > http [ACK] Seq=887 Ack=192 Win=65345 Len=0
216.109.127.16	TCP	[TCP ZeroWindow] [TCP Dup ACK 32#1] 1379 > http [
192.168.4.27	TCP	http > 1381 [SYN, ACK] Seq=0 Ack=1 Win=65535 Len=0

FIGURE 14-1 Ethereal capture showing a DNS query and response

Step 5   Click the initial query line in Ethereal and look in the lower box. This is a detailed breakdown of the frame. It is important to note that the entire DNS query takes up exactly one frame and only one IP packet. This tells you that the DNS query is a UDP protocol. Why would the makers of DNS use UDP instead of TCP?

_____

_____

Step 6   Go through both of the DNS frames in detail and answer these questions.

What port does DNS use? What port will the response to the DNS query use? What is the IP address for www.cheese.com? What are the name servers for www.cheese.com? What are the IP addresses for these name servers?

_____

_____

Step 7   Close Ethereal and run the **IPCONFIG /displaydns** command. Can you find the listing for www.cheese.com? What about the name servers for www.cheese.com?

 30 MINUTES

Lab Exercise 14.02: DHCP Troubleshooting

DHCP is the primary method of TCP/IP addressing for client systems. The creation of TCP/IP removed the tedium of changing IP settings on every client in your network whenever changes needed to take place.

DHCP is far more flexible than you might think at first glance. In this lab, we'll watch some DHCP in action and see how changes to your IP settings can create some unique situations.

Learning Objectives

In this lab, you will perform a number of dynamic and static IP configurations on a Windows client. You will use the Ethereal program to inspect the DHCP process. At the end of this lab, you should be able to:

- Recognize how DHCP requests work between a DHCP client and DHCP server

- Customize a Windows client to use DHCP and static IP information for unique situations

- Recognize some typical DHCP problems and know how to deal with them

Lab Materials and Setup

The materials you'll need for this lab are

- A Windows 2000 or XP system using DHCP

- Optional: Access to two DHCP servers to create DHCP conflicts

Getting Down to Business

Your employer's downtown office is having some very strange problems with some of its systems' IP addresses. Some systems are intermittently getting Automatic Private IP Addressing (APIPA) addresses, signifying no connection to a DHCP server, while other systems get an IP address that is not part of your network ID! You head over to the office to check things out and to get rid of this problem.

Step 1   Run Ethereal on a DHCP client system, but do not start capturing frames. Go to a command prompt and run **ipconfig /release**. Go back to Ethereal and start capturing frames. Return to your command prompt and run **ipconfig /renew**. When the renewal is successful, stop capturing frames.

Step 2   You should find five frames labeled as DHCP under the Protocol column, as shown in Figure 14-2. Note that there are four distinct UDP frames: DHCP Discover, DHCP Offer, DHCP Request, and DHCP ACK.

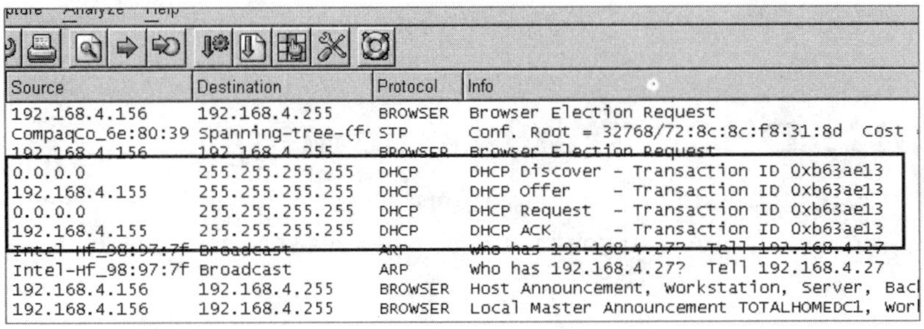

FIGURE 14-2 Ethereal capture of a DHCP request

Step 3   The first frame, DHCP Discover, is a broadcast (255.255.255.255) from your client (0.0.0.0). Remember that at this moment, your client does not have a DHCP address. This is where your system is trying to locate a DHCP server. What port does DHCP use? Go into the bootstrap protocol details of this frame. Did your system request a particular IP address? If yes, why do you think it did so?

_____

_____

Step 4   The second frame is DHCP Offer. What IP address did this come from? Go into the frame's details. What is the IP address the DHCP server is offering? What other IP information is being offered by the DHCP server?

_____

_____

Step 5   The third frame is DHCP Request. This frame is almost identical to DHCP Discover. This step is not intuitive. Why should the DHCP client make a second request if the DHCP server has already responded with all the information it needs?

_____

_____

Step 6   The final step is DHCP ACK. This is the step where the client confirms the IP information. The DHCP server will not start the DHCP lease until it gets this ACK command from the client. Based on this fact, speculate why this frame is sent to the broadcast address instead of the DHCP server's IP address.

_____

_____

Step 7   Going back to the downtown office, you notice that some of the systems have completely different IP addresses than the ones your DHCP server is designed to lease to clients. The different addresses do not start with 169.254. What could be the problem? How could you use Ethereal to test your conclusions?

_____

_____

 45 MINUTES

Lab Exercise 14.03: Fun with TCP/IP Tools

Every Windows system comes with some number of utilities to help you diagnose problems with DNS, DHCP, and WINS. These utilities, although very useful, have two drawbacks. First, different versions of Windows have different utilities; second, many troubleshooting scenarios require using multiple tools, and the order in which you use them is not always obvious.

Learning Objectives

In this lab, you will review the tools shown in Chapter 14 and understand their functions in greater detail.

- Describe the function and use of the following commands: PING, NETSTAT, and NBTSTAT.

Lab Materials and Setup

The materials you'll need for this lab are

- Pencil and paper
- A Windows 9x system with access to a DNS, DHCP, and WINS server
- A Windows 2000/XP system with access to a DNS, DHCP, and WINS server

Getting Down to Business

It's your first day on the job and you're assigned to work with an experienced tech to get comfortable with the many systems on the network. While working with this tech to diagnose a network problem, you notice he uses some of the commands you've seen before, but in ways that are unfamiliar to you. You ask him to show you some of these commands.

→ **Note**

You'll be making heavy use of the help functions of these commands in order to use some of these more advanced functions! When in doubt, type the command and add a /? to the end!

Step 1   You've been asked to move a Windows XP system to a new office. When you plug the new system into the wall outlet, it cannot access the network and the link lights are off. The experienced tech runs to the equipment room to connect this cable run to the switch. Before he leaves, he types in this command:

ping 192.168.4.1 -t

and tells you "Let me know when I get a reply!" 192.168.4.1 is the IP address for the default gateway. What does the -t option do? Why would it be handy in this situation? Is there a PING switch that lets you set the number of pings to a fixed number? Can you use PING to test DNS?

_____

_____

Step 2   Compare the PING command on a Windows XP system to the PING command on a Windows 98 system. How are they different?

_____

_____

Step 3 The next call sends you to a system that you suspect may have a Trojan horse virus. Before running your company's standard antivirus program, your experienced tech wants to run NETSTAT. Why would he want to do this? You run NETSTAT without any switches, and he tells you to run it with the -a switch. What does the -a switch do that NETSTAT alone cannot?

_____

_____

Step 4 While running NETSTAT -n switch, you see connections to foreign systems using these ports. Use the Internet to determine what program is using these port numbers and fill in the following table.

Port Number	Application Using this Port Number
80	_____
139	_____
445	_____
1214	_____
1863	_____
5190	_____

Step 5 Which switch do you run with NBTSTAT to determine if you are using a WINS server? Explain the information you see and how it would enable you to determine whether a WINS server was used or not.

_____

_____

Step 6 There are two switches you run with NBTSTAT to determine what other systems are currently accessing your shared resources. What are they and what is the difference between the two?

_____

_____

 45 MINUTES

Lab Exercise 14.04: DNS/DHCP/WINS Troubleshooting

When you're exposed to problems that you suspect might be related to DNS, DHCP, or WINS, you need to take the time to determine what tools are at your disposal. Next, you think about the problem—combining the known errors with what you understand about how DNS, DHCP, or WINS works—and come up with a way to test your hypothesis.

There's rarely one single method or one "right answer" in solving these types of problems. You have to be flexible and to accept that you may need to make a number of attempts before you come up with a solution. A combination of patience and persistence is the key to these types of problems. Oh!—one more item to consider. Have you ever heard the old adage, "When you see hoof prints, think horses, not zebras?" In other words, don't assume a problem is more complex than the symptoms describe. Many times, suspected DNS, DHCP, or WINS problems are actually different problems hidden under symptoms that make you think they might be related to one of those three. Consider yourself warned!

Learning Objectives

In this lab, you will review the TCP/IP tools provided by different versions of Windows and then use those tools to diagnose potential DNS, DHCP, or WINS errors.

- Describe the different TCP/IP tools provided in Windows 9x vs. 2000/XP.

- Properly use these tools in different troubleshooting scenarios.

Lab Materials and Setup

The materials you'll need for this lab are

- Pencil and paper

- A Windows 9x system with access to a DNS, DHCP, and WINS server

- A Windows 2000/XP system with access to a DNS, DHCP, and WINS server

Getting Down to Business

What a nightmare! You just got a call from a new customer, complaining that his company's new network is a complete mess. Seems that one of the company's employees was boasting just a bit too much when she claimed she could take this mix of Windows 9x and Windows XP systems and get a network going from the ground up! This is your first exposure to this network, and you have no idea about anything other than the following:

There are 12 Windows 98 systems, 14 Windows XP Professional systems, and 6 Windows XP Home systems. These systems were previously used in a number of different networks. There are two Windows

Server 2003 systems, both of them domain controllers, one of which is configured for DNS, DHCP, and WINS serving. This latter server has a statically configured IP address of 192.168.4.100/24 and a default gateway of 192.168.4.1. The web browser on this server can access any web page on the Internet. Initially, this server system was tested at another location, but you've been assured it successfully served DNS, DHCP, and WINS for a previous network, a domain called TEST.LOCAL. The DHCP server is set to distribute the entire IP address range of 192.168.4/24, a default gateway of 192.168.1.1, and a DNS server of 192.168.4.100. The other server's main role is to share files. It is also on the TEST.LOCAL domain, and has a static IP address of 192.168.4.12/24 and a default gateway of 192.168.1.1.

> ➜ **Note**
>
> Each step in this lab assumes a different scenario! Do not assume that something that takes place in one step is also valid for another step unless explicitly stated.

Step 1 None of the client system's web browsers work. Give a series of steps that you would take to track down the problem. You may assume that the entire network is on a single collision domain and that all systems are physically connected. Use the PING, TRACERT, and IPCONFIG/WINIPCFG commands. Defend those steps.

_____

_____

_____

_____

_____

Step 2 Inspect the DHCP server's IP settings. Explain the problems with the DHCP server's settings and provide recommendations for correcting any errors you might see.

_____

_____

_____

> **➜ Note**
>
> From this point forward you may assume that the DHCP server is properly configured based on your recommendations.

Step 3   After reconfiguring the DHCP settings, you notice that almost all of the systems have strange IP settings, from APIPA addresses to a number of other IP addresses. What do you need to do to make sure all of the systems use the DHCP-supplied settings?

_____

_____

Step 4   Five systems are generating the error "Duplicate name exists on network." What causes this error? Would the presence of a WINS server help repair this issue? What would you do to fix this problem?

_____

_____

Step 5   Opening My Network Places/Network Neighborhood is an amazing experience. Different systems show different information, but every system shows at least two networks. You want only one domain. What's going on here? What can you do to fix this?

_____

_____

_____

Step 6   How do you feel about the name TEST.LOCAL? Is it acceptable? Why or why not? What questions would you have to ask about the network to confirm the acceptability of this name?

_____

_____

_____

_____

Step 7 After finally getting the systems organized, you suddenly find that one system cannot access the address www.ibm.com. It was able to access this web site just a few minutes ago. What commands would you run, and why would you run them to diagnose the problem?

_____

_____

Lab Analysis

1. Explain the relationship between the HOSTS file and DNS, and give an example of how they might conflict.

    _____

    _____

2. Explain the concept of DNS root servers, and show how a Windows 2003/XP network not connected to the Internet might still need a DNS root server.

    _____

    _____

3. Can a host have both static and DHCP settings? Give an example. What takes place if a host has a static setting during a DHCP lease request?

    _____

    _____

4. Explain APIPA and show how it can be helpful in a network.

    _____

    _____

5. You recently explained WINS to a friend. He remarks that his four-system home network, all running Windows 98 and the TCP/IP protocol, works just fine, and he's sure that there is no WINS server running. Why does he not need a WINS server?

_____

_____

Key Terms Quiz

Use the vocabulary terms from the list below to complete the sentences that follow. Not all of the terms will be used.

APIPA	IPCONFIG
Cache	Name resolution
DHCP server	NBTSTAT
DNS server	NetBIOS
Domain Name Service (DNS)	NETSTAT
Dynamic Host Configuration Protocol (DHCP)	NSLOOKUP
DHCP ACK	PING
DHCP Discover	Windows Internet Naming Service (WINS)
DHCP Offer	WINS server
DHCP Request	

1. Use the _____ command to query a DNS server.

2. The _____ command would show you the current TCP sessions on your system.

3. You can run the _____ command with the -t switch to make it run continually.

4. DNS deals with _____ between FQDNs and IP addresses.

5. Without a _____, NetBIOS machines must use broadcasting to resolve their IP addresses to NetBIOS names.

6. The final step in the five-step DHCP lease process is _____.

7. An IP address starting with 169.254 is an _____ address.

Chapter 15

Network Operating Systems

Lab Exercises

Taking TCP/IP out of the LAN and moving it out to the Internet requires a re-examination of a number of concepts, components, and software you've already seen. For example, you've studied the concept of routing in some detail, but now you need to look at routing from the perspective of the Internet to understand how the big routers make the big connections possible.

In addition, this chapter covers LAN technology, in particular NAT and proxy serving. These two technologies are critical for the protection of any private network you want to connect to the Internet. In this chapter, you'll install and configure both NAT and proxy serving programs to see how they work in the real world.

30 MINUTES

Lab Exercise 15.01: Working with Routing Tables

Routing tables provide TCP/IP nodes and routers with the ability to move data successfully from one node or network to another as efficiently as possible. Every TCP/IP host system has some form of routing table. Client systems have relatively simple routing tables, while routers may or may not have complex routing tables. Whatever their size, being comfortable reading and understanding routing tables is the key to understanding exactly how IP packets move around large networks, including the Internet.

In this exercise, you'll be given a number of network scenarios involving routers, subnets, and networks. From this information, you'll build routing tables that will fulfill the needs of that particular network.

Learning Objectives

In this lab, you will examine the basic characteristics of routing table functions. By its end, you will be able to:

- Define the individual components of a generic routing table
- Create a route based on given information
- Diagnose and correct improper static routes in routers or hosts

Lab Materials and Setup

The only materials you need for this lab are a pencil and paper.

Getting Down to Business

Your boss has just handed you a fairly large assignment. ABC Company has opened a second office in the city and connected that network to your company network via a T1 connection. The two routers, labeled A and B, are attached to the T1 connection and to the hub in each network, as shown in Figure 15-1. Your job is to oversee the configuration of static routes in all routers to ensure that every system on the greater WAN can connect. This network does not connect to the Internet—yet!

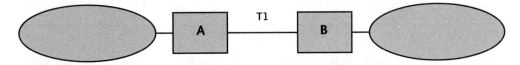

FIGURE 15-1 Diagram of a network

Step 1   Come up with network IDs for the two local networks. You will use DHCP, but NAT must not be used. You do not need to concern yourself with subnetting. Why is subnetting not needed for this network?

_____

_____

_____

_____

Step 2   Assume you chose to use the network ID of 192.168.1/24 for Network A and 212.43.2/24 for Network B. Draw a diagram, circling and identifying the subnets over Figure 15-1.

Step 3   T1 connections also have IP addresses. Whoever installed the T1 system gave the T1 connection on Router A the address 10.12.14.1/24 and the T1 connection on Router B 10.12.14.2/24. In essence, this places these two routers into their own little subnet of 10.12.14/24, as shown in Figure 15-2.

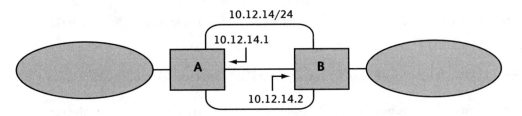

FIGURE 15-2 A router subnet

Why can't you make the T1 connections part of the subnets you created in Step 1?

_____

_____

_____

_____

The next two questions require you to define (on paper only) the static routes for your routing tables. The routes you will make follow the format you saw for Windows routing tables in Chapter 15 of the textbook. You will define these routes by filling out this template as you answer the following questions.

Network Destination	Subnet Mask	Gateway	Interface	Metric
_____	_____	_____	_____	_____

→ **Note**

Remember, "255" means an exact match, while "0" means any value!

Step 4   Concentrating on Router B, confirm the fact that it has two interfaces, an Ethernet connection to the local network and a T1 connection to Router A. Define the standard first route for the routing table: any IP address with any subnet mask goes out the T1 connection.

✔ **Hint**

Router A is Router B's default gateway.

Network Destination	Subnet Mask	Gateway	Interface	Metric
_____	_____	_____	_____	_____

Step 5   Define the route for Router B that forwards all traffic for Network B out to that network.

Network Destination	Subnet Mask	Gateway	Interface	Metric
_____	_____	_____	_____	_____

Step 6   Router B does not need any routing information about Network A. Why is this the case?

_____

_____

 45 MINUTES

Lab Exercise 15.02: Running ICS and NAT

Network Address Translation (NAT) is a powerful technology that enables many network clients on a TCP/IP network to share a single Internet connection. Most popular Internet gateway routers on the market have built-in NAT functionality, and the latest versions of Windows also provide the NAT service. Windows 2000 Server and Server 2003 both have NAT support capable of connecting large numbers of clients to the Internet simultaneously, while the workstation versions of Windows since Windows 98 SE provide the popular Internet Connection Sharing (ICS) service—essentially a stripped-down version of NAT designed for small networks.

Let's take a quick review of the main selling points of NAT by watching ICS in action.

Learning Objectives

In this lab, you will explain the function of Network Address Translation (NAT). By its end, you will be able to:

- Configure a small network to use Windows ICS

Lab Materials and Setup

The materials you need for this lab are

- A pencil and paper

- A Windows PC (XP preferred; at least 98 SE or later) with two network connections: Internet connectivity via modem or NIC and a second NIC to act as the internal network interconnection

- A small network of one or two other systems (optional)

Getting Down to Business

Your Aunt Bessie and Uncle Pete each have Windows XP Professional computers in their home. They want to share their new cable modem connection but don't want to "bother" (as your Aunt Bessie says) with the extra complication and cost of a SOHO router. They would also like to get a new laser printer (the printer uses a USB port) and have some way to share it. Both of their systems are in the same room in their home, and both systems have functional 100BaseT NICs that they currently do not use. You decide to use ICS.

Step 1   Draw a quick network diagram using a small 100BaseT switch to connect all devices. Include the new laser printer and the Internet connection.

Step 2   Given that so many routers offer both DHCP and NAT, many people confuse the two or think they are dependent upon each other. How would you respond to these areas of confusion?

_____

_____

Step 3   Aunt Bessie is a pretty smart cookie and fairly astute in computing and networking—she has spent years listening to you ramble on about computer "stuff," and by this point has a basic grasp of IP addressing, default gateways, and subnet masks. She wants to understand about Windows XP ICS. Tell her the features of ICS and why she might like it or not like it. Include the following information:

- Benefits of ICS

- Potential drawbacks

- Hardware requirements

- Alternatives to ICS

Do not include Internet Connection Firewall (ICF) in this description!

_____

_____

_____

_____

Step 4   Follow these steps to activate ICS on your Windows XP Professional system:

1.   Select Start | My Network Places, and click the *View network connections* link.

2.   Alternate-click the network connection that you will share and select Properties.

3.   On the network connection's Properties dialog box, click the Advanced tab.

4.   In the section labeled Internet Connection Sharing, select the checkbox labeled, *Allow other network users to connect through this computer's Internet connection*, and click the OK button.

What are the results of these steps? What's the local NIC's IP address? (The local NIC connects to your LAN, not the Internet.) Is it static or dynamic? Why is this the case?

_____

_____

_____

Step 5   How does activating ICS on your PC affect the other systems on your network?

_____

_____

✔ **Hint**

Configuring ICS on a networked PC turns that PC into a DHCP server.

Step 6   Run IPCONFIG. What are the DNS server settings? Where did that information come from?

_____

_____

 30 MINUTES

Lab Exercise 15.03: Running a Proxy Server

Proxy servers were once very popular in networks, but have lost that status due to easy-to-configure firewalls and other applications. Nevertheless, nothing can cache web pages or change TCP/UDP ports like a proxy server, which makes them popular for those networks that find these features handy.

Proxy servers manifest themselves as programs you run on a system. In fact, some proxy server programs run on any operating system. Some Windows-based programs include proxy serving as part of a more comprehensive (and cost-enhancing) package such as Microsoft's ISA server. Others, like FreeProxy, written by Greg Robson-Garth, are freeware and run on almost every version of Windows.

Learning Objectives

In this lab, you will review the functions of a proxy server and run a sample proxy server in a Windows environment. By the end of the lab, you will be able to:

- Describe the function of proxy serving

- Describe typical options that come with proxy servers

- Successfully implement a complete proxy serving solution in a Windows network

Lab Materials and Setup

The materials you'll need for this lab are

- A pencil and paper

- Two or more Windows PCs (98, 2000, or XP) networked together with Internet access

- A copy of FreeProxy (http://www.alphalink.com.au/~gregr/freeproxy.htm)

→ Note

This lab is not designed to teach you how to use the FreeProxy program. The goal is to show you how proxy serving works. It is assumed you can find certain configurations on your own or use the help that comes with FreeProxy to get the answers you need. Don't be afraid to poke around.

Getting Down to Business

Your customer wants a method that will protect his networked systems from hacking, as well as monitor what web sites his employees visit. You think that a proxy server is the tool he needs.

Step 1 Install FreeProxy on any system on your network. Note the IP address of the system running FreeProxy. Start the FreeProxy program, as shown in Figure 15-3. Note that this is *not* the proxy server—FreeProxy calls this the Control Centre. Start the FreeProxy service by clicking the Start/Stop button. Run FreeProxy as a service on Windows 2000/XP and in the console in Windows 9x.

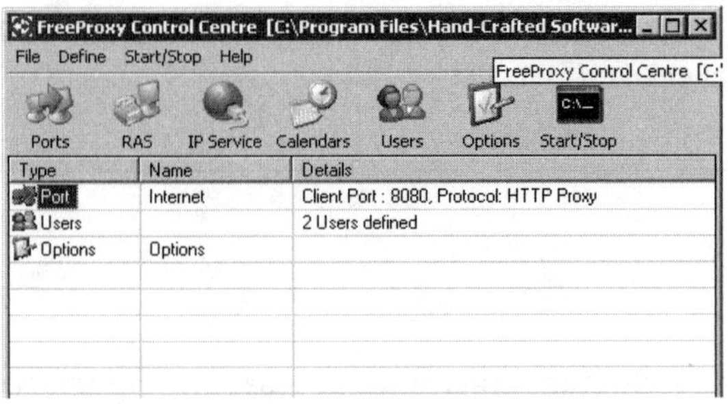

FIGURE 15-3 The FreeProxy Control Centre

Step 2   FreeProxy is preconfigured to proxy serve HTTP requests using port 8080. Start Internet Explorer on another system. Make sure it is able to access web pages on the Internet. Go to Internet Options (the exact location of the Internet options varies from version to version) and select the Connections tab. Click the LAN Settings button and configure the browser to use your newly installed proxy server by entering its IP address and port 8080. Close Internet Explorer and then reopen it. Does it access a web page? If so, the proxy server is running. If you were not successful, where would you look for errors to get this working?

_____

_____

Step 3   Use the Ports feature to create an FTP proxy. Use port number 2523. FTP requires a few special settings—match your settings to those shown in Figure 15-4 to ensure a successful FTP proxy setup.

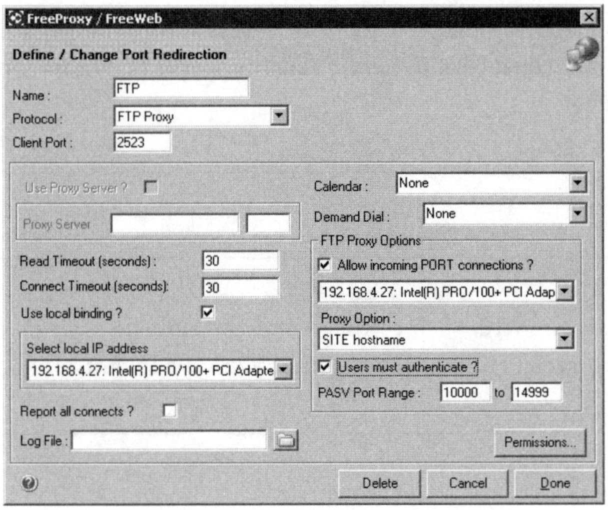

FIGURE 15-4 Setting up FTP in FreeProxy

Internet Explorer is also a rudimentary FTP client. What must you do in your other system's Internet Options to enable FTP proxy to work with the proxy server?

_____

_____

Step 4   Many people confuse proxy serving with routers. Routers must have at least two interfaces. FreeProxy, like most proxy servers, only needs a single NIC to connect to a LAN and to connect that LAN to an external network, such as the Internet. Draw or describe the path that a single HTTP packet takes as it leaves the client system and goes to a remote web site.

_____

_____

Step 5   FreeProxy has an optional RAS setting to support dial-up networking. In this case, the system running the proxy server is also the system acting as the Internet connection. Describe the path that a single HTTP packet takes as it leaves the client system and goes to a remote web site.

_____

_____

Lab Analysis

1.   In the first lab, you manually edited routing tables. These routes, which will never change, are called static routes. However, many routers are capable of dynamic routing. Explain dynamic routing and why it is so important for the Internet.

_____

_____

2.   If you had a Windows system with more than one NIC, each connected to the Internet, which one would Windows use if you opened a web browser? Could you change it? Would you want to?

_____

_____

_____

_____

3. Multiple DHCP servers on one network can cause the network to fail. What would happen to a network connected to two routers, each capable of NAT?

_____

_____

_____

_____

4. FreeProxy is a fine, but rather simple, proxy server. What other features could you add to this proxy server?

_____

_____

_____

_____

5. How would a proxy server protect computers on a network from hackers?

_____

_____

Key Terms Quiz

Use the vocabulary terms from the list below to complete the sentences that follow. Not all of the terms will be used.

Border Gateway Protocol (BGP-4)

Dynamic routing

Electronic mail (e-mail)

Enhanced Interior Gateway Routing Protocol (EIGRP)

File Transfer Protocol (FTP)

HyperText Transport Protocol (HTTP)

HyperText Transport Protocol over SSL (HTTPS)

Interior Gateway Routing Protocol (IGRP)

Internet Message Access Protocol (IMAP)

Network Address Translation (NAT)

Open Shortest Path First (OSPF)

Post Office Protocol version 3 (POP3)

Proxy server

Router

Routing table

Secure Sockets Layer (SSL)

Simple Mail Transport Protocol (SMTP)

Simple Network Management Protocol (SNMP)

Static route

Telnet

1. For _____ to work, you must configure your TCP/IP applications to use them.

2. _____ enables the use of private addressing for networks that connect to the Internet.

3. RIP is one method of _____.

4. Every host system running TCP/IP has a(n) _____.

5. The _____ is an alternative to POP3.

6. The _____ dynamic routing protocol uses "Hello" messages.

7. SSH's encryption capability is quickly making _____ obsolete.

8. Any device that directs IP packets is by definition a(n) _____.

9. _____ never change in a routing table unless they are manually edited.

10. A(n) _____ e-mail server stores your incoming e-mail until you are ready to download it into your e-mail client.

Chapter 16

Remote Access

Lab Exercises

One of the most important skills of the modern network tech is the ability to create and maintain remote network connections of all types. All modern network operating systems enable network techs to connect users to private networks running some sort of Remote Access Service (RAS), and also to that big network *of* networks, the Internet. On a larger scale, you may be called upon to connect entire networks to each other via one of the various high-speed *backbone* technologies, such as T-carrier lines or a packet-switched technology.

As more and more organizations see the value of going global, you'll find yourself as a Network+ certified technician called upon to make informed recommendations for client connectivity and WAN bridging. The following exercises will help you develop an appreciation and methodology for these tasks. Let's get started.

 30 MINUTES

Lab Exercise 16.01: Remote Connectivity Options for Local Area Networks

It wasn't that long ago that the Internet was considered by many to be simply a passing fad. Well, to paraphrase a line from *The Simpsons*, "Fad or not, the Internet is here to stay."

One of your most basic tasks as a Network+ certified technician is to ensure Internet connectivity for a local area network (LAN). PCs have had the capability to connect to remote networks for some time now, but the explosion of the Internet has really put remote networking on the map, so to speak. You have a number of options available, and it's up to you to know which options best suit a particular network environment. In this lab exercise, you'll examine the remote connectivity options for a LAN.

Learning Objectives

In this lab, you will examine your remote connectivity options. By its end, you will be able to:

- Describe the various options available for configuring remote connectivity with RAS services and the Internet

Lab Materials and Setup

The only materials you'll need for this lab will be a pencil and some paper.

Getting Down to Business

Your client, Dr. Peter Simione, wants to connect his office's networked computers to the Internet, and also wants to be able to test access to his office PC from his home office or from remote locations while traveling to retrieve and update data files. If this remote access test is successful, he wants to enable remote access for his employees and partners. He wants you to explain the options and requirements available to meet these goals.

Step 1 Explain the difference between a dedicated and a dial-up RAS or Internet connection. Provide at least one example of each type of connection.

_____

_____

Step 2 Describe the specifications for a remote connection via Public Switched Telephone Network (PSTN). Include the following information:

- Hardware requirements
- Software requirements
- Data throughput speed
- Internet connection sharing capabilities

_____

_____

Step 3 Describe the specifications for a remote connection via Integrated Services Digital Network (ISDN). Include the following information:

- Hardware requirements
- Software requirements
- Data throughput speed
- Distance limitations
- Internet connection sharing capabilities

_____

_____

Step 4   Describe the specifications for a remote connection via Asymmetric Digital Subscriber Line (ADSL) and Symmetric Digital Subscriber line (SDSL). Include the following information:

- Hardware requirements

- Software requirements

- Data throughput speeds for both ADSL and SDSL

- Distance limitations

_____

_____

Step 5   Describe the specifications for a remote connection via cable. Include the following information:

- Hardware requirements

- Software requirements

- Data throughput speed

- Distance limitations

- Internet connection sharing capabilities

_____

_____

Step 6   Describe the specifications for a remote connection via satellite. Include the following information:

- Hardware requirements

- Software requirements

- Data throughput speed

- Distance limitations

- Internet connection sharing capabilities

_____

_____

Step 7   Based on your client's goals, make a recommendation for Internet and RAS access.

_____

_____

 45 MINUTES

Lab Exercise 16.02: Extending a LAN to a WAN

Many organizations require dedicated WAN connectivity in order to share data between users at remote sites or grant access to a centrally located resource, such as a database. With that in mind, you should also be familiar with the options for connecting a LAN to another LAN across a high-speed network link to make a wide area network (WAN) connection.

Learning Objectives

In this lab, you will examine the various WAN technology solutions available. By its end, you will be able to:

- Explain the specifications of the various WAN technology solutions

- Make an informed recommendation of a WAN technology implementation to a client

Lab Materials and Setup

The only materials you will need for this lab are a pencil and some paper.

Getting Down to Business

Your client, Gulf Coast Helicopters & Airplane, is a private aircraft charter corporation servicing the petrochemical industry in the greater Gulf Coast region. The company has its base of operations in Pearland, Texas, with satellite bases in Corpus Christi and Angleton, Texas, and Houma, Louisiana. Currently, each location has its own network and maintains its own set of records and data. Growth within the company has given the owners reason to link the LANs together. Their goals are as follows:

- Each location requires dedicated connectivity to the base of operations in order to access a centralized flight dispatch database running on a server at headquarters.

- The WAN connection needs to have sufficient throughput to accommodate the flight dispatch database data (text formatted data), e-mail, and FTP and Web access, as well as occasional transfers of large graphics (photos of aerial surveillance activity).

- Cost is an issue, so the solution should be relatively inexpensive and require a minimum of additional equipment to implement.

With those goals in mind, explain to the owners the various WAN connectivity options available, and make a recommendation that suits their goals.

Step 1 Explain the difference between a local area network (LAN) and a wide area network (WAN). List the common technologies that network techs use to link LANs to WANs, and describe the common parts of these WAN connection technologies.

_____

_____

_____

Step 2 Describe the specifications for T-class copper carriers. Include the following information:

- Types of T-class carrier technologies
- Hardware requirements
- Signal method
- Number of channels
- Data throughput speed
- Typical usage

_____

_____

Step 3 Describe the specifications for fiber carriers. Include the following information:

- Types of fiber carrier technologies
- Hardware requirements
- Signal method
- Data throughput speed
- Typical usage

_____

_____

Step 4 Describe the specifications for the various packet switching technologies. Include the following information:

- Types of packet switching technologies

- Data throughput speed
- Typical usage

_____

_____

Step 5   Given your client's goals, which data carrier and packet switching technologies do you recommend that they implement?

_____

_____

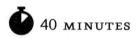 40 MINUTES

Lab Exercise 16.03: Connecting Clients to Remote Access Service Servers and the Internet

As I mentioned earlier, PCs have long been able to connect to remote servers, although it hasn't always been easy. Network techs used to have to jump through a number of hoops to get even the simplest Internet or RAS connection up and running. Modern network operating systems and Plug-and-Play hardware have simplified the process tremendously.

In this exercise, you'll run through the steps to connect to the Internet and to private network RAS servers via dial-up, VPN, or a dedicated connection such as xDSL. You'll also look at how to share an Internet connection on your network. Let's get started.

Learning Objectives

In this lab, you will review the methods for establishing Internet and RAS connectivity from a Windows network client. By its end, you will be able to:

- Understand the various procedures for connecting a Windows PC to a RAS and the Internet via an ISP

Lab Materials and Setup

The only thing you will need for this lab is a PC running Windows XP Professional.

Getting Down to Business

You've previously explained the various Internet and RAS connectivity options and requirements to your client, Dr. Peter Simione. He now wants you to demonstrate the steps to configure a client connection so he can train his staff.

Step 1   Windows XP Professional's New Connection Wizard provides one-stop shopping for network connection configuration. Follow these steps to configure a new remote network connection:

1. Start the wizard by opening your Network Connections folder (Start | My Network Places | View network connections) and then clicking the *Create a new connection* link listed under Network Tasks. Click the Next button to get to the Network Connection Type screen shown in Figure 16-1.

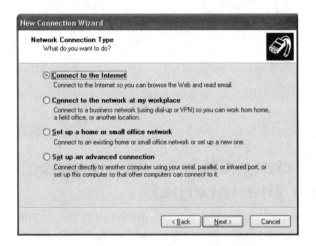

FIGURE 16-1 New Connection Wizard, Network Connection Type screen

2. Specify the type of network connection you want to configure: Internet connection, RAS or VPN connection, LAN connection, or a direct connection to another PC via serial, parallel, or infrared port.

3. For this example, select *Connect to the Internet* and click the Next button. The next screen gives you the option of selecting a new ISP, setting up a connection manually (with account info, dial-up numbers, and so on), or using a setup CD provided by your ISP. Select *Set up my connection manually*, and click Next.

4. Your next step is to specify how you will connect to the Internet. Your choices are dial-up modem using PSTN or ISDN, broadband DSL or cable using PPPoE, or dedicated broadband. Select the appropriate choice and click Next.

5. Specify a name for the Internet connection at the next screen (for example, the name of your ISP). This name appears as a label for the Internet connection icon in your Network Connections folder. Once you've typed a name, click Next again.

6. Type the telephone number that your PC dials to connect to your ISP at the next screen, and click the Next button again when you're finished.

7. At the Internet Account Information screen, type in your ISP-supplied user name and password. Note the three options that are configurable with a checkbox for this account information: *Use this account name and password when anyone connects to the Internet from this computer*, *Make this the default Internet connection*, and *Turn on Internet Connection Firewall for this connection*. Click Next to continue.

8. At the last screen, review your configuration information, and select whether or not to add a shortcut to this network connection on your desktop. Click Finish to complete the configuration.

What are the results?

_____

_____

Step 2   The steps to configure a network connection directly to a RAS server via dial-up are very similar to the steps for connecting to an ISP.

1. Start the New Connection Wizard, and at the Network Connection Type screen, select *Connect to the network at my workplace*, and click the Next button.

2. At the Network Connection screen, shown in Figure 16-2, select *Dial-up connection* and click Next.

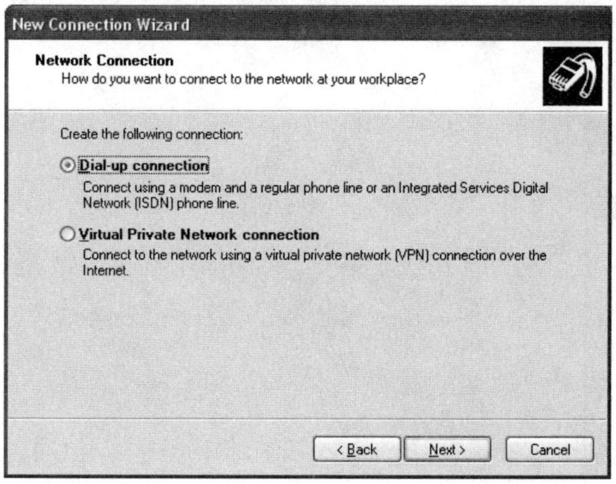

FIGURE 16-2 Network Connection wizard, connect to RAS via Dialup or VPN

3. Specify a name for the RAS connection at the next screen. This name appears as a label for the RAS connection icon in your Network Connections folder. Once you've typed a name in, click Next again.

4. Type the telephone number to dial to connect to the dial-up RAS server at the next screen, and then click the Next button to continue.

5. At the last screen, review your configuration information (and select whether or not to add a shortcut to this network connection on your desktop) and click Finish to complete the configuration.

    What are the results?

_____

_____

Step 3   Follow these steps to configure a VPN connection to a private RAS server.

1. Start the New Connection Wizard, and at the Network Connection Type screen, select *Connect to the network at my workplace*, and click the Next button.

2. At the Network Connection screen, select *Virtual Private Network connection* and click Next.

3. Specify a name for the VPN connection at the next screen. This name appears as a label for the VPN connection icon in your Network Connections folder. Once you've typed a name in, click Next again.

4. At the Public Network screen, shown in Figure 16-3, you must specify a network connection (for example, an Internet or RAS connection) for the VPN to use.

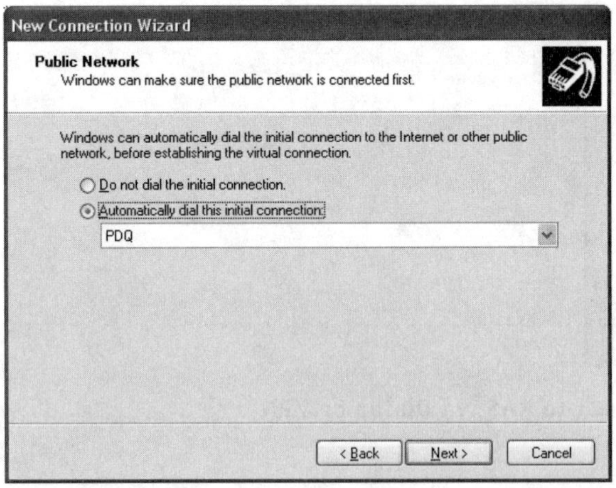

Figure 16-3 Specify a network connection for the VPN to use

Your choices are *Do not dial the initial connection* (choosing this option requires that you manually select a network connection for the VPN to use when you initiate the VPN connection) and *Automatically dial this initial connection* (choosing this option causes the VPN to initiate the dial-up connection automatically when the VPN connection is started). Once you've selected an option, click Next to specify your VPN server.

5. At the VPN Server Selection screen, type the host name or IP address of your company's VPN server, and click Next.

6. At the last screen, review your configuration information (and select whether or not to add a shortcut to this network connection on your desktop). Click Finish to complete the configuration.

What are the results?

_____

_____

Step 4   True dedicated connections are configured directly on the terminal adapter hardware that you use to connect to your ISP or RAS server. However, the Windows XP Professional New Connection Wizard provides an interface for configuring high-speed cable or DSL connections using PPPoE. Follow these steps to configure this type of dedicated connection:

1. Start the New Connection Wizard, and at the Network Connection Type screen, select *Connect to the Internet*, and click the Next button.

2. Select the *Set up my connection manually* option and click the Next button, then at the Internet Connection screen, select *Connect using a broadband connection* that requires a user name and password. Click Next again, and type in a name for this dedicated connection.

3. Click Next, and enter your broadband Internet account information (that is, your user name, password, and connection availability options).

4. Click Next one more time to get to the final screen and review your settings, then click Finish to complete the wizard.

What are the results?

_____

_____

Step 5   For all the steps that go into configuring any type of Internet connection, configuring Internet Connection Sharing (ICS) for a particular Internet connection couldn't be simpler. To enable sharing of any Internet connection configured on a system, follow these steps:

1.   Locate the Internet connection's icon in the Network Connections folder, alternate-click it, and select Properties.

2.   In the connection's Properties dialog box (shown in Figure 16-4), click the Advanced property sheet tab and check the box labeled *Allow other network users to connect through this computer's Internet connection*, and then click OK.

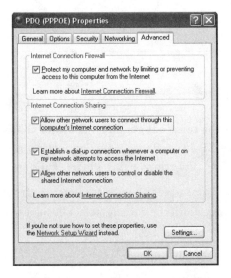

FIGURE 16-4 Configure Internet Connection Sharing on the Internet connection's Properties page

What are the results?

_____

_____

Step 5   Configuring Windows XP Professional to accept incoming connections from remote PCs is practically as easy as configuring outgoing connections.

1.   Start the New Connection Wizard, and at the Network Connection Type screen, select *Set up an advanced connection*, and click the Next button.

2.   At the next screen, select the option to *Accept incoming connections*, as shown in Figure 16-5, and click Next.

3. At the Devices for Incoming Connections screen, select the appropriate device (such as a modem or xDSL/cable router) and click the Next button.

4. Select whether to allow or disallow VPN connections on this computer. Note that the PC must have a public IP address to enable a VPN connection. Select the appropriate choice and client and then click Next.

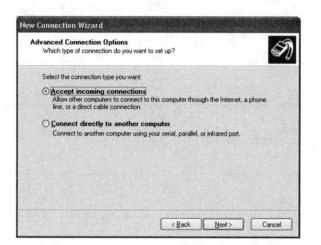

FIGURE 16-5 Configure an Internet connection to enable a PC to accept incoming connections from remote users.

5. At the next screen, specify the local user accounts that are permitted to connect to this PC remotely and click Next.

6. Specify the software (protocols and services) that you want to enable for incoming connections. Typically, unless you have specific needs (such as the need to support a remote NetWare connection using IPX/SPX), you can accept the default settings and click Next.

7. Click Finish to complete the wizard.

What are the results?

_____

_____

Lab Analysis

1. Which of the following authentication protocols offers the least security? Explain why.

    a. Password Authentication Protocol (PAP)

    b. Microsoft Challenge Handshake Protocol (MS-CHAP)

    c. Extensible Authentication Protocol (EAP)

    d. Shiva Password Authentication Protocol (SPAP)

    _____

    _____

2. List at least three reasons why SLIP has been supplanted by PPP.

    _____

    _____

3. What means do VPN connections use to secure the session?

    _____

    _____

4. List at least three services provided to a network by a PC configured to run ICS.

    _____

    _____

5. Briefly describe how packet switching technology works, and list three examples of packet-switching implementation.

    _____

    _____

Key Terms Quiz

Use the vocabulary terms from the list below to complete the sentences that follow. Not all of the terms will be used.

Asymmetric DSL (ADSL)

ATM

B-channel

Basic Rate Interface (BRI)

Channel Service Unit/Data Service Unit (CSU/DSU)

D-channel

Dedicated connections

Dedicated lines

Digital subscriber line (DSL)

Frame Relay

Integrated Services Digital Network (ISDN)

Internet Connection Sharing (ICS)

Layer 2 Tunneling Protocol (L2TP)

Modulator/demodulator (modem)

Network Address Translation (NAT)

Optical carrier (OC)

Plain old telephone system (POTS)

Point-to-Point Protocol (PPP)

Point-to-Point Tunneling Protocol (PPTP)

PPP over Ethernet (PPPoE)

Public Switched Telephone Network (PSTN)

Remote Access Server (RAS)

Serial Line Internet Protocol (SLIP)

Symmetric DSL (SDSL)

Synchronous Digital Hierarchy (SDH)

Synchronous Optical Network (SONET)

Synchronous Transport Signal (STS)

T1 line

T3 line

Terminal adapter (TA)

Virtual private network (VPN)

V92 standard

Wide area network (WAN)

X.25

1. A device that converts digital signals to analog and then back again is called a
   _____.

2. A _____ connects a T1 line to the LAN, usually via a router.

3. _____ and _____ use the same technology and
   equipment to carry digital data on copper telephone lines; they only differ in the speed at
   which they enable users to upload data.

4. _____ is a standard for optical transport published by the American
   National Standards Institute (ANSI).

5. A typical ISDN _____ setup consists of two B-channels and one D-channel,
   with an aggregate throughput of 128 Kbps.

Chapter 17
Protecting Your Network

Lab Exercises

Network protection covers many different security aspects, from using proper passwords for logons to encryption and firewalls. Given the many options available, these labs concentrate on a number of free products that demonstrate technology and techniques for protecting your network. In the first lab, you will install and use public key encryption of e-mail using the popular PGP software program. The next two labs cover the same issue—software firewalls—but show how even this fairly narrow topic can manifest itself in very different programs.

45 MINUTES

Lab Exercise 17.01: Public Keys with PGP

Public key encryption is embedded in many TCP/IP applications, from secure web sites to VPNs and e-mail. But how does public key encryption manifest itself? What does a public or private key look like? The answer to this varies depending on the application, but e-mail stands out among the many applications as one place where you'll see public and private keys.

E-mail benefits dramatically from encryption. After all, it's not difficult for someone to intercept your e-mail—and we're not just talking about hackers. The administrator of your POP/SMTP server can easily access the e-mail on the server, or even configure the server to forward your e-mail to another account for him to read at his leisure. Encrypting your e-mail on your local system before you send it won't stop these people from intercepting your e-mail, but it certainly keeps them from reading it!

E-mail also benefits from digital signatures. It is surprisingly easy to *spoof* e-mail—to make the e-mail address of the person sending the e-mail look like someone other than the true sender. With digital signatures, you can check incoming e-mail to confirm that it truly does come from the person whose name is in the "from:" line of the e-mail.

Easily the most popular public key encryption tool for e-mail is the venerable PGP (Pretty Good Privacy), created by Phil Zimmerman. PGP has become so popular that most people consider it the *de facto* standard for e-mail encryption. PGP comes in both commercial and freeware (for personal use only) versions.

Here's how public key encryption works in a nutshell. You have two keys, called your *key pair*: a public key and a private key. You make the public key available to anyone who wants to send a message to you. The sender uses your public key to encrypt a message; you then decrypt the message with your private key. Only your private key can decrypt messages encrypted with your public key. Similarly, if you want to send an encrypted message to someone, you must obtain his or her public key. Simple enough in theory, right? Let's put it into practice.

In this exercise, you'll be introduced to the PGP program and go through the processes of creating your own private/public key pair. Then you'll encrypt and decrypt an e-mail message.

Learning Objectives

In this lab, you will examine the basic characteristics of public key encryption from the standpoint of e-mail using PGP. By the end of the lab, you will be able to:

- Create a personal public/private key pair using PGP

- Encrypt and send an e-mail

- Decrypt and read an encrypted e-mail

Lab Materials and Setup

The materials you'll need for this lab are

- A copy of the freeware PGP Desktop program, available at http://www.pgp.com/products/free-ware.html. Remember that web addresses can and do change from time to time! If this link doesn't work, go to www.pgp.com and search for "freeware" to find this program.

- Two Windows systems (any version) configured with an e-mail client. Each system must have a legitimate POP3/SMTP e-mail account and be able to send e-mails to each other.

- Adobe Acrobat Reader installed on one of the PCs. You can get the free software at www.adobe.com.

> **→ Note**
>
> The folks at PGP work hard to keep their products up-to-date. As a result, the current version of the PGP freeware is subject to change. This lab was developed using PGP Desktop freeware version 8.1. Also, this lab is not designed to teach you how to use PGP—the goal is to teach you concepts of public key encryption and digital signatures with e-mail. Not every feature of PGP will be discussed and there is a level of expectation in the lab that the student can successfully locate particular settings—even if that means you might have to read a help file to do so.

Getting Down to Business

You've just received a call from the accounting department. It seems that one of your customers is now using PGP to encrypt e-mail and the folks in accounting cannot read the e-mails. The customer's response was simple: "Go buy a copy of PGP for each of your accountants, or at least for anyone you want reading these e-mails!" Your job is to explain the use of PGP to your boss and then show the accountants how to use PGP. You download and install the freeware version of PGP Desktop on two separate machines and proceed to present PGP to your boss to convince him of the need to use PGP.

Step 1 Install PGP on both systems. The installation is straightforward, with a couple of exceptions. Extract the two installation files, PGP8.exe and PGP8.exe.sig, and double-click the former to start installing (see Figure 17-1). Click Yes at the License Agreement dialog box and Next at the Read Me dialog box—you can take a moment to read the Release Notes here, if you like. This brings you to the User Type dialog box (see Figure 17-2). This dialog box asks you if you already have PGP keyrings or if you're a new user. Be sure to select the *No, I'm a New User* radio button and then click Next. I'll go over keyrings a little later in this lab.

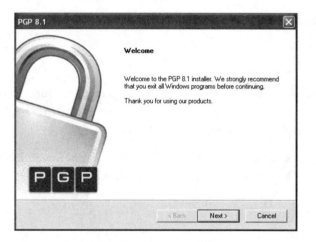

FIGURE 17-1 Installing PGP Desktop

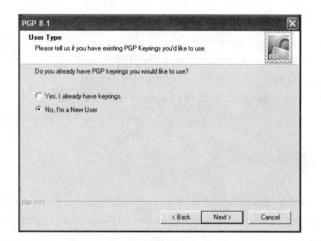

FIGURE 17-2 User Type dialog box

After being prompted about an installation folder, you'll reach the second non-intuitive screen, the Select Components dialog box (Figure 17-3). This dialog box prompts you to install optional plug-ins for encrypting a portion of your hard drive and different e-mail clients. These plug-ins are extremely handy, but they don't work with the freeware version, so deselect them! Finish the rest of the installation as you would any other software installation. You'll be prompted to reboot your computer at the completion.

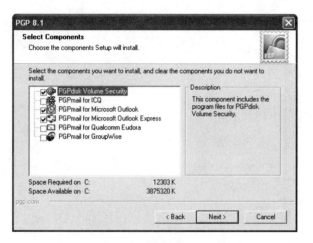

FIGURE 17-3 Select Components dialog box

Step 2 When you reboot the computer, PGP brings up the PGP License Authorization dialog box (Figure 17-4). Click on the Later button to use the freeware version.

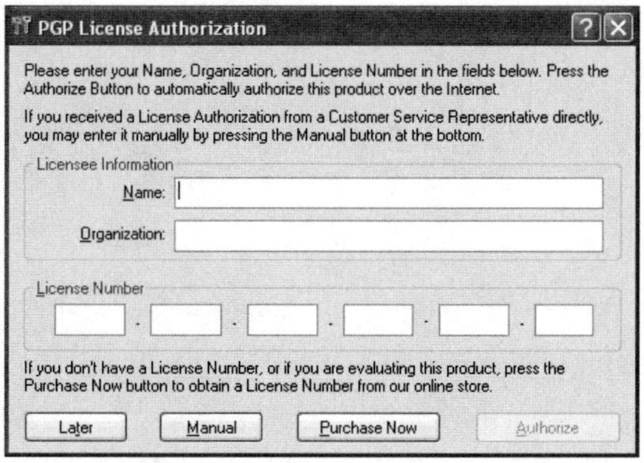

FIGURE 17-4 PGP License Authorization dialog box

Because you can't do anything with PGP without having your set of keys, that's the very next step. PGP automatically runs the PGP Key Generation Wizard so you can generate your personal public/private key pair. The Wizard will prompt for a name and an e-mail address (Figure 17-5). Be sure to use the true e-mail address for the e-mail account on each system. The wizard will also prompt you for a passphrase for access to the private key it's about to generate for you (Figure 17-6). The passphrase prevents anyone who walks up to your system from gaining access to your private key.

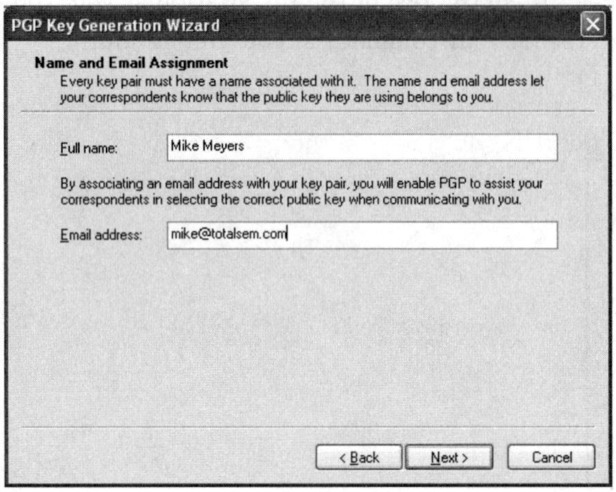

FIGURE 17-5 PGP Key Generation Wizard in action

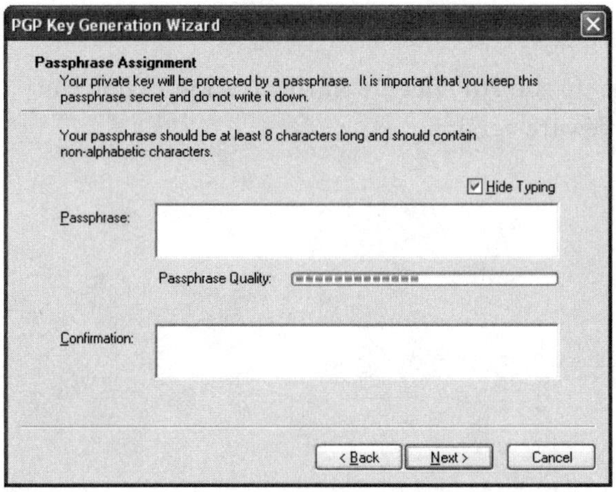

FIGURE 17-6 Passphrase generation

When you click Finish to complete the Wizard, PGP adds your newly created key pair to your keyring. The keyring stores your key pair and all the public keys you (will) have.

→ **Note**

The names for PGP options invariably lose their spaces over time. You'll see key ring and keyring, key pair and keypair, key server and keyserver. Either use is acceptable.

PGP installs three options in the Start menu under All Programs | PGP: Documentation, PGPkeys, and PGPmail. The documentation is excellent and you should take a moment to read through at least the first part of the "PGP User's Guide." You will need to refer to this manual to answer some of the questions in this lab. The "Intro to Crypto" article is also pretty cool, if you have the time.

The freeware version of PGP Desktop manifests itself as two programs: your keyring (PGPkeys) and your e-mail encryption/decryption/signing tool, PGPmail. Figure 17-7 shows both of these programs running in Windows XP. Your keyring is very important! With PGP, you'll soon begin to acquire a large number of other user's public keys—the keyring is your handy one-stop location for storing others' public keys and for sending out your public key to others.

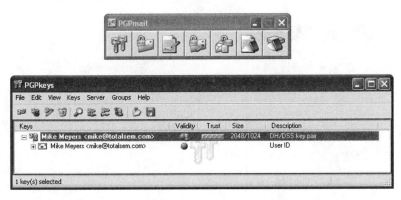

FIGURE 17-7 PGPkeys and PGPmail in Windows XP

Make sure to go through this process on both systems! Note that PGP installs an icon into your toolbar to make opening either of these programs faster.

Step 3 Open PGPkeys. Locate your public key. Send your public key to the e-mail account on the other system. When the key from the other account comes into your e-mail, import that key into your keyring. What steps must you take to import the key into your keyring? Why must each system send a public key to the other?

_____

_____

_____

_____

Step 4   Open PGPkeys and locate the option to send a key to a server. Send it to ldap://keyserver.pgp.com. Why would you want to send your public key to a key server?

_____

_____

Step 5   Create an e-mail to encrypt. Do not send it. Instead, with the e-mail still open, alternate-click the PGP icon in your system tray and move your mouse over the Current Window menu option. Select Encrypt, as shown in Figure 17-8.

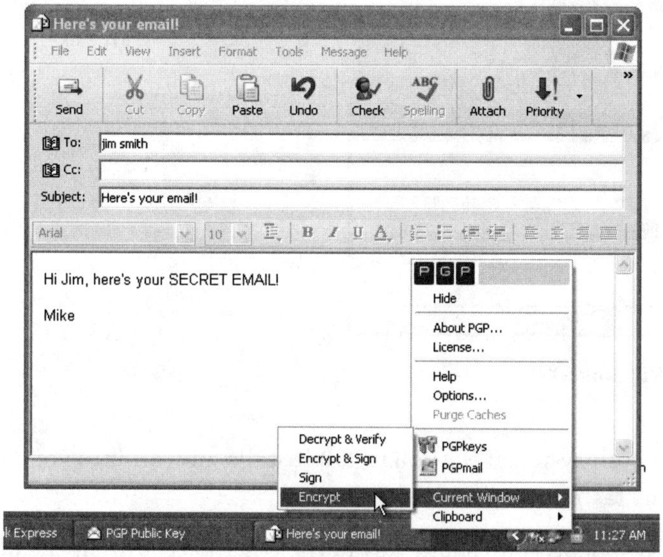

FIGURE 17-8   PGP encryption steps

Why does PGP then bring up another dialog box for the recipient? What does the encrypted mail look like? Does the subject of the e-mail change in any way?

_____

_____

_____

Step 6   When you receive the encrypted e-mail from the other system, open it. Then alternate-click the PGP icon in your system tray and move your mouse over the Current Window menu option and select Decrypt & Verify. Were you successful?

_____

_____

_____

 45 MINUTES

Lab Exercise 17.02: Running ZoneAlarm

The introduction of widespread broadband connectivity also opened up systems to hacking, especially in homes with single systems directly connected to cable modems or DSL lines. Hackers had an easy time of attacking these systems, given that they had no firewall protection and were always connected to the Internet.

In response to this threat, a number of companies began to create software firewalls—programs designed to run on and protect a single system from external attacks and to prevent unauthorized access of the Internet from the system itself. Many companies have created excellent software firewalls, one of the most popular being the powerful (and free!) ZoneAlarm by Check Point Software Technologies Ltd.

Generally, software firewalls have grown dramatically in terms of power and ease of use. Yet like any program, they all have their quirks that sometimes challenge even good techs to understand how to use them effectively.

Learning Objectives

In this lab, you'll learn how to describe the function of a software firewall. By its end, you'll be able to:

- Describe how software firewalls work, showing both their weaknesses and their strengths

- Configure and optimize the ZoneAlarm firewall

Lab Materials and Setup

The materials you need for this lab are

- A Windows PC (XP preferred) with Internet connectivity

- A copy of the freeware ZoneAlarm (www.zonealarm.com)

Getting Down to Business

Three of your company's new hires are telecommuting, and your job is to set up their home systems to use the Internet via cable modems. When you go to the first person's home to set up a VPN connection, you see that he has no firewall between his single system and the cable modem. You decide to install the freeware version of ZoneAlarm.

Step 1 Assume for a moment that the telecommuters access your company's network via a VPN connection. Why would a firewall still make sense, even though VPN connections have password protection and encryption?

_____

_____

_____

Step 2 Install ZoneAlarm. ZoneAlarm divides the IP information coming into and going out of your system into two zones: the trusted zone and the Internet zone. Read the documentation and then explain this zone concept and why it might make a handy method of configuring your software firewall.

_____

_____

_____

Step 3 Once ZoneAlarm is running, begin using the Internet with your web browser, e-mail, and any other TCP/IP applications you might have on your system. ZoneAlarm will show a number of alerts similar to the ones displayed in Figure 17-9. Track the different types of alerts that come up. How many ports, program names, or IP addresses are familiar?

_____

_____

_____

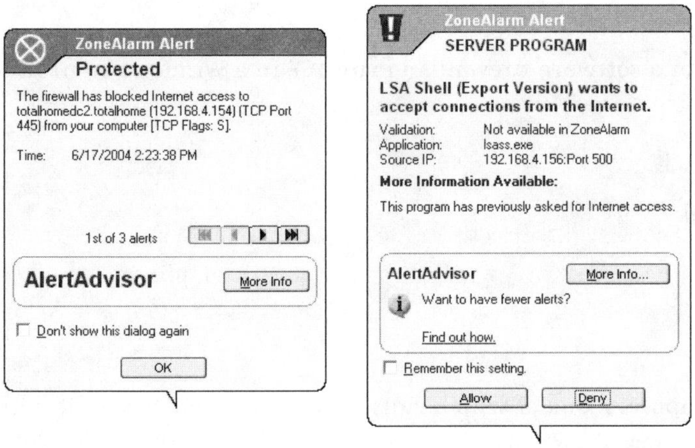

FIGURE 17-9 Sample ZoneAlarm alerts

Step 4 ZoneAlarm does a fairly good job of protecting your system just from the default settings. Give some examples of warnings that might come up that would signal a potential threat to your PC.

_____

_____

_____

Step 5 Suppose you want to add a web server to this system. Go through the steps necessary to configure ZoneAlarm to enable your system to run this web server successfully. Describe what you did.

_____

_____

45 MINUTES

Lab Exercise 17.03: Using ICF

The popularity of software firewalls motivated the folks at Microsoft to build a software firewall into Windows XP called Internet Connection Firewall (ICF). Though certainly not as robust as many third-party firewalls, ICF has the distinct advantage of being built in and therefore ready to go without the need to install more software.

Learning Objectives

In this lab, you will review the functions of a software firewall and run ICF in a Windows environment. By its end, you'll be able to:

- Describe the function of ICF

- Configure ICF for a small network

Lab Materials and Setup

The materials you need for this lab are

- A small network of Windows computers, one of which runs Windows XP and connects both to the Internet and to the other networked systems

Getting Down to Business

Hey! It's your Aunt Bessie again! She's been really happy with the ICS setup you did for her a couple of chapters ago, but she's now having a number of problems on her system. A quick check shows she has no firewall. Being the frugal person that she is, Aunt Bessie asks you to install a firewall for her. You pick ICF—because it's there!

Step 1   You really can't install ICF since it comes with XP. How do you activate ICF? (Clue: Head over to Network Connections in the Control Panel!)

_____

_____

Step 2   Can you run ICF without using Internet Connection Sharing (ICS)? Speculate why Microsoft would do this.

_____

_____

_____

_____

Step 3   Could you run a web server on a system "behind" the system running ICF? What would you need to do?

_____

_____

Step 4   Your cousin Timmy wants to operate a game server behind the system running ICF. This game server needs ports 7777 and 7787. Can you open these ports in ICF to allow a system to act as a game server? What steps would you need to take?

_____

_____

Lab Analysis

1. In the first lab, you used public key encryption. In order to encrypt your e-mail, you first had to send the other person your public key. Why could the person with your public key simply encrypt and decrypt using that key instead of having to send you their public key?

    _____

    _____

2. If you were a hacker, how could you get a person's private key? Could you use social engineering techniques to get access?

    _____

    _____

    _____

3. Compare ICF to ZoneAlarm. If you had a small network and you wanted to provide all of the systems access to the Internet via one system, which product would you choose and why?

_____

_____

_____

4. With the popularity of small SOHO routers, why would someone want to use software firewalls for a small network? What if they had a web server? Would that change your opinion? What would you say to convince a person to use one or the other?

_____

_____

_____

_____

5. ZoneAlarm comes in multiple commercial versions, as well as a free version. Go to the ZoneAlarm web site and determine the differences. Explain the differences between the two and why someone might choose the commercial version instead of the free version.

_____

_____

Key Terms Quiz

Use the vocabulary terms from the list below to complete the sentences that follow. Not all of the terms will be used.

Authentication

Demilitarized zone (DMZ)

Denial-of-service (DoS) attack

Digital certificate

Digital signature

Encryption

External threat

Firewall

Hacker

Honey pot

Internal threat

Internet Connection Firewall (ICF)

IPSec

Kerberos

Key pair

Keyring

Network Address Translation (NAT)

Network threat

Packet filtering

Port blocking

Port filtering

Private key

Public key

Secure Sockets Layer (SSL)

Social engineering

Zombie attack

1. A user with improperly configured file access permissions who accidentally deletes an important file is a classic example of an _____.

2. When using PGP, you encrypt e-mails with the recipient's _____.

3. A hacker posing as an IT support person and calling a user to get their user name and password is an example of _____.

4. The data that verifies a public key is legitimate is called a _____.

5. You can confirm that an e-mail is truly from the person sending it if they use a _____ and you have previously been given a copy of their public key.

6. Microsoft's built-in software firewall that comes with Windows XP is called
   _____.

7. Any device that filters TCP/IP traffic based on IP address or port number is by definition a
   _____.

8. Any device that directs IP packets is by definition a _____.

9. When using PGP, you decrypt e-mails you receive with your _____.

10. _____ enables a gateway system to convert IP addresses, thereby hiding
    the IP addresses of your local network from the Internet.

Chapter 18

Interconnecting Network Operating Systems

Lab Exercises

Much to the chagrin of Microsoft, Novell, Apple, *et al*, computer users just won't stick with a single OS. From the largest global corporations to the small office/home office (SOHO) market, you're unlikely to find a completely homogeneous computer environment. For example, if you toured the luxurious Total Seminars compound, you'd find systems running just about every recent version of Microsoft Windows, including Windows 98 SE, Me, NT Server, 2000 Professional, 2000 Server, Server 2003, XP Home Edition, and XP Professional Edition. You'd also find a few Macs running OS 9, OS X 10.1, 10.2 Jaguar, and 10.3 Panther, a couple of Novell NetWare file servers (different versions), a couple of Linux systems (different distros), and even a few old curiosities like a Texas Instruments 286 laptop running DOS 3.0 and an Apple Macintosh SE running OS 6.

In this chapter, you'll review the basics of interconnecting different network operating systems. Let's get started.

 30 MINUTES

Lab Exercise 18.01: Connecting to Windows

Microsoft Windows dominates much of the networking world, so you can count on being called upon to interconnect Windows servers and desktop systems with network clients of all makes and models. You've already covered much of the process for connecting Windows-to-Windows. Now let's look at how to make a link to a Windows system from a system running another NOS.

Learning Objectives

In this lab, you will review the methods for connecting computers running different network operating systems to resources shared on Windows systems. By the end of this lab, you will be able to:

- Describe the requirements and methods for connecting to shared resources on Windows PCs

Lab Materials and Setup

The materials you need for this lab are

- A PC running Windows 2000 Professional or Windows XP Professional with a local printer installed

- A PC running Windows 2000 Server or Windows Server 2003 with a local printer installed

- An Apple Macintosh system running OS X 10.1 or later and using TCP/IP

- An Apple Macintosh system running OS X 10.1 or earlier and using AppleTalk

- Internet connectivity

Getting Down to Business

Your client, Mullins Community College, wants to connect their small art department's computers to their Windows network. The art department uses systems running different versions of Macintosh. Older Macs use AppleTalk, while newer ones run TCP/IP. They also want you to configure a Windows system with printer support for a UNIX file server.

Step 1   In the chart that follows, describe the level of native support each version of Windows has for the listed client network operating systems:

Windows Version	Apple Macintosh	UNIX/Linux
Windows 9x	_____	_____
Windows NT Workstation/2000 Professional/XP Professional	_____	_____
Windows NT Server/2000 Server/Server 2003	_____	_____

Step 2   You need to share your Windows XP Professional workstation's printer with the UNIX system. Follow these steps to install Print Services for UNIX:

1.   Choose Start | My Network Places, and then select View network connections from the Network Tasks options. On the menu bar, choose Advanced, and select Optional Network Components to start the Windows Optional Networking Components Wizard, shown in Figure 18-1.

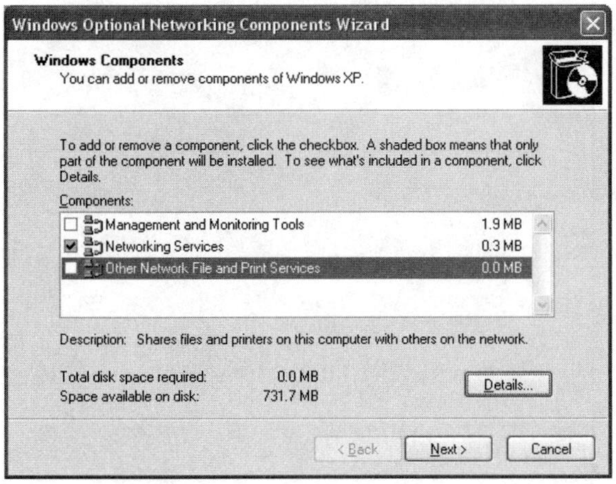

FIGURE 18-1 The Windows Optional Networking Components Wizard

2. Select the Other Network File and Print Services checkbox and click the Details button.

3. In the dialog box that opens, select the Print Services for Unix checkbox (it's the only option available), and click the OK button to close the dialog box.

4. Click the Next button to configure the selected network components. Depending on how you originally installed Windows XP Professional, you may be prompted to insert the installation CD-ROM to extract the LPDSVC.DLL (Line Printer Daemon driver) file from the \i386 folder.

5. Use the LPQ utility to check the status of the UNIX line printer queue by opening a command-line window and typing **lpq –S *servername* –P *printername*** and pressing ENTER. For example, if your PC is named Workstation1 and your printer is shared as Printer1, you would enter **lpq –S workstation1 –P printer1** and press ENTER.

    What are the results?

    _____

    _____

Step 3   Follow these steps to connect to a Windows system from Macintosh OS X 10.1 or later using TCP/IP:

1. From the Finder menu bar, click Go, and select Connect to Server.

2. The Connect to Server dialog box shows a list of available servers on the network. Choose an available server from the list, as shown in Figure 18-2, or manually type in a server name or address and click the Connect button. Note that the Address field indicates that Server Message Block (SMB) is the default transport.

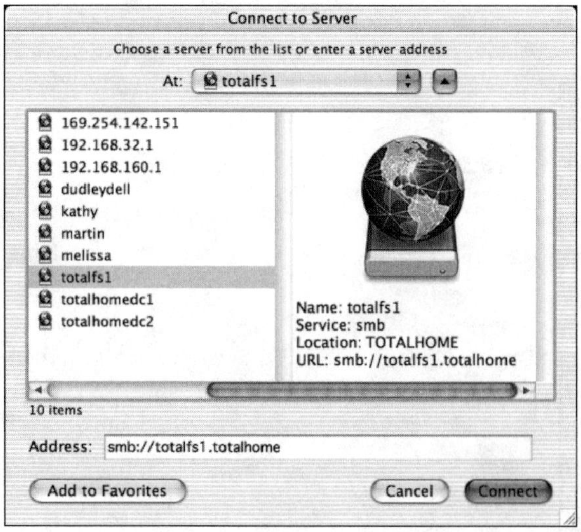

Figure 18-2 The OS X Connect to Server dialog box

3. When prompted, enter the user name and password for a valid account on the Windows server, and then select a shared resource to mount and click OK.

What are the results?

Step 4   To integrate the Macintosh OS 9 systems running AppleTalk with the Windows server system, you need to install the AppleTalk protocol, File Services for Macintosh (FSM), and Print Services for Macintosh (PSM) on the server. I've covered the steps for installing network protocols previously, so I won't rehash them here. To configure a Windows Server 2003 system with FSM and PSM, follow these steps:

1. Click Start | Control Panel | Network Connections.

2. From the menu bar of the Network Connections window, click Advanced and select Optional Networking Components.

3. In the Windows Optional Networking Components Wizard, select the option labeled Other Network File and Print Services and click the Details button.

4. In the Other Network File and Print Services dialog box, select the checkboxes for File Services for Macintosh and Print Services for Macintosh, as shown in Figure 18-3, and click the OK button to close the dialog box.

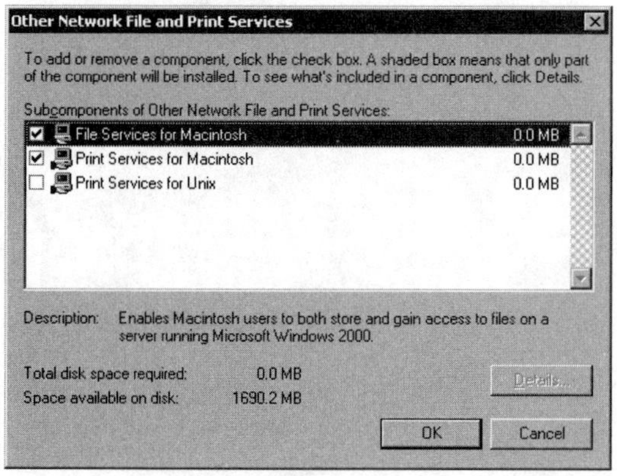

Figure 18-3 The Other Network File and Print Services dialog box with File Services for Macintosh and Print Services for Macintosh selected

5. Back in the Windows Optional Networking Components Wizard, click Next to complete the installation process. If prompted, insert the Windows 2000 Server/Server 2003 installation CD-ROM.

What are the results?

✔ **Hint**

You can also add optional networking components by going to the Control Panel and using the Add/Remove Windows Components applet.

Step 5 Once you've installed services for Macintosh onto your Windows server system, you need to configure the file server properties (such as the server name, logon message, authentication options, and so on) and create Macintosh-accessible shares. Follow these steps to access the configuration utility:

1. Open the Computer Management MMC and alternate-click the Shared Folders node icon.

2. Select Configure File Server for Macintosh from the pop-up menu.

3. Note the three configuration property sheets: Configuration, File Association, and Sessions, as shown in Figure 18-4.

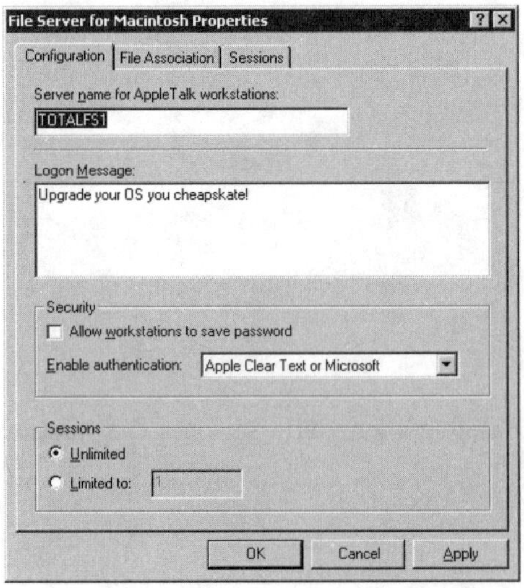

FIGURE 18-4 File Server for Macintosh Properties

Describe the configuration options for each of these property sheets. What are your authentication options? How do you control and interact with active Macintosh sessions?

Step 6 By default, only the Microsoft User Authentication Module (UAM) Volume folder (created when Macintosh services are installed) is accessible to AppleTalk clients. This volume is not configured to permit write access to clients. To create a shared folder accessible to AppleTalk clients, follow these steps:

1. Open the Computer Management MMC and expand the Shared Folders node icon.

2. Alternate-click the Shares subnode icon and select New File Share from the pop-up menu.

3. In the Create Shared Folder dialog box, enter (or browse to) the path to the shared folder on the server. Enter the share name, the description, and the Macintosh share name. Then specify that the shared folder is accessible from Macintosh clients by selecting the Apple Macintosh checkbox, as shown in Figure 18-5.

Figure 18-5 Create a shared folder for Macintosh clients

4. Click the Next button. At the next screen, configure the level of network share permissions for the shared folder (the default is *All users have full control*) and click Finish.

   What are the results?

Step 7   To connect a Macintosh client to the newly created network share using AppleTalk, follow these steps:

1.   From the Finder menu bar, click Go, and select Connect to Server.

2.   Select AppleTalk from the list of available networks, and then choose the Windows server running Services for Macintosh, as shown in Figure 18-6. Note that the Address field indicates that Apple File Protocol is the default transport.

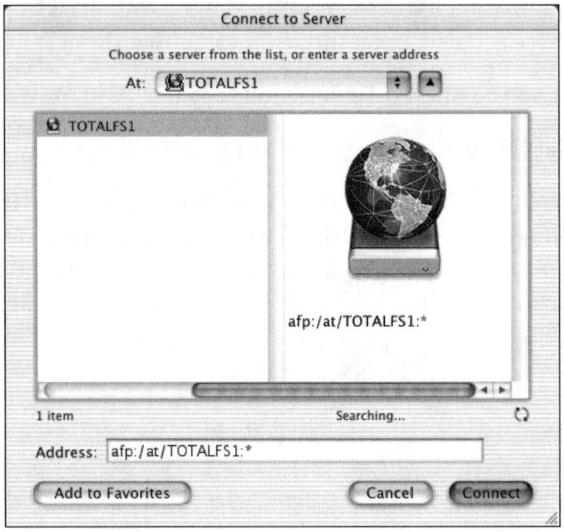

FIGURE 18-6 The OS X Connect to Server dialog box showing AppleTalk servers on the network

3.   When prompted, enter the user name and password for a valid account on the Windows server, and then select the shared folder created earlier and click OK.

What are the results?

_____

_____

Step 8   To connect Macintosh systems to Windows via terminal emulation, Microsoft's Remote Desktop Connection (RDC) client for Macintosh enables OS X 10.2.8 and later systems to establish terminal sessions with Windows server systems running Terminal Services and Windows XP Professional systems running the Remote Desktop service. To install and use the RDC client, follow these steps:

→ **Note**

This option is not available in Windows XP Home Edition.

1. Go to http://www.microsoft.com/mac/downloads.aspx and download the appropriate version of the client software (for example, to install the English language version of the client software, download the **RDC102EN.DMG** file).

2. Once downloaded, double-click the file to expand it, and then open the Remote Desktop Connection volume created on the Macintosh desktop. Copy the Remote Desktop Connection folder to a permanent location on your Macintosh system's hard disk (for instance, in Applications/Utilities).

3. Start the RDC client by navigating to the Remote Desktop Connection folder and double-clicking the Remote Desktop Connection client icon. By default, the only visible configuration option is blank text box—labeled Computer—where you can enter the name or IP address of a computer running Terminal Services or Remote Desktop. (Once you've added one or more PCs to the text box and connected successfully, by the way, you'll see those names or IP addresses as options when you run the RDC client.) Click Options to expand the full configuration options menu, as shown in Figure 18-7.

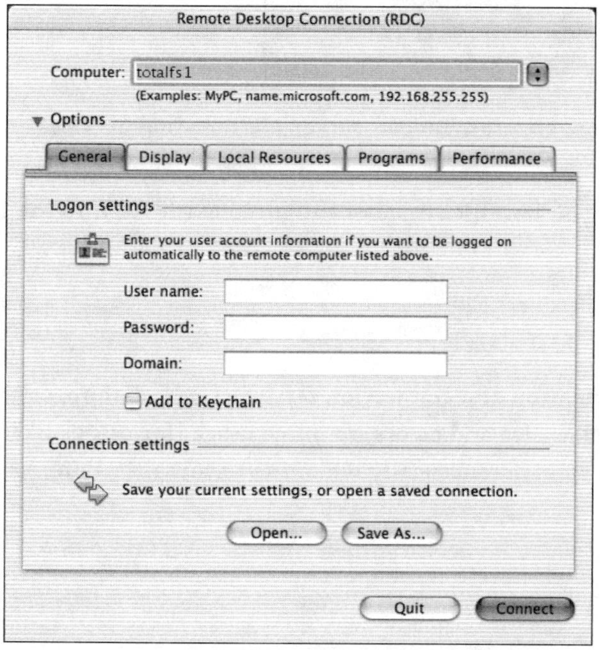

FIGURE 18-7 Microsoft Remote Desktop Connection (RDC) client configuration options

4. Type the NetBIOS name, DNS name, or IP address of the Windows system running Terminal Services (or Remote Desktop) and click the Connect button. Once connected, a terminal window opens showing the desktop of the remote system and a logon dialog box, as shown in Figure 18-8.

Figure 18-8 Microsoft RDC for Macintosh connected to Windows server via Terminal Services

5. Type in a valid logon name and password (if you haven't already configured this data into the RDC client options). What are the results?

→ Note

With the full options menu, you can configure logon and connection settings (LAN, dial-up, or broadband), logon settings, the terminal window size and colors, resource usage (for things like printers and disk drives), which programs to start automatically when the terminal session begins, and performance settings.

 40 MINUTES

Lab Exercise 18.02: Connecting to NetWare

Novell NetWare is still going strong as a server-class NOS. You'll run into NetWare systems of all vintages chugging away in server closets all over the world. Interconnecting these with Windows, UNIX/Linux, or Macintosh systems can be challenging, given the many choices available. In this exercise, you'll examine the various ways to connect client systems to Novell NetWare servers.

Learning Objectives

In this lab, you will examine the methods you have available for connecting to Novell NetWare servers. By its end, you will be able to:

- Describe the methods and procedures for interconnecting Novell NetWare

Lab Materials and Setup

The materials you'll need for this lab are

- A PC running Windows 2000 Professional or Windows XP Professional

- A PC running Windows 2000 Server or Windows Server 2003

Getting Down to Business

Your client, Howard, Fine, & Howard Psychiatric Services, needs to integrate several new Windows workstation clients with a pair of older (version 3.14) NetWare servers. They also want you to explain the options available for integrating their NetWare servers with a newly purchased Windows Server 2003 system.

Step 1 Review the protocols and methods available for connecting Windows client systems to the NetWare server systems. What protocols can interconnect older and newer versions of Novell NetWare with Windows systems? When is one protocol or method preferred over another? Which method offers the most centralized administrative control?

Step 2 You need to connect your Windows XP Professional client system to an older NetWare server that uses IPX/SPX. As you know, to connect to older NetWare servers, you need to install the NWLink IPX/SPX protocol and the NetWare client. You have the option of installing either the Microsoft client or the Novell client software. In fact, the installation wizard is smart enough to help you along depending on whether you install the Microsoft Client for NetWare first or the NWLink IPX/SPX protocol first. If you install the Microsoft Client for NetWare software, the installation wizard automatically installs NWLink IPX/SPX along with it. If you install NWLink IPX/SPX first, then the client software is not automatically installed, leaving you with the option of using either the Microsoft or Novell client software. For this example, assume your network client is going to use the Microsoft Client for NetWare. Follow these steps to install the Novell NetWare networking client and protocol software:

1. Open the Network Connections folder (choose Start | My Network Places | View network connections), then alternate-click the Local Area Connection icon and select Properties.

2. On the General property sheet, click the Install button.

3. From the Select Network Component Type dialog box, select Client and click the Add button.

4. In the Select Network Client dialog box, pick the Client Service for NetWare (it's your only choice) and click the OK button.

5. You'll be prompted to restart your computer to complete the installation. Click the No button to restart later and check the settings of your Local Area Connection.

   What are the results?

   _____

   _____

Step 3   Restart the system and note the results. What is different about the logon procedure now that NWLink and the Client for NetWare are installed?

_____

_____

Step 4   For the most part, that's all there is to installing client support for NetWare; however, if your network has specific needs that go beyond the basic installation (such as using IPX routing), you may need to adjust your internal network number and/or frame type settings. Follow these steps to do so:

1. Open the Network Connections folder (choose Start | My Network Places | View network connections), then alternate-click the Local Area Connection icon and select Properties.

2. On the General property sheet, highlight the listing for NWLink IPX/SPX/NetBIOS Compatible Transport Protocol and click the Properties button. This opens the NWLink IPX/SPX/NetBIOS Compatible Transport Protocol dialog box shown in Figure 18-9.

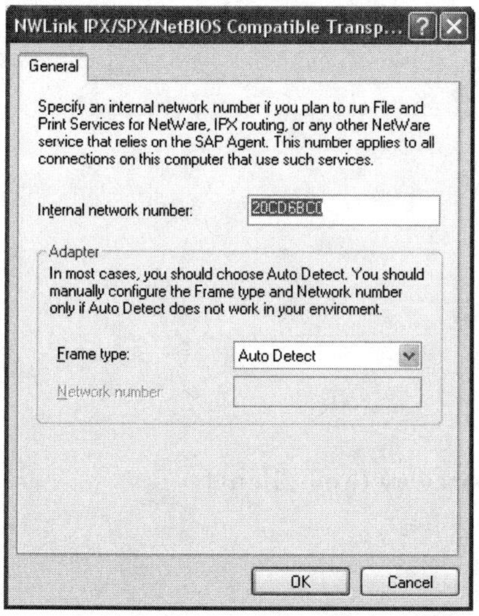

FIGURE 18-9 The NWLink IPX/SPX/NetBIOS Compatible Transport Protocol properties dialog box

3. Note the configuration options and explain when it is appropriate to change from the default to a manual setting.

_____

_____

Step 5 As an alternative to installing CSNW on each Windows system that requires access to a Net-Ware server, GSNW runs on a single Windows NT Server, 2000 Server, or Server 2003 system. Networked Windows client systems then access folders shared on the NetWare server via the gateway service running on the Windows server system. To configure a Windows Server 2003 system with GSNW, follow these steps:

1. Choose Start | Control Panel | Network Connections.

2. Alternate-click the Local Area Connection icon and select Properties.

3. On the General property sheet, click the Install button, and then in the Select Network Component Type dialog box, select Client and click Add.

4. Select Gateway (and Client) Services for NetWare, as shown in Figure 18-10, and click the OK button.

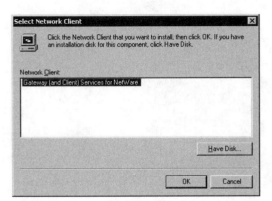

FIGURE 18-10 The Select Network Client dialog box showing Gateway (and Client) Services for NetWare

5. Follow the prompts to complete the installation, restarting the Windows server system when prompted.

What are the results?

_____

_____

Step 6 To enable the gateway service on the Windows server, open the Control Panel and double-click the GSNW icon to open the Gateway Service for NetWare applet, shown in Figure 18-11.

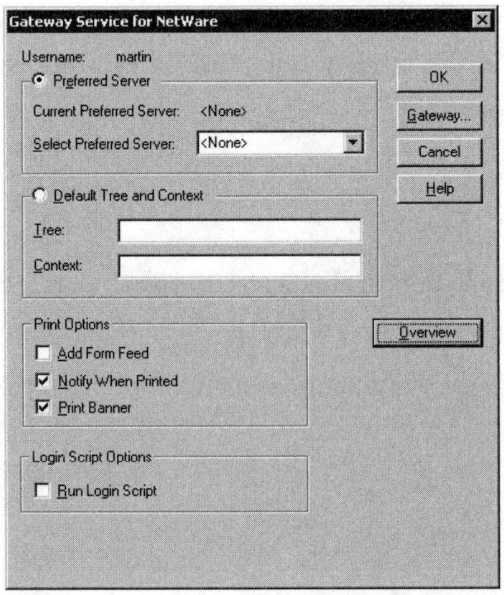

FIGURE 18-11 The Gateway Service for NetWare applet

Follow these steps to configure the gateway service:

1. Click the Gateway button to start the Configure Gateway dialog box, shown in Figure 18-12.

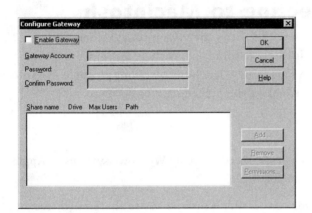

FIGURE 18-12 The Configure Gateway dialog box

2. Click the checkbox labeled Enable Gateway, and then enter a default gateway account name and password (this is a user account that all users who access the NetWare server use to authenticate).

3. Click the Add button to open the New Share dialog box, shown in Figure 18-13.

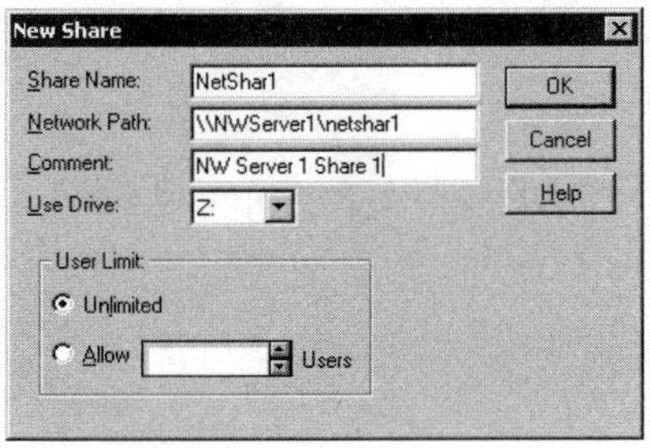

FIGURE 18-13 The New Share dialog box

Here, enter the share name (the name that Windows clients will use to access the resource on the NetWare server), network path (the UNC path to the volume shared on the NetWare server—for example, \\NWServer1\netshar1), any descriptive comments, a local drive letter to connect to the NetWare volume, and a user limit number (if any). Click OK to close all dialog boxes.

What are the results?

_____

_____

 25 MINUTES

Lab Exercise 18.03: Connecting to Macintosh

Apple Macintosh systems of old were super-easy to network with other Macintosh systems, but could be quite a pain to get to work with other NOS types. Third-party solutions, such as DAVE, were often the way to go to get Mac systems to talk to, say, Windows machines. The latest versions of Apple Macintosh OS X make interconnecting considerably easier. Let's look at the procedures for doing so.

Learning Objectives

In this lab, you will review the requirements and methods for connecting Windows systems to Apple Macintosh systems. By the end of this lab, you will be able to:

- Describe the requirements and methods for connecting Windows PCs to shared printers and folders on Apple Macintosh systems using the AppleTalk protocol and TCP/IP

Lab Materials and Setup

The materials you'll need for this lab are

- A PC running Windows 2000 Professional or Windows XP Professional

- An Apple Macintosh system running OS X 10.1 or later and using TCP/IP

Getting Down to Business

You are visiting a client's office site with your trusty Windows 2000 Professional laptop and need to print some documents to a printer that uses the AppleTalk protocol. You also need to connect to a Macintosh OS X 10.2.8 system to copy some data files.

Step 1   Follow these steps to install AppleTalk onto your system:

1.   Open the Network Connections folder (choose Start | Settings | Network and Dial-up Connections), then alternate-click the Local Area Connection icon and select Properties.

2.   On the General property sheet, click the Install button.

3.   From the Select Network Component Type dialog box, select Protocol, and click the Add button.

4.   In the Select Network Protocol dialog box, pick the AppleTalk Protocol and click the OK button.

    What are the results?

_____

_____

→ **Note**

The AppleTalk protocol on Windows client systems is only used to enable printing between Windows and Macintosh systems. AppleTalk (combined with FSM and PSM) on Windows server systems enables full network communication between Macintosh and Windows server systems. AppleTalk is no longer supported on Windows XP Home or Professional Editions.

Step 2   In the Local Area Connection properties dialog box, select the AppleTalk protocol and click the Properties button. What are your configuration options for the AppleTalk protocol?

_____

_____

Step 3   To finish configuring support for printing to an AppleTalk printer, you must create a new printer port on the Windows system. Follow these steps to do so:

1. Start the Add Printer Wizard by clicking Start | Settings | Printers, and double-clicking the Add Printer icon.

2. Click Next, and then at the Local or Network Printer dialog box, select the radio button for Local printer.

3. Clear the checkbox labeled *Automatically detect and install my Plug and Play printer*, and click the Next button.

4. At the Select the Printer Port dialog screen, select the *Create a new port* radio button. Select the AppleTalk Printing Devices option, shown in Figure 18-14, and then click Next.

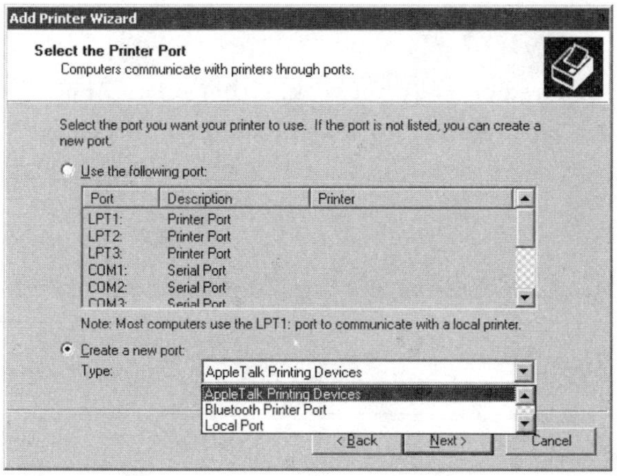

Figure 18-14 Adding the AppleTalk Printing Devices port to Windows 2000

5. The Add Printer Wizard then scans your network for AppleTalk print devices and displays available devices, as shown in Figure 18-15. Select the appropriate AppleTalk device and click OK.

FIGURE 18-15 The Available AppleTalk Printing Devices dialog box

6. You may be asked whether or not you wish to capture the printer port, thereby turning your Windows 2000 PC into the network print server for the AppleTalk print device. Click No to continue.

7. At the next screen, select the make and model of the AppleTalk print device and select any other driver options (keep existing drivers or replace the driver with a new one), and click Next again.

8. Enter a name for the AppleTalk printer (or keep the default), and select whether to use this device as the default printer for the Windows PC, and click Next again.

9. Select whether or not to share the printer and click Next.

10. Enter any descriptive text or notes for the printer and continue to finish the wizard.

    What are the results?

➜ **Note**

This step assumes you have an AppleTalk printer shared on your network, either on an Apple Macintosh client or a Windows server system with File Services for Macintosh, Print Services for Macintosh, and AppleTalk installed.

Step 4 Modern Macintosh systems (OS X 10.1 and later) make file and printer sharing much simpler by using TCP/IP and the Samba service. Follow these steps to connect a Windows system to a Mac network share:

1. On the Macintosh system, open System Preferences (Apple menu | System Preferences) and click the Sharing icon under the Internet & Network category.

2. On the Services tab, select the checkboxes labeled Personal File Sharing and Windows File Sharing, as shown in Figure 18-16.

FIGURE 18-16 Starting the Personal File Sharing and Windows File Sharing services in Macintosh OS X

3. As with Windows NT/2000/XP systems, users need a valid user account to log onto Macintosh OS X. In System Preferences, click the Accounts icon under the System category.

4. Select an account and click the Edit User button. In the user account properties dialog box, make sure the *Allow user to log in from Windows* checkbox is selected, as shown in Figure 18-17, and click Save.

5. From your Windows system, browse to the Macintosh OS X system by name or IP address, and enter a valid user name and password when prompted.

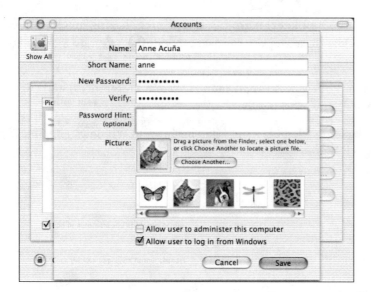

FIGURE 18-17 A Macintosh OS X user account with the *Allow user to log in from Windows* option selected

What are the results?

_____

_____

Lab Analysis

1. You are the administrator of your office LAN. Your Windows XP Professional workstation is part of a Windows 2000 Active Directory domain. How can you configure services and use tools that reside on your Windows 2000 Server domain controller from your Windows XP Professional workstation?

_____

_____

2. What service must be installed on a Windows 2000 or XP Professional workstation to enable it to share its printer with UNIX systems?

_____

_____

3. Without using third-party solutions, how do you enable Windows PCs to access files on an Apple Macintosh OS X 10.2 Jaguar system?

_____

_____

4. Describe the difference between using CSNW and GSNW to connect Windows clients to Novell NetWare servers.

_____

_____

5. What two properties of the Windows NWLink IPX/SPX protocol must be configured properly to ensure communication with NetWare servers?

_____

_____

Key Terms Quiz

Use the vocabulary terms from the list below to complete the sentences that follow. Not all of the terms will be used.

AppleShare IP

AppleTalk Configurator

Client for NetWare Networks

Client Service for NetWare (CSNW)

Client32

DAVE

eDirectory

File Services for Macintosh (FSM)

Gateway Services for NetWare (GSNW)

Gateway Services for UNIX

Mac OS X

Macintosh NetWare Client

Microsoft Windows Services for UNIX (MWSU)

Native File Access

Netatalk

Novell Directory Services (NDS)

PC MACLAN

Print Services for Macintosh (PSM)

Samba

Services for UNIX (SFU)

Terminal Services

VNC

WinFrame/MetaFrame

1. _____ is a service application that enables UNIX/Linux and Macintosh OS X (10.1 and later) to support the Server Message Block (SMB) file sharing protocol and thus connect to Windows network resources.

2. The component of Microsoft Windows Services for UNIX (MWSU) that enables a Windows server to provide connectivity for network clients to UNIX servers is called _____.

3. _____ and _____ are two examples of third-party applications that enable computers running Macintosh OS to connect to Windows networks.

4. Client Service for NetWare differs from Microsoft Client for NetWare in that it supports both NetWare 3 binderies and _____.

5. _____ are examples of terminal emulation applications.

Chapter 19

The Perfect Server

Lab Exercises

The most important and the most expensive part of every network is the data stored on your servers. Loss of data costs organizations millions (some say billions) of dollars every year in lost productivity. The perfect server is a conglomeration of specialized hardware and software that, combined with strict maintenance systems and data backups, does not allow your data to go away. The labs in this chapter are designed to get your hands dirty in some of the commoner issues that take place in buying, configuring, and supporting those perfect servers.

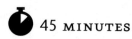 45 MINUTES

Lab Exercise 19.01: Working with RAID

Hardware RAID, once the exclusive domain of high-end servers, is now a common extra on many motherboards and pre-built systems. These mainstream RAID implementations generally stick with the basics, providing RAID 0, 1, and sometimes 0+1. You'll find few frills, but mainstream RAID is better than nothing!

Most server systems sport dedicated hardware RAID to provide proper redundancy for the most expensive part of any network-irreplaceable data. These server-level RAID implementations support RAID 0, 1, and 5 at least, and also include cool features such as hot-swapping of drives, automatic failover (where a ready spare immediately starts to rebuild the RAID array in case of failure), and e-mail or voice failure notification.

Software RAID is not a viable solution for serious server systems. The workload placed on the CPU to handle RAID duties (that in hardware RAID are handled by the RAID controllers) are simply not responsive enough for any but the simplest RAID configurations.

The software RAID provided with Windows 2000 Server and Server 2003, however, is an excellent tool to understand how RAID works. The goal of this lab is to inspect different types of RAID configurations, focusing on software RAID in Windows. You will see what you need to do to install and maintain a RAID array, and what to do in case of a drive failure in a RAID array.

→ **Note**

Windows 2000 Server and Server 2003 support software-based RAID 0, RAID 1, and RAID 5 configurations using Microsoft's proprietary Dynamic Disk technology. Windows 2000 Professional and XP Professional only support software RAID 0 and RAID 1 configurations.

Learning Objectives

In this lab, you will examine some software RAID solutions and determine how to do the following:

- Configure RAID for RAID 0, 1, or 5

- Perform basic drive maintenance

- Rebuild arrays in case of failure

Lab Materials and Setup

The materials you'll need for this lab are

- A pen and some paper

- One Windows 2000 Server or Server 2003 system. The operating system is installed on the primary master ATA drive. This system must then have three more identical ATA hard drives that can be added to standard ATA controllers. (You may remove any other ATA devices such as CD Media or DVD drives to make room for the hard drives.) This system also needs some form of hardware RAID, preferably an ATA add-in card with RAID-5 support and another three drives.

→ **Note**

The same three ATA drives connected to the standard controllers may also be used to connect to the hardware RAID controller.

Getting Down to Business

After yet another disastrous hard drive failure, you've finally got the boss to a point where she is willing to consider adding RAID to your small office network. You need to take three steps to get RAID up and running on your Windows servers: first, explain RAID to the boss. She's fairly technical and has an idea what RAID is, but needs details. Second, develop a RAID solution for your office. Third, install and support your RAID solution choice.

→ **Note**

This lab assumes a basic familiarity with the Windows Disk Management applet.

Step 1 Create a table summarizing RAID 0, RAID 1, RAID 5 and RAID 0+1 for your boss. Use the following as a template.

RAID Level	Short description	Benefits	Drawbacks	Minimum drives
0	_____	_____	_____	_____
1	_____	_____	_____	_____
5	_____	_____	_____	_____
0+1	_____	_____	_____	_____

Step 2 Install your three ATA drives to the standard ATA controllers on your Windows Server system to match the following configuration.

Primary Master (or first boot disk)—Windows Server operating system

Primary Slave (or second boot disk)—ATA drive 1 (Disk 1)

Secondary Master (or third boot disk)—ATA drive 2 (Disk 2)

Secondary Slave (or fourth boot disk)—ATA drive 3 (Disk 3)

Go into Disk Management and confirm that the three ATA drives are completely blank. Remove any volumes or partitions if any exist. Initialize each drive and then convert them to Dynamic Disks. Do this in one of the following ways:

- Use the Initialize and Convert Wizard that pops up automatically when you start Disk Management.

- Manually open Disk Management, alternate-click one of the three drives, and select Initialize. Then alternate-click one of the three disks and select Convert to Dynamic Disk. Repeat the process to initialize and convert the other two drives. The result should look like Figure 19-1.

What are the results? Include the capacities of the drives.

_____

_____

Step 3 Now follow these steps to create a stripe set using Disk 1 and Disk 2:

1. Open Computer Management, expand the Storage node, and click on the Disk Management icon.

2. Alternate-click an unconfigured disk volume and select New Volume from the pop-up menu to start the New Volume Wizard.

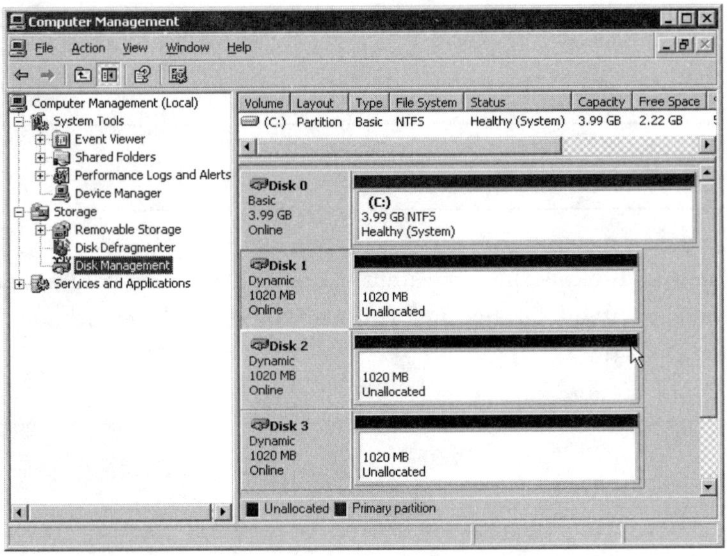

FIGURE 19-1 Four ATA drives in Disk Management (Windows Server 2003)

3. Click Next, then at the Volume Type screen, select Striped (different versions of server have different names here but it should be obvious), and click Next.

4. Select the volumes you wish to stripe and configure the volume size (to save time, configure the size of the striped set to something small, such as 250 MB), then follow the prompts to assign a drive letter to the volume and specify a format (FAT, FAT32, or NTFS).

5. After you've configured these parameters, click Finish to create a new striped volume set.

What are the results? What is the total capacity of the stripe set? Could you have made a stripe set using Disk 1, Disk 2, and Disk 3?

_____

_____

Step 4 Now follow these steps to create a mirror set:

1. First, delete the striped set by alternate-clicking on it and selecting Delete Volume from the pop-up menu.

2. Repeat steps 1 and 2 from the previous procedure, only this time choose Mirror Set in the Select Volume Type dialog screen.

3. Follow the prompts to create a mirror set across Disk 1 and Disk 2.

What are the results? What is the total capacity of the mirror set? Could you have made a mirror set using Disk 1, Disk 2, and Disk 3?

_____

_____

Step 5   Now delete the mirrored volumes and follow the same steps to create a spanned volume set using Disk 1 and Disk 2. What is the total capacity of the spanned volume? Could you have made a spanned volume using Disk 1, Disk 2, and Disk 3?

_____

_____

Step 6   Delete the spanned volume and follow the previous steps to create a RAID 5 set using all three disks. What is the total capacity of the RAID 5 set? Could you have made a RAID 5 set using only Disk 1 and Disk 2?

_____

_____

Step 7   Shut down the system, remove one of the three drives from the RAID 5 set, and then reboot the system. What are the results? Can you still access the RAID set? What is the process to replace the bad drive in a real-world environment?

_____

_____

Step 8   Delete the software RAID 5 set and reconfigure your system to use the hardware RAID.

1.   First, install and configure drivers for your RAID controller following the manufacturer's instructions.

2.   Disconnect the three drives from the standard ATA controllers and reconnect them to the RAID controller.

3.   Restart the system and, using the manufacturer's RAID administration utility, configure two of the drives as a mirror set.

Restart the system and go into Disk Management. How does the mirrored set you just created manifest itself? How does the mirror set manifest in My Computer?

_____

_____

Step 9 Now, following the RAID controller manufacturer's instructions, delete the mirror set and configure a RAID 5 array.

1. Once you've done this, restart the system and then go into Disk Management and partition and format the drive(s) in the RAID 5 array.

2. Verify the RAID set is working by copying files onto the hardware RAID 5 set.

3. Shut down the system and remove one of the drives from the RAID 5 set. Restart the system.

Can you still access the RAID set? Speculate what the process would be to replace the bad drive in a real-world environment.

_____

_____

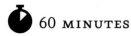 60 MINUTES

Lab Exercise 19.02: Tape Backups

There are two types of network administrators in the real world: those who perform dependable tape backups and those who are unemployed. In keeping with the philosophy that the most important part of a network is the data, your tape backup is the point of last defense when RAID arrays fail, when users accidentally delete that critical database, or when viruses corrupt your file server.

It's hard to find any but the smallest of organizations that fail to use some form of tape backup. In a world where DVD drives can store a few gigabytes of data, why do we still use tape backups, a technology that has remained hasn't changed significantly in over 40 years? Well, the latest tape backup formats have the ability to store many tens of gigabytes of data per tape, all at a cost that no other media can even begin to approach.

This lab looks at tape backup technologies as well as the more popular backup strategies used in the real world. Let's go!

Learning Objectives

In this lab, you'll learn to perform the following:

- Describe the latest tape drive technologies and capacities

- Run a backup using Windows Backup

- Develop a practical tape backup strategy for a small business

Lab Materials and Setup

The materials you'll need for this lab are

- A pencil and some paper

- A Windows PC (2000 or XP). A tape drive and tapes are handy but not necessary

Getting Down to Business

Your new employer, Eenie-Meanie, Chili-Beanie Corporation (EMCB Corp.), has just suffered through a major data loss. Your predecessor, who no longer works for EMCP Corp., failed to back up properly the file server that stores the daily account receivable database. A nasty system crash destroyed the hard drive—and an entire week's worth of accounts receivable data, almost 1400 records, were lost and required 200 man hours of manual re-entering. The mood at EMCB Corp. is not good, to say the least.

Your first job is to review their tape backup system from ground up. You are to report your evaluation of the current system to your supervisor. Based on your evaluation, you will then purchase the correct backup tape equipment for your office and devise a reliable backup strategy.

Step 1   You begin your evaluation by taking an inventory of the existing backup equipment and evaluating the current backup strategy. Here's what you discover:

1. The existing tape backup is an old QIC/Travan tape drive that uses tapes with a capacity of 2 GB uncompressed. Even though no one makes Travan tapes of this size anymore, your predecessor bought over 200 used Travan tapes off of eBay a few years ago. It all seems in good working order.

2. Almost all of the critical business of the company is focused around three databases. Each database manifests itself as a large file. ACCOUNTS.MDB is almost 1 GB, and is continually updated throughout every business day. PRODUCT.MDB is slightly more than 500 MB, and is modified only about once a month. CUSTOMER.MDB is around 300 MB, and is modified by salespeople as needed—usually once a week.

Given this information, explain to the boss why the current tape backup is acceptable or unacceptable in terms of technology and capacity.

_____

_____

Step 2   Develop a backup strategy for these databases using the existing hardware. Define a weekly backup using either full, incremental, or differential methods and explain your reasons.

_____

_____

Step 3   The company has a number of files, mainly word documents, created by users. The users save them in a number of locations on their personal systems. How would you have the users organize these files so they may also be backed up?

_____

_____

Step 4   The office's main productivity software suite is Microsoft Office. Microsoft Outlook is used extensively for e-mail and to keep track of appointments, contacts, and customer calls. Currently, however, there is no plan in place to back up the vital Outlook database files (.PST files). Explain to the boss how users could keep backups of their critical Outlook information.

_____

_____

Step 5   The Word documents and the backups of the Outlook .PST files take up another 4 GB of data. Explain to the boss why you can still use the old Travan tapes, but also explain why a new, higher capacity tape backup would make more sense.

_____

_____

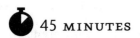 45 MINUTES

Lab Exercise 19.03: Working with Anti-Virus Software

Everyone uses anti-virus software today, but how many of us simply install some program without truly understanding what is taking place? In this lab, we will inspect a popular and free (for personal use) anti-virus program called avast! (www.avast.com) and compare it to other anti-virus programs such as Symantec's Norton AntiVirus, McAfee VirusScan, and AVG Anti-Virus.

Learning Objectives

In this lab, you will review the common functions of anti-virus programs used for individual systems.

- Describe the main components of an anti-virus program

- Show how to configure typical anti-virus options

Lab Materials and Setup

The materials you need for this lab are

- A Windows 2000 or XP Professional PC with Internet connectivity and Microsoft Outlook installed and configured with a fully functional SMTP/POP3 account.

- This computer should also have a copy of any popular instant message program, such as MSN, Yahoo! Messenger, ICQ, or AIM. The program needs a functional account.

- A copy of the freeware avast! anti-virus software, available at www.avast.com.

→ **Note**

Alwil Software, the creators of avast!, only allow use of the freeware version for home use. avast! is used in this lab because 1) it is very powerful, and 2) Alwil isn't concerned with anyone using their free product on a temporary basis. Alwil supplies a number of superb commercial anti-virus programs for organizations.

Getting Down to Business

This emergency customer call is a rather ugly scene. It seems the entire office was attacked by a number of viruses, causing system slowdowns and data loss. Despite repeated cries of "but we use anti-virus programs!" from the manager of the office, you realize that you've got a big cleanup job to do. First you'll need to clean out the viruses from all of the computers. Second, you'll need to install an anti-virus program and explain to the manager how it works and how to use the anti-virus software properly.

Step 1 Download and install avast! freeware edition, using the Custom install. Notice the different types of protection avast offers. What are they? (You may need to go to the avast! web site for details.) Would everyone need all these features?

_____

_____

Step 2   Like most anti-virus programs, avast! will prompt you to reboot your computer for a boot-time scan. Why do all anti-virus programs want to do this?

_____

_____

Step 3   The office manager is confused. She says, "We already have an anti-virus program!" and shows you a copy of Spybot's Search and Destroy (www.spybot.info), which is running on every system. Research this freeware program and write a memo to the office manager boss explaining the difference between this program and avast!.

_____

_____

Step 4   Open up the avast! On-Access Protection program by double-clicking the avast! icon on the system tray (it looks like a blue ball with the letter "a"). You may be prompted for a license key. If you're prompted for a key, just click the Demo button. This will allow you to use avast! for 60 days—plenty of time for this lab! You should see a Details button at the bottom of the screen—click it to see something similar to Figure 19-2.

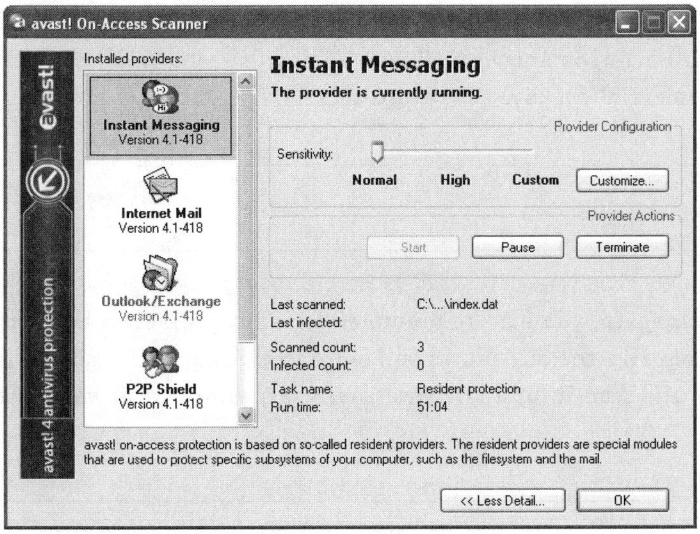

Figure 19-2 The avast! On-Access Protection dialog box

Go through each of what avast! calls Providers. The Providers are

- Instant Messaging
- Internet Mail
- Outlook/Exchange
- P2P Shield,
- Standard Shield

Explain each of these to the office manager and help her determine the ones the office might need.

_____

_____

Step 5 Open Task Manager and note the CPU usage. Try sending e-mail with attachments and sending files over your IM program. Does the computer seem to slow down? Is there a substantial increase (>15 percent) in CPU usage in Task Manager? Explain to the office manager why this is happening.

_____

_____

Step 6 Get on the Internet and compare the freeware avast! to another anti-virus program such as Symantec's Norton AntiVirus, McAfee VirusScan, or AVG Anti-Virus by going to each company's web site. What features do you see in the commercial package that avast! lacks?

_____

_____

Step 7 Start avast! from the Start menu (again, you may be prompted for a license). Close the Simple User Interface—you should see a dialog box like the one shown in Figure 19-3. Scan all the files in the My Documents Folder. Grab a floppy disk and scan it for any viruses. Why is scanning removable media important?

_____

_____

FIGURE 19-3 The avast! main screen

Step 8 All anti-virus programs need ongoing updates to ensure they recognize the latest virus. Show the office manager how to update the anti-virus program.

→ **Note**

Procedures for completing this step will vary depending on the anti-virus application.

Lab Analysis

1. In the RAID lab you used ATA drives. Traditionally, SCSI drives were the only practical option for RAID and only in the last few years has RAID using ATA drives become available. Describe why SCSI dominated RAID for many years, and then explain what happened to ATA technology to make it a common RAID solution.

2. Windows Server versions support RAID 0, 1, and 5 but do not support RAID 2, 3, or 4. In fact, it is very difficult to find any RAID solution—hardware or software—that uses RAID 2, 3, or 4. Describe these levels of RAID and speculate as to why Microsoft, as well as almost all hardware vendors, never adopted these RAID levels.

3. A number of newer tape backup technologies are starting to supplant DAT and DLT tape backups. Research technologies such as Ultrium LTO and Super DLT and determine their capacities, cost of drives, and cost of tape cartridges. Can you find any other tape backup technologies?

_____

_____

4. There are dozens of commercial backup programs that can inspect your system and back up critical information such as e-mail, web favorites, and critical system files, and then save them to tape, CD-RW, or even hard drives. Do some research and see if you can find a program that would suit a typical home system's needs. What aspects were most important to you?

_____

_____

Key Terms Quiz

Use the vocabulary terms from the list below to complete the sentences that follow. Not all of the terms will be used.

Bimodal/bipartite virus

Boot sector virus

Checksum

Digital audio tape (DAT)

Digital linear tape (DLT)

Disk striping

Disk striping with parity

Drive duplexing

Drive mirroring

Enhanced Integrated Drive Electronics (EIDE)

Executable virus

Host bus adapter (HBA)

Hot-swapping

Just a Bunch of Disks (JBOD)

Macro virus

Network attached storage (NAS)

Parallel Advanced Technology Attachment (PATA)

Quarter-inch tape (QIC)/Travan tape

Random Array of Independent/Inexpensive Disks (RAID)

SCSI chain

Serial ATA (SATA)

Storage area network (SAN)

Small Computer System Interface (SCSI)

Stealth virus

Trojan virus

Uninterruptible power supply (UPS)

Worm

1. A virus that propagates over the Internet is typically classified as a(n) _____.

2. _____ hard drives use a narrow, seven-wire data cable.

3. A(n) _____ provides a few minutes of power to your server in the event of power loss.

4. The technique of using two or more drives instead of a single drive for increased data protection or speed is known as _____.

5. The original ATA cabling standard is called _____ to differentiate it from the newer SATA cabling standard.

6. A _____ chain consists of a maximum of 16 devices.

7. RAID 0 is also known as _____.

8. Both _____ and _____ fit under the RAID-1 standard.

9. One major benefit of SATA over PATA is that SATA drives are designed for _____.

10. _____ backup hardware stores up to 70 GB of data.

Chapter 20

Zen and the Art of Network Support

Lab Exercises

I'm a big fan of movies. Science-fiction movies and thrillers, in particular, are likely to put me in a theater seat. One of the things that drive me crazy about these movies, however, is the manner in which they present computer technology. If we're to believe what we see onscreen, network techs never need more than three attempts to crack a password, any security policy can be bypassed by typing in something like *override* at a command prompt, and worst of all, network techs never need to actually *work* at their skills. To quote one particularly egregious example, "I just see the code in my head. I can't explain it." The keystrokes flow, as if by magic, and without so much as a system reboot our hero (or villain) has averted a disaster (or caused one).

Well, I guess I don't have to tell you that it's *not* that way in the real world! Real network techs in the real world don't just "see the code," but I don't suppose people would pay money to see a movie where the hero backs up the system data, isolates the network problem through careful analysis and testing, implements his fix, and then meticulously documents the solution, would they?

In this chapter, we'll wrap things up by looking at those un-cinematic but essential skills that Network+-certified network techs in the real world need to master in order to tackle real-world network problems. Let's get started.

🕐 25 MINUTES

Lab Exercise 20.01: Network Troubleshooting Toolkit

Toolkits for implementing fixes to network problems vary in their contents, and may include everything from a simple Philips-headed screwdriver to a costly Time Domain Reflectometer. The only tool you really need to determine the cause of network failure is always at hand. Your own know-how and experience are the only troubleshooting tools you need to unpack when you reach a worksite. Cable testers, crimpers, Sniffers, TDRs, and reverse-flux capacitors all have their time and place, but before you break out any hardware, fire up the software in your head. Talk to the users who are having trouble connecting to the network. Establish the symptoms that they and their network client workstations are experiencing. Determine possible solutions. Once you've laid the groundwork, then it's time to open up the toolbox and impress lookers-on with your gadgetry.

Learning Objectives

In this lab, you will examine the tools that network techs use to establish causes of network connection failures. By its end, you will be able to:

- Describe the network troubleshooting tools and methods that enable network technicians to determine the causes of network problems

- Demonstrate the use of Windows Performance Monitor to gather network performance data

Lab Materials and Setup

The materials you'll need for this lab are

- A pencil and some paper

- A networked Windows XP Professional PC

Getting Down to Business

You've been hired as a network support technician for Robot Monkey Butler Hypermedia, Ltd., a medium-sized software publishing company. Your supervisor, Robin McElfresh, informs you that your predecessor had quit unexpectedly, leaving very little documentation about the network, and that a number of support request tickets remain unresolved. Further, you are told that many employees are hesitant to make support requests due to the previous network technician's brusque nature, and are simply "living with" network connectivity problems. This, in turn, is harming productivity. Your task now is to resolve any open support request tickets, to establish a good relationship with the network users so they won't hesitate to make support requests, and to discover any network connectivity issues that have gone unreported.

Step 1 Prioritize the following five network support requests, and provide explanations for your decisions:

Support Issue	Priority (1–5)	Explanation
A user in the Marketing department is unable to access e-mail via Outlook, but is able to access e-mail via the company's ISP web site. No other users are having trouble with e-mail.	_____	_____
One of your customer service representatives is unable to access a support document database on the company's main file server, and has had to use printed support documents to handle customer tech support calls.	_____	_____
No backups have been made of the data on your company's central file server for over two weeks.	_____	_____

Support Issue	Priority (1–5)	Explanation
A member of the sales staff reports that the company's RAS server connection is unreliable and has cut him off numerous times when he connects to the network from on the road to update sales records. He has therefore had to provide this information to an assistant over the telephone, incurring long-distance charges.	_____	_____
The CEO reports that she keeps getting offensive popup windows every time she connects to the Internet, and that her browser's homepage keeps getting redirected to a pornographic web site.	_____	_____

✔ **Hint**

Prioritizing support issues is highly subjective, so student answers will vary.

Step 2　One of your users calls you to report that he is unable to access the Internet. Read through the following questions and decide which ones are likely to elicit useful information and which are likely to delay the troubleshooting process. Provide explanations for your answers, and suggest alternate questions where appropriate.

Question	Usefulness (Y/N)	Explanation
"What did you change on the computer?"	_____	_____
"When were you last able to access the Internet?"	_____	_____
"Why do you need to get on the Internet?"	_____	_____
"Are you able to access our local network?"	_____	_____
"Have you tried to ping the router's IP address?"	_____	_____
"Are you getting any specific error messages when you try to go online?"	_____	_____

Step 3　Your predecessor had put in a purchase order for a Sniffer protocol analyzer, a rather expensive piece of equipment. His justification was that he suspected that a network client's NIC was malfunctioning, and the Sniffer was necessary in order to isolate the particular NIC causing the problem. Your supervisor has not yet approved the purchase order, and would like your opinion before doing so.

Provide a recommendation, pro or con, for the purchase of the protocol analyzer hardware, and explain your recommendation.

_____

_____

Step 4 Your company has recently purchased a suite of adjoining offices in their building. Your predecessor had installed network cabling into the new suite of offices and connected the cables to a patch panel in your server room; however, neither the cable drop outlets nor the patch panel connections are labeled. What should you do to identify which cable drops correspond to the patch panel connections?

_____

_____

Step 5 One of the users on your network reports that she cannot access any network resources. You attempt to ping her PC, but are unsuccessful. Upon questioning, she tells you the following:

- She had no problems accessing network resources during the previous day.

- She has not changed any settings on the PC.

- She received an error message when she tried to log on using her domain account, but was successful when logging onto the PC with a local account.

- The NIC on her PC does not have any problems indicated in Device Manager.

You decide to visit her office, and notice that her desk has been moved to the other side of the room. She tells you she did this to cut down on the glare coming through her office window, but that she left all PC cables plugged in "exactly as they were." What should you do next?

_____

_____

Step 6 You have recommended to your supervisor that you be allowed to use the built-in Windows Task Manager and Performance Monitor tools to gather performance data to establish a performance baseline for your company's network. She would like you to demonstrate the process. Follow these steps to gather sample network performance data on a Windows XP Professional PC using Task Manager:

1. Press CTRL-ALT-DELETE once to bring up the Windows Security dialog box, and then click the Task Manager button.

> **→ Note**
>
> Alternatively, you can alternate-click a blank space on your Taskbar and select Task Manager from the popup menu.

2. Click the Networking property sheet tab to display the performance graph for the local area connection, shown in Figure 20-1.

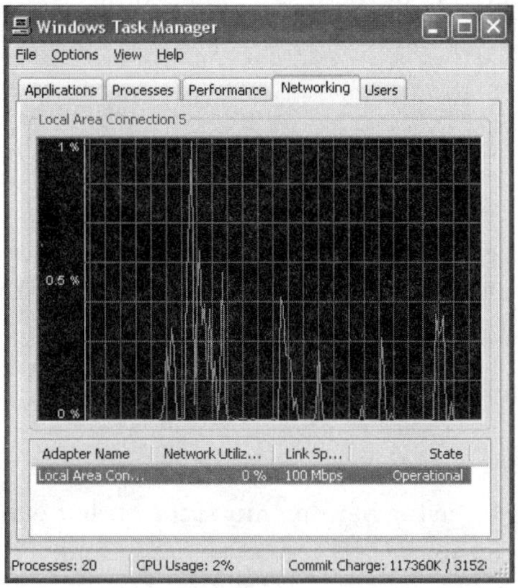

FIGURE 20-1 Windows Task Manager's Networking performance graph

3. With the Task Manager running, open Windows Explorer and connect to a remote PC on your network. Copy a large file or folder to, or from, the remote PC.

What are the results?

_____

_____

Step 7   Follow these steps to gather sample network performance data on a Windows XP Professional PC using Performance Monitor:

1. Open Performance Monitor by choosing Start | Control Panel, then click the Performance and Maintenance link and select Administrative Tools. Finally, click the icon for the Performance MMC to start Performance Monitor, shown in Figure 20-2.

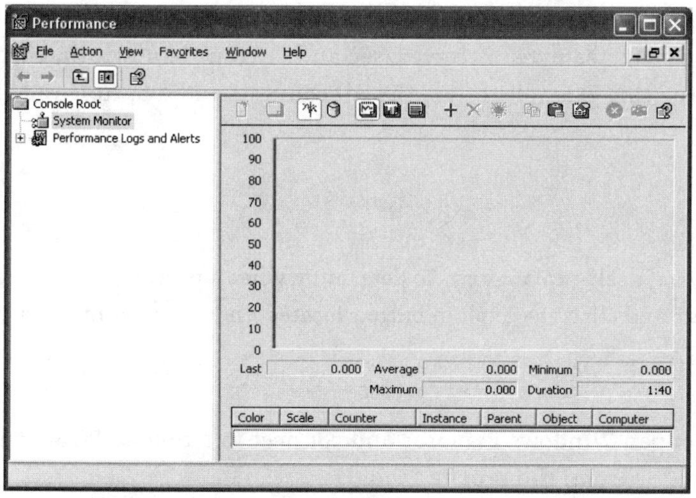

FIGURE 20-2 Windows XP Professional Performance Monitor

➜ **Note**

Alternatively, open Performance Monitor by clicking Start | Run, typing **perfmon**, and pressing ENTER.

2. Alternate-click the System Monitor graph area and select Add Counters from the popup menu to open the Add Counters dialog box.

3. Click the Performance object menu to see a list of all the possible performance objects that you can monitor on the system. Note that performance objects exist for many networking services and protocols, including TCP, IP, UDP, ICMP, the Browser service, Server service, Redirector, and many more. For this example, select the Network Interface performance object, as shown in Figure 20-3.

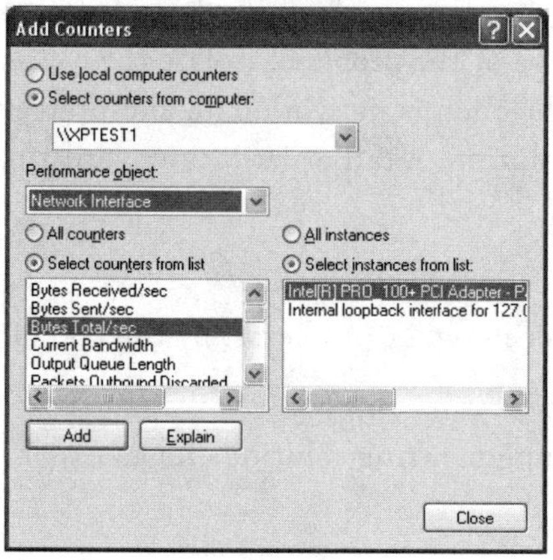

FIGURE 20-3 Performance Monitor, Network Interface performance object added

4. Now note the individual counter objects available for the Network Interface performance object. You can select specific counter objects, such as Bytes Received/sec and Current Bandwidth, depending on the data you wish to gather. For this example, select the All counters radio button and click the Add button. Then click Close.

→ **Note**

The function of counter objects isn't always self-explanatory. To determine what a particular counter object does, highlight the object and click the Explain button located under the counter list.

5. With Performance Monitor running, open Windows Explorer and connect to a remote PC on your network. Copy a large file or folder to, or from, the remote PC.

    What are the results?

    _____

    _____

 35 MINUTES

Lab Exercise 20.02: Network Troubleshooting Process

Troubleshooting is as much an art as it is a science. Like any art, there's more to it than just talent alone. Technique plays as much a part in troubleshooting as skill. The knowledgeable network technician doesn't just throw every fix available at a problem and hope that one of them will work. This wastes the time of both the tech and the client. Rather, the good network tech relies on his or her knowledge, skill, and troubleshooting technique to establish the symptoms and scope of the problem, isolate the cause, and implement the solution—while simultaneously preserving the client's network data and protecting the network from further harm as a result of the implemented solution. A tall order by any yardstick!

Learning Objectives

In this lab, you will review the process by which you troubleshoot network problems. By the end of the lab, you will be able to:

*   Describe the appropriate troubleshooting process for implementing solutions for network problems

Lab Materials and Setup

The only materials you'll need for this lab are a pencil and some paper.

Getting Down to Business

Pleased with your performance, your employer, Robot Monkey Butler Hypermedia, Ltd., wants you to develop a regular backup schedule and create a procedures manual on network troubleshooting.

Step 1 Your supervisor asks you to explain how the backup software knows which files to back up each night. In the space provided here, describe the function of the archive bit attribute and how it affects an automated backup schedule.

_____

_____

Step 2 In the following chart, fill in the appropriate information describing each backup type:

Backup Type	Data Backed Up	Archive Bit Set (Y/N)	When Used
Normal	_____	_____	_____
Copy	_____	_____	_____
Incremental	_____	_____	_____
Differential	_____	_____	_____
Daily	_____	_____	_____

Step 3 You need to plan a data backup strategy for your company's main file server system. You want to run a large normal backup once a week and also back up data that has changed every night. You need to store the backup tape in a safe location before leaving, so you want to use the method that takes the least amount of time to perform the backup operation. Restoration time isn't an issue. Which strategy is best for you?

_____

_____

Step 4 In the following chart, arrange the separate network error diagnostic and troubleshooting steps in their proper order:

Troubleshooting Process Step	Step Number (1–8)
Establish what has changed that might have caused the problem	_____

Troubleshooting Process Step	Step Number (1–8)
Test the solution	_____
Identify the most probable cause	_____
Establish the symptoms	_____
Implement a solution	_____
Isolate the cause of the problem	_____
Document the solution	_____
Recognize the potential effects of the solution	_____

Step 5 To simplify troubleshooting for your network, you have decided to create and distribute a troubleshooting checklist using the patented Mike Meyers Four-Layer Model. In the following chart, fill in a description for each layer and list the appropriate utilities and tools that function at each layer.

Layer	Description	Utilities and Tools
Hardware	_____	_____
Protocols	_____	_____
Network	_____	_____
Shared Resources	_____	_____

→ **Note**

Student answers will vary. Remember that Mike's Four-Layer Model is a practical network troubleshooting tool, not an industry standard. There's room for debate and flexibility!

Lab Analysis

1. Several of your users report that they are having trouble accessing resources on the network and have experienced timeout errors. In your server closet, you notice that your hub's activity light is steadily blinking. You suspect that one of your network client's NICs is stuck in transmit mode. How do you identify which network client is malfunctioning?

_____

_____

2. Your TCP/IP network uses Windows XP Professional systems configured to receive IP addresses from a Windows 2000 Server system running the DHCP service in the range 192.168.10.1 to 192.168.10.225 with a subnet mask of 255.255.255.0. File servers are configured with static IP addresses in the range of 192.168.10.226 to 192.168.10.254 with a subnet mask of 255.255.255.0. Some of your users report that they are unable to connect to any of the network's file servers, although they are able to browse to several of the other Windows XP Professional network client systems. You run IPCONFIG from several of the client systems that are experiencing this problem, and note that the systems' IP addresses are in the range of 169.254.x.x, with a subnet mask of 255.255.0.0. What is causing this discrepancy? What steps should you take to correct it?

_____

_____

3. Clients on your network are able to access resources on your LAN, receive e-mail, and access most web sites, but are unable to connect to a specific web site. How do you determine where the problem lies?

_____

_____

4. You have just completed an extensive network upgrade for a client, including installing several new file servers and upgrading existing network client workstations and network hubs and switches. Before turning your clients loose on your new network environment, what two things should you do?

_____

_____

5. While consulting with a client, you discover that they don't perform regular backups of their important data files to removable media. Instead, they use a third-party program that creates a full copy of the NOS and data files. This copy is stored on a separate hard disk on the file server. Is this solution acceptable? If not, can you suggest an alternate data backup solution?

_____

_____

Key Terms Quiz

Use the vocabulary terms from the list below to complete the sentences that follow. Not all of the terms will be used.

Archive bit	Network Monitor (NetMon)
Backups	Normal backup
Baselines	Object
Console monitor	Performance Monitor (PerfMon)
Copy backup	Protocol analyzer
Counter	Software tools
Daily backup (daily copy backup)	System logs
Daily copy	System Management Software Suite
Differential backup	Touchy tools
Hardware tools	Troubleshooting model
Incremental backup	Troubleshooting process
Mike's Four-Layer Model	Troubleshooting scenarios
NetWare Loadable Module (NLM)	Troubleshooting tools
Network analyzer	View

1. A(n) _____ is a measurement of normal performance parameters used to compare performance under stress conditions.

2. Windows _____ is a utility that measures the behavior of services, protocols, and hardware components.

3. A(n) _____ backup clears the archive bit of each file backed up, while a _____ backup leaves the archive bit untouched.

4. After experiencing a system crash, check the _____ for clues as to the cause of the failure.

5. If a file's _____ attribute is set to 1 (on), this tells the backup software that the file has changed and should be backed up.

Glossary

5-4-3 RULE A general rule for approximating the correct size of a collision domain. In a collision domain, no two nodes may be separated by more than five repeaters, four segments, and three populated segments.

10BASE2 An Ethernet LAN designed to run on common coax RG-58 cabling, almost exactly like the coax for cable television. It runs at 10 megabits per second and has a maximum segment length of 185 meters. Also known as *Thinnet* or *Thin Ethernet*. It uses baseband signaling and BNC connectors.

10BASE5 The original Ethernet LAN, designed to run on specialized coax cabling. It runs at 10 megabits per second and has a maximum segment length of 500 meters. Also known as *Thicknet* or *Thick Ethernet*, 10Base5 uses baseband signaling running on RG-8 coaxial cable. It uses DIX connectors and external transceivers, known as *AUI connectors*.

10BASEFL Fiber-optic implementation of Ethernet that runs at 10 megabits per second using baseband signaling. Maximum segment length is 2 kilometers.

10BASET An Ethernet LAN designed to run on UTP cabling, 10BaseT runs at 10 megabits per second. The maximum length for the cabling between the NIC and the hub (or the switch, the repeater, and so forth) is 100 meters. It uses baseband signaling.

16-BIT Able to process 16 bits of data at a time.

24-BIT COLOR Also referred to as *true color*, this uses 3 bytes per pixel to represent a color image in a PC. The 24 bits enable up to 16,777,216 colors to be stored and displayed.

100BASEFX An Ethernet LAN designed to run on fiber-optic cabling. It runs at 100 megabits per second and uses baseband signaling.

100BASET A generic term for any Ethernet cabling system that is designed to run at 100 megabits per second on UTP cabling. It uses baseband signaling.

100BASET4 This is an Ethernet LAN designed to run on UTP cabling. It runs at 100 megabits per second and uses four pairs of wires on CAT 3 or better cabling.

100BASETX This is an Ethernet LAN designed to run on UTP cabling. It runs at 100 megabits per second and uses two pairs of wires on CAT 5 cabling. It uses baseband signaling.

100BASEVG Also called *100BaseVGAnyLAN*. Uses CAT 3 cabling and an access method called Demand Priority.

110-PUNCHDOWN The most common connection used on the back of an RJ-45 jack.

110-PUNCHDOWN TOOL A specialized tool for connecting UTP wires to an RJ-45 jack.

286 Also called *80286*. Intel's second-generation processor. The 286 had a 16-bit external data bus and a 24-bit address bus. It was the first Intel processor to achieve protected mode.

386 Also called *80386DX*. Intel's third-generation processor. The 386 DX had a 32-bit external data bus and a 32-bit address bus.

386SX Also called *80386SX*. This was a hybrid chip that combined the 32-bit functions and modes of the 80386DX with the 16-bit external data bus and the 24-bit address bus of the 80286.

486DX Intel's fourth-generation CPU. Essentially, an 80386DX with a built-in cache and math coprocessor.

486DX/2, 486DX/3, 486DX/4 486 CPUs that operate externally at one speed and internally at a speed that is two, three, or four times faster. Although the internal speed can be more than two times as fast as the external speed, these CPUs are known collectively as *clock doublers*.

486SX A 486DX without the functional math coprocessor.

586 This is an unofficial, generic term that describes the Intel Pentium family of CPUs, as well as comparable CPUs made by other manufacturers.

802.3 ETHERNET *See* Ethernet.

802.11 *See* IEEE 802.11.

802.11A A wireless standard that operates in the frequency range of 5 GHz and offers throughput of up to 54 Mbps.

802.11B The most popular wireless standard, 802.11b operates in the frequency range of 2.4 GHz and offers throughput of up to 11 Mbps.

802.11G The newest wireless standard in general use, 802.11g operates in the frequency range of 2.4 GHz and offers throughput of up to 54 Mbps.

1000BaseT Gigabit Ethernet. This is an Ethernet LAN designed to run on UTP cabling. It runs at 1000 megabits per second and uses two pairs of wires on CAT 5e or better cabling. It uses baseband signaling.

8086/8088 These were the first generation of Intel processors to be used in IBM PCs. The 8086 and 8088 were identical with the exception of the external data bus: the 8086 had a 16-bit bus, while the 8088 had an 8-bit bus.

8086 MODE *See* Real Mode.

8237 This is the part number for the original DMA controller. Although long obsolete, the name is still often used in reference to DMA usage.

8259 This is the part number for the original IRQ controller. Although long obsolete, the name is still often used in reference to IRQ usage.

16450, 16550, 16550A, 16550AF, 16550AFN These are incremental improvements in UARTs. The 16550AFN is considered the most sophisticated UART available today. Note: The 16450 should not be used with any modem faster than a 14.4 Kbps modem.

ACCESS The reading or writing of data. Also a verb meaning "to gain entry to data." Most commonly used in connection with information access via a user ID and qualified by an indication of the kinds of access permitted. For example, "read-only access" means that the contents of the file may be read, but not altered or erased.

ACCESS TIME The time interval measured from the moment that data is requested to the moment it is received. Most commonly used in measuring the speed of storage devices.

ACCOUNT A registered set of rights and/or permissions to an individual computer or to a network of computers.

ACPI (ADVANCED CONFIGURATION AND POWER INTERFACE) A power management specification that far surpasses its predecessor, APM, by providing support for hot swappable devices and better control of power modes.

ACTIVE DIRECTORY Microsoft's directory service, introduced with Windows 2000.

ACTIVE MATRIX A type of liquid crystal display that replaced the passive matrix technology used in early portable computer displays.

ACTIVITY LIGHT An LED on a NIC, hub, or switch that blinks rapidly to show data transfers over the network.

ADDRESS BUS The wires leading from the CPU to the Northbridge that enable the CPU to address RAM. Also used by the CPU for I/O addressing.

ADDRESS RESOLUTION PROTOCOL (ARP) A protocol in the TCP/IP suite used with the command-line utility of the same name to determine the MAC address that corresponds to a particular IP address.

ADDRESS SPACE The total amount of memory addresses that an address bus can contain.

AD-HOC MODE Each wireless node in ad-hoc mode is in direct contact with every other node in a decentralized free-for-all. Wireless network ad-hoc mode is similar to the wired network *mesh topology*.

ADMINISTRATIVE TOOLS A group of Control Panel applets, including Computer Management, Event Viewer, and Performance, that enable you to handle routine administrative tasks in Windows 2000, Windows XP, and Windows Server 2003 systems.

ADMINISTRATOR The person whose job it is to maintain a computer system or network.

ADMINISTRATOR ACCOUNT A user account that has unrestricted access to all system functions, services, and data. A default administrator account, such as the appropriately-named Administrator account in Windows, is created when the NOS is installed on the PC.

ADSL (ASYMMETRIC DIGITAL SUBSCRIBER LINE) *See* Asymmetric Digital Subscriber Line (ADSL).

AGP (ACCELERATED GRAPHICS PORT) A 32-bit expansion slot designed by Intel specifically for video, which runs at 66 MHz and yields a throughput of 254 megabytes per second, at least. Later versions (2X, 3X, 4X) give substantially higher throughput.

AIX (ADVANCED INTERACTIVE EXECUTIVE) IBM's version of UNIX, which runs on 386 or better PCs.

ALGORITHM A set of rules for solving a problem in a given number of steps.

ALTERNATING CURRENT (AC) A type of electricity where the flow of electrons alternates direction, back and forth, in a circuit.

ALU (ARITHMETIC LOGIC UNIT) The circuit that performs CPU math calculations and logic operations.

AMD (ADVANCED MICRO DEVICES) The manufacturer of chipsets and microprocessors. AMD produces CPUs for computers worldwide.

AMPERES (AMPS OR A) The unit of measure for amperage, or electrical current.

AMPLIFIER A device that strengthens electrical signals, enabling them to travel farther.

ANALOG A type of device that uses a physical quantity, such as length or voltage, to represent the value of a number. By contrast, digital storage relies on a coding system of numeric units.

ANALOG VIDEO Picture signals represented by a number of smooth transitions between video levels. Television signals are analog, whereas digital video signals assign a finite set of levels. Because computer signals are digital, video must be converted into analog form before it can be shown on a computer screen. All modern CRTs use analog video standards based on the VGA standard. *See* VGA (Video Graphics Array).

ANDING A Boolean logic function used by TCP/IP to determine if IP addresses are local or remote. In the ANDing process, IP addresses and subnet masks are reduced to their binary values and compared. Any combination of bits set to 1 ("on") yields a result of 1. Any other combination (e.g., 1 + 0, 0 + 1, or 0 + 0) yields a result of 0. *See* Boolean logic.

ANSI (AMERICAN NATIONAL STANDARDS INSTITUTE) The body responsible for standards, such as ASCII.

ANSI CHARACTER SET The ANSI-standard character set that defines 256 characters. The first 128 are ASCII, and the second group of 128 contain math and language symbols.

ANTI-ALIASING In computer imaging, a blending effect that smoothes sharp contrasts between two regions, that is, jagged lines or different colors. This reduces the jagged edges of text or objects. In voice signal processing, it refers to the process of removing or smoothing out spurious frequencies from waveforms produced by converting digital signals back to analog.

API (APPLICATION PROGRAMMING INTERFACE) A software definition that describes operating system calls for application software; conventions defining how a service is invoked.

APM (ADVANCED POWER MANAGEMENT) The BIOS routines that enable the CPU to selectively turn on and off selected peripherals.

APPLETALK A network protocol suite invented to run on Apple computers. Modern Macintosh systems still support AppleTalk, but most Macintosh systems use TCP/IP rather than AppleTalk.

APPLICATION A program designed to perform a job for the user of a PC. A word processor and a spreadsheet program are typical applications.

APPLICATION LAYER *See* OSI Seven-Layer Model.

APPLICATION SERVERS Servers that provide clients access to software or other applications that run on the server only. Examples include web servers, e-mail servers, and database servers.

ARCHIVE To copy programs and data onto a relatively inexpensive storage medium (disk, tape, and so forth) for long-term retention.

ARCHIVE BIT An attribute of a file that shows whether the file has been backed up since the last change. Each time a file is opened, changed, or saved, the archive bit is turned on. Some types of backups will turn off this archive bit to indicate that a good backup of the file exists on tape.

ARCNET (ATTACHED RESOURCE COMPUTER NETWORK) The original ARCnet standard defined a true star topology, in which both the physical and logical topology work as a star. ARCnet uses token passing to get frames from one system to another. ARCnet runs at 2.5 megabits per second.

ARGUMENT A value supplied to a procedure, a macro, a subroutine, or a command that is required to evaluate that procedure, macro, subroutine, or command. Synonymous with *parameter*.

ARP (ADDRESS RESOLUTION PROTOCOL) *See* Address Resolution Protocol (ARP).

ARPANET The first practical network ever created. It was conceived by an organization called the Advanced Research Projects Agency (ARPA).

ASCII (AMERICAN STANDARD CODE FOR INFORMATION INTERCHANGE) The industry standard 8-bit characters used to define text characters, consisting of 96 uppercase and lowercase letters, plus 32 nonprinting control characters, each of which is numbered. These numbers were designed to achieve uniformity among different computer devices for printing and the exchange of simple text documents.

ASPECT RATIO The ratio of width to height of an object. In television, this is usually a 4:3 ratio, except in the new HDTV standard, which is 16:9.

ASPI (ADVANCED SCSI PROGRAMMING INTERFACE) A series of tight standards that enable SCSI devices to share a common set of highly compatible drivers.

ASSEMBLER A program that converts symbolically coded programs into object-level, machine code. In an assembler program, unlike a compiler, there is a one-to-one correspondence between human-readable instructions and the machine-language code.

ASYMMETRIC DIGITAL SUBSCRIBER LINE (ADSL) A fully digital, dedicated connection to the telephone system that provides download speeds of up to 9 megabits per second and upload speeds of up to 1 megabit per second.

ASYNCHRONOUS COMMUNICATION A type of communication in which the receiving devices must send an acknowledgement or ACK to the sending unit to verify a piece of data has been sent.

ASYNCHRONOUS TRANSFER MODE (ATM) A network technology that runs at speeds between 25 and 622 megabits per second using fiber-optic cabling or CAT 5 UTP.

AT (ADVANCED TECHNOLOGY) The model name of the second-generation, 80286-based IBM computer. Many aspects of the AT, such as the BIOS, CMOS, and expansion bus, have become de facto standards in the PC industry.

ATA (AT ATTACHMENT) A type of hard drive and controller. ATA was designed to replace the earlier ST506 and ESDI drives without requiring the replacement of the AT BIOS. These drives are more popularly known as IDE drives. *See* ST506, ESDI, and IDE. The **ATA/33** standard has drive transfer speeds up to 33 MB/s; the **ATA/66** up to 66 MB/s; the **ATA/100** up to 100 MB/s; and the **ATA/133** up to 133 MB/s.

ATAPI (AT ATTACHMENT PACKET INTERFACE) A series of standards that enables mass storage devices other than hard drives to use the IDE/ATA controllers. Extremely popular with CD-media, DVD-media, and removable media drives like the Iomega Zip drive. *See also* EIDE.

AT BUS The 16-bit expansion bus used in the IBM Personal Computer and the 32-bit bus of computers using the Intel386 and 486 microprocessors.

ATHLON A family of fifth, sixth, and seventh generation CPUs produced by AMD. Includes the Athlon, Athlon XP, and Athlon 64.

ATM (ASYNCHRONOUS TRANSFER MODE) *See* Asynchronous Transfer Mode (ATM).

AUI CONNECTOR An AUI or Attachment Unit Interface is the standard connector used with 10Base5 Ethernet. This is a 15-pin female DB connector, also known as *DIX*.

AUTHENTICATION A process that proves good data traffic truly came from where it says it originated by verifying the sending and receiving users and computers.

AUTHORITATIVE DNS SERVERS DNS servers that hold the IP addresses and names of systems for a particular domain or domains in special storage areas called *Forward Lookup Zones*.

AUTOEXEC.BAT A batch file that DOS executes when you start or restart the system. AUTOEXEC.BAT is not necessary, but when you're running a computer to which you've attached several devices and several different software applications, the file is essential for efficient operation. AUTOEXEC.BAT files commonly include PATH statements that tell DOS where to find application programs and commands to install a mouse or operate your printer.

AUTOMATED SYSTEM RECOVERY (ASR) A utility included with Windows XP that enables a user to create a complete system backup.

AUTOMATIC PRIVATE IP ADDRESSING (APIPA) A feature of later Windows operating systems that enables TCP/IP clients to self-configure an IP address and subnet mask in the Class B Private IP range (169.254.x.x, with a subnet mask of 255.255.0.0) automatically when a DHCP server isn't available.

AUTOMATIC SKIP DRIVER (ASD) A utility for preventing "bad" drivers from running the next time that you boot your computer. This utility examines startup log files and removes problematic drivers from the boot process.

BACKBONE A generalized term defining a primary network cabling and hardware systems that connect networks.

BACKGROUND PROCESSING Users may use a terminal for one project and concurrently submit a job that is placed in a background queue that the computer will run as resources become available. Also refers to any processing in which a job runs without being connected to a terminal.

BACKSIDE BUS The set of wires that connect the CPU to Level 2 cache. The backside bus first appeared in the Pentium Pro, and most modern CPUs have a special backside bus. Some busses, such as that in the later Celeron processors (300A and beyond), run at the full speed of the CPU, whereas others run at a fraction of this speed. Earlier Pentium IIs, for example, had backside busses running at half the speed of the processor. *See also* Frontside Bus and External Data Bus.

BACK UP To save important data in a secondary location as a safety precaution against the loss of the primary data.

BACKWARD-COMPATIBLE Compatible with earlier versions of a program or earlier models of a computer.

BANDWIDTH A piece of the spectrum occupied by some form of signal, whether it is television, voice, fax data, and so forth. Signals require a certain size and location of bandwidth to be transmitted. The higher the bandwidth, the faster the signal transmission, thus allowing for a more complex signal such as audio or video. Because bandwidth is a limited space, when one user is occupying it, others must wait their turn. Bandwidth is also the capacity of a network to transmit a given amount of data during a given period.

BANK The total number of SIMMs that can be simultaneously accessed by the MCC. The "width" of the external data bus divided by the "width" of the SIMM sticks.

BASEBAND Digital signaling that has only one signal (a single signal) on the cable at a time. The signals must be in one of three states: one, zero, or idle.

BASELINE A measurement of a network's (or system's) performance when all elements are known to be working properly.

BASIC (BEGINNERS ALL-PURPOSE SYMBOLIC INSTRUCTION CODE) A commonly used personal-computer language first developed at Dartmouth during the 1960s and popularized by Microsoft.

BASIC DISKS A hard disk drive partitioned in the classic way in Windows 2000/XP/2003, with a master boot record (MBR) and partition table.

BASIC RATE INTERFACE (BRI) The basic ISDN configuration, which consists of two B channels (which can carry voice or data at rate of 64 Kbps) and one D channel (which carries setup and configuration information, as well as data, at 16 Kbps).

BASIC SERVICE SET (BSS) In wireless networking, a single access point servicing a given area.

BAUD One analog cycle on a telephone line. In the early days of telephone data transmission, the baud rate was often analogous to bits-per-second. Due to advanced modulation of baud cycles as well as data compression, this is no longer true.

BBS (BULLETIN BOARD SYSTEM) A term for dial-up online systems from which users can download software and graphics, send and receive e-mail, and exchange information. Usually run by individuals from their homes. Although once very popular, BBS sites are rapidly disappearing because of the popularity of the Internet.

BIMODAL (BIPARTITE) VIRUS A type of virus that combines the characteristics of boot sector and executable viruses.

BINARY NUMBERS A number system with a base of 2, unlike the number systems most of us use that have bases of 10 (decimal numbers), 12 (measurement in feet and inches), and 60 (time). Binary numbers are preferred for computers for precision and economy. Building an electronic circuit that can detect the difference between two states (on-off, 0–1) is easier and more inexpensive than one that could detect the differences among ten states (0–9).

BINDERY Security and account database used by default on Novell NetWare 3.*x* servers and available to NetWare 4.*x*, 5.*x*, and 6.*x* servers.

BINDING The process of determining which NICs use which protocols for which transactions. Every protocol installed on a system must be bound to one or more NICs, and every NIC must be bound to one or more specific protocols.

BIOS (BASIC INPUT/OUTPUT SYSTEM) Classically, the software routines burned onto the system ROM of a PC. More commonly seen as any software that directly controls a particular piece of hardware. A set of programs encoded in read-only memory (ROM) on computers. These programs handle startup operations and the low-level control for hardware such as disk drives, the keyboard, and the monitor.

BIT (BINARY DIGIT) A single binary digit, typically represented by 1s and 0s. Any device that can be in an on or an off state.

BLUETOOTH Bluetooth is a radio-frequency standard that creates a small wireless network between PCs and peripheral devices such as PDAs and printers, input devices like keyboards and mice, and consumer electronics like cell phones, home stereos, televisions, and home security systems. Bluetooth uses a spread-spectrum broadcasting method, switching among any of the 79 frequencies available in the 2.45-GHz range.

BNC CONNECTOR Stands for *British Naval Connector* (or *Bayonet Connector*). A cylindrical-shaped connector used for 10Base2 coaxial cable. All BNC connectors have to be locked into place by rotating the locking ring 90 degrees.

BOOLEAN LOGIC Boolean logic (named for the 19th-century mathematician George Boole) is a mathematical process in which all values are reduced to either true or false: or in binary, 1 or 0. The TCP/IP ANDing process is an example of Boolean logic.

BOOT To initiate an automatic routine that clears the memory, loads the operating system, and prepares the computer for use. The term *boot* is derived from the phrase "pull yourself up by your bootstraps." PCs must do that because RAM doesn't retain program instructions when the power is turned off. A "cold boot" occurs when the PC is physically switched on, while a "warm boot" enables the system to reset itself without putting a strain on the electronic circuitry. To perform a warm boot, you press the CTRL, ALT, and DELETE keys at the same time, a ritual commonly known as the "three-fingered salute."

BOOTP (BOOTSTRAP PROTOCOL) This is a component of TCP/IP that allows computers to discover and receive an IP address from a DHCP server prior to booting the OS. Other items that may be discovered during the BOOTP process are the IP address of the default gateway for the subnet and the IP addresses of any name servers.

BOOT SECTOR The first sector on an IBM-PC hard drive or floppy disk, track 0. The bootup software in ROM tells the computer to load whatever program is found there. If a system disk is read, the program in the boot record directs the computer to the root directory to load MS-DOS. *See* ROM.

BOOT SECTOR VIRUS A type of virus that changes the code in the master boot record (MBR) of the hard drive. The virus resides in memory and attempts to infect the MBRs of other drives by spreading to removable media and networked machines.

BORDER GATEWAY PROTOCOL (BGP) An exterior gateway routing protocol that enables groups of routers to share routing information so that efficient, loop-free routes can be established.

BPS (BITS PER SECOND) A measurement of how fast data is moved from one place to another. A 28.8 modem can move 28,800 bits per second.

BRIDGE A device that connects two networks and passes traffic between them based only on the node address, so that traffic between nodes on one network does not appear on the other network. For example, an Ethernet bridge only looks at the Ethernet address. Bridges filter and forward packets based on MAC addresses and operate at Level 2 (the Data Link layer) of the OSI seven-layer model.

BROADBAND Analog signaling that sends multiple signals over the cable at the same time. The best example of broadband signaling is cable television. The zero, one, and idle states (*see* Baseband) exist on multiple channels on the same cable.

BROADCAST A broadcast is a packet addressed to all machines. In TCP/IP, the general broadcast address is 255.255.255.255.

BROADCAST ADDRESS The address a NIC attaches to a frame when it wants every other NIC on the network to read it.

BROWSER A software program specifically designed to retrieve, interpret, and display web pages.

BUFFER Electronic storage, usually DRAM, that holds data moving between two devices. Buffers are used anywhere there is a situation where one device may send or receive data faster or slower than the other device with which it is communicating. For example, the BUFFERS statement in DOS is used to set aside RAM for communication with hard drives.

BUG A programming error that causes a program or a computer system to perform erratically, produce inconsistent results, or crash. This term was coined when a real bug was found in a circuit of one of the first ENIAC computers.

BUILDING ENTRANCE The building entrance is where all the cables from the outside world (telephone lines, cables from other buildings, and so on) come into a building.

BUS A series of wires connecting two or more separate electronic devices, enabling those devices to communicate.

BUS TOPOLOGY A network topology in which all computers connect to the network via a central bus cable.

BYTE Eight contiguous bits, the fundamental data unit of personal computers. Storing the equivalent of one character, the byte is also the basic unit of measurement for computer storage. Bytes are counted in powers of two.

CAB FILES Short for "cabinet files." These files are compressed and most commonly used during Microsoft operating system installation to store many smaller files, such as device drivers.

CABLE DROP A cable drop is the location where the cable comes out of the wall.

CABLE MODEM High-speed home Internet access that runs through a coax cable laid by a cable company.

CABLE TESTER A device that tests the continuity of cables. Some testers also test for electrical shorts, crossed wires, or other electrical characteristics.

CACHE A special area of RAM that stores the data most frequently accessed from the hard drive. Cache memory can optimize the use of your systems.

CACHED-LOOKUP The *A* list kept by a DNS server of IP addresses it has already resolved, so it won't have to re-resolve a FQDN name it has already checked.

CACHE MEMORY A special section of fast memory chips set aside to store the information most frequently accessed from RAM.

CACHE-ONLY DNS SERVERS (CACHING-ONLY DNS SERVERS) DNS servers that do not have any Forward Lookup Zones. They will resolve names of systems on the Internet for the network, but are not responsible for telling other DNS servers the names of any clients.

Capturing A process by which a printer uses a local LPT port that connects to a networked printer is called *capturing a printer*. This is usually only done to support older programs that are not smart enough to know how to print directly to a UNC-named printer; it's quite rare today.

Card Generic term for anything that you can snap into an expansion slot.

CAT 3 Category 3 wire, an EIA/TIA standard for UTP wiring that can operate at up to 16 megabits per second.

CAT 4 Category 4 wire, an EIA/TIA standard for UTP wiring that can operate at up to 20 megabits per second. This is not widely used, except in older Token Ring networks.

CAT 5 Category 5 wire, an EIA/TIA standard for UTP wiring that can operate at up to 100 megabits per second.

CAT 5e Category 5e wire, an EIA/TIA standard for UTP wiring with improved support for 100 megabits per second using two pairs, and support for 1000 megabits per second using four pairs.

CAT 6 Category 6 wire, an EIA/TIA standard for UTP wiring with improved support for 1000 megabits per second.

Category (CAT) Rating A variety of grades called *categories* help network installers get the right cable for the right network technology. CAT ratings are officially rated in megahertz (MHz), indicating the highest frequency bandwidth the cable can handle.

CD-R (Compact Disc—Recordable) An improvement on CD-ROM technology that allows for a single write onto the media.

CD-ROM (Compact Disc Read-Only Memory) A read-only compact storage disc for audio or video data. Recordable devices, such as CD-Rs and CD-RWs, are updated versions of the older CD-ROM players.

CD-RW (Compact Disc Read/Write) A technology that enables repeated writing and erasing of data to a compact disc designed for such an activity (a CD-RW disc).

CHAP (Challenge Handshake Authentication Protocol) CHAP is the most common remote access protocol. It has the serving system challenge the remote client, which must provide an encrypted password.

Chat A multiparty, real-time text conversation. The Internet's most popular version is known as Internet Relay Chat

(IRC), which many groups use to converse in real time with each other.

Checksum A simple error-detection method that adds a numerical value to each data packet, based on the number of data bits in the packet. The receiving node applies the same formula to the data and verifies that the numerical value is the same; if not, the data has been corrupted and must be re-sent.

Chipset Electronic chips that handle all of the low-level functions of a PC, which in the original PC were handled by close to 30 different chips. Chipsets usually consist of one, two, or three separate chips to handle all of these functions.

CHS (Cylinder/Heads/Sectors per Track) The initials for the combination of the three critical geometries used to determine the size of a hard drive: cylinders, heads, and sectors per track.

CISC (Complex Instruction-Set Computing) A CPU design that enables the processor to handle more complex instructions from the software at the expense of speed. The Intel x86 series (386, 486, Pentium) for PCs are CISC processors.

Cladding The exterior casing of a network cable. With fiber-optic cabling, the cladding makes the light reflect down the fiber.

Classful Subnet A subnet that falls into a pre-defined subnet class; for example, 255.255.0.0 is a Class B subnet.

Classless Subnet A subnet that does not fall into the common categories such as Class A, Class B, and Class C.

Client A computer program that uses the services of another computer program; software that extracts information from a server. Your autodial phone is a client, and the phone company is its server. Also, a machine that accesses shared resources on a server.

Client/Server A relationship in which client software obtains services from a server on behalf of a user.

Client/Server Application An application that performs some or all of its processing on an application server rather than on the client. The client usually only receives the result of the processing.

Client/Server Network A network that has dedicated server machines and client machines.

Clipboard A temporary storage space from which captured data can be copied or pasted into other documents.

Clock An electronic circuit using a quartz crystal to generate evenly spaced pulses at speeds of millions of cycles per second. The pulses are used to synchronize the flow of information through the computer's internal communication channels. Most of the chips on a PC synchronize to this clock. The speed of the clock's signal is called the *clock rate*.

CLUSTER 1. Groups of sectors organized by the operating system to store files. The number of sectors in a cluster is dependent on the size of the partition and the file system used. When an operating system stores a file on disk, it writes those files into dozens or even hundreds of clusters. 2. A pair or group of computers that function as a single unit.

CMOS (COMPLIMENTARY METAL-OXIDE SEMICONDUCTOR) Originally, the type of nonvolatile RAM that held information about the most basic parts of your PC such as hard drives, floppies, and amount of DRAM. Today, actual CMOS chips have been replaced by "Flash" -type non-volatile RAM. The information is the same, however, and is still called *CMOS*, even though it is now almost always stored on Flash RAM.

COAX Short for coaxial. Cabling in which an internal conductor is surrounded by another, outer conductor, thus sharing the same axis.

CODE A set of symbols representing characters (for example, ASCII code) or instructions in a computer program (a programmer writes *source* code, which must be translated into *executable* or *machine* code for the computer to use). Used colloquially as a verb—*to code* is to write computer code—and as a noun, "He writes clean/sloppy/bad code."

COLLISION The result of two nodes transmitting data packets at the same time on a multiple access network such as the Ethernet. Data packets that collide become corrupted and are unusable

COLLISION DOMAIN A set of Ethernet segments that receive all traffic generated by any node within those segments. Repeaters, amplifiers, and hubs do not create separate collision domains, but bridges, routers, and switches do.

COLLISION LIGHT A light on some older hubs and NICs that flickers to indicate when a network collision is detected.

COM 1. In Microsoft operating systems, a device name that refers to the serial communications ports available on your computer. 2. When used as a program extension, .COM indicates an executable program file limited to 64K.

COMMAND A request, typed from a terminal or embedded in a file, to perform an operation or to execute a particular program.

COMMAND.COM In DOS and Windows 9x, a file that contains the command processor. This file must be present on the startup disk for DOS to run. COMMAND.COM is usually located in the root directory of your hard drive. Windows NT, 2000, and XP use CMD.EXE instead of COMMAND.COM.

COMMAND PROCESSOR The part of the operating system that accepts input from the user and displays any messages, such as confirmation and error messages.

COMMON UNIX PRINTING SYSTEM (CUPS) A printing system based on the Internet Printing Protocol (IPP) standard that supports any printer language, although it is most commonly associated with the PostScript language.

COMMUNICATIONS PROGRAM A program that makes a computer act as a terminal to another computer. Communications programs usually provide for file transfer between microcomputers and mainframes.

COMPRESSION The process of reducing the size of files, allowing them to be stored using less space and transmitted using less bandwidth. Different compression applications use different methods to reduce file size, such as removing blank spaces, redundant characters, and so on.

COMPUTER A device or system that is capable of carrying out a sequence of operations in a distinctly and explicitly defined manner. These operations are frequently numeric computations or data manipulations, but they also include data input and output. The capability to branch within sequences is its key feature.

CONCENTRATOR A device that brings together at a common center connections to a particular kind of network (such as Ethernet), and implements that network internally.

CONFIG.SYS An ASCII text file in the root directory that contains configuration commands. CONFIG.SYS enables the system to be set up to configure high, expanded, and extended memories by the loading of HIMEM.SYS and EMM386.EXE drivers, as well as drivers for non-standard peripheral components.

CONNECTIONLESS PROTOCOL A protocol that does not establish and verify a connection between the hosts before sending data; it just sends the data and hopes for the best. This is faster than connection-oriented protocols. UDP is an example of a connectionless protocol.

CONNECTIONLESS SESSION A networking session in which packets are sent without first creating a connection-oriented session. Network protocols use connectionless sessions only for data that won't cause problems if it doesn't make it to the intended recipient.

CONNECTION-ORIENTED PROTOCOL A protocol that establishes a connection between two hosts before transmitting data and verifies receipt before closing the connection between the hosts. TCP is an example of a connection-oriented protocol.

CONTIGUOUS Adjacent; placed one next to the other.

CONTROL PANEL A collection of Windows applets (small, specialized programs) that are used to configure various hardware, software, and services in a system.

CONTROLLER CARD A card adapter that connects devices, like a disk drive, to the main computer bus/motherboard.

CONVENTIONAL MEMORY In any IBM PC-compatible computer, the first 640 KB of the computer's RAM.

COPY BACKUP A type of backup similar to Normal or Full, in that all selected files on a system are backed up. This type of backup does *not* change the archive bit of the files being backed up.

CPU (CENTRAL PROCESSING UNIT) The "brain" of the computer. The microprocessor that handles the primary calculations for the computer. Intel and American Micro Devices (AMD) are the largest (practically the *only*) CPU manufacturers, producing CPUs with names such as Pentium 4 and Athlon XP.

CRC (CYCLICAL REDUNDANCY CHECK) A mathematical method that is used to check for errors in long streams of transmitted data with high accuracy. Before data is sent, the main computer uses the data to calculate a CRC value from the data's contents. If the receiver calculates a different CRC value from the received data, the data was corrupted during transmission and is re-sent. Ethernet packets have a CRC code.

CRIMPERS Also called *crimping tool*. The tool used to secure a connector, such as an RJ-45 connector, onto the end of a cable.

CROSS-LINKED FILES A file-storage error that occurs when the file allocation table indicates that two files claim the same disk cluster. These occur when the system is abnormally halted.

CROSSOVER CABLE A special UTP cable used to connect hubs or to connect network cards without a hub. Crossover cables reverse the sending and receiving wire pairs from one end to the other.

CROSSOVER PORT Special port in a hub that crosses the sending and receiving wires, thus removing the need for a crossover cable to connect the hubs. *See* Uplink Port.

CROSS-PLATFORM SUPPORT This refers to standards created to enable terminals (or now operating systems) from different companies to interact with one another.

CROSSTALK Electrical signal interference between two cables that are in close proximity to each other.

CRT (CATHODE RAY TUBE) The tube of a monitor in which rays of electrons are beamed onto a phosphorescent screen to produce images. Monitors are sometimes called *CRT Displays*.

CSMA/CA (CARRIER SENSE MULTIPLE ACCESS WITH COLLISION AVOIDANCE) This access method is used mainly on Apple networks and is also implemented on wireless networks. With CSMA/CA, before hosts send out data, they send out a signal that checks to make sure that the network is free of other signals. If data is detected on the wire, the hosts wait a random time period before trying again. If the wire is free, the data is sent out.

CSMA/CD (CARRIER SENSE MULTIPLE ACCESS WITH COLLISION DETECTION) The access method Ethernet systems use in LAN technologies, enabling packets of data to flow through the network and ultimately reach address locations. Known as a *contention* protocol, hosts on CSMA/CD networks send out data without checking to see if the wire is free first. If a collision occurs, then both hosts wait a random time period before retransmitting the data.

CSU/DSU (CHANNEL SERVICE UNIT/DATA SERVICE UNIT) A piece of equipment that connects a leased line from the telephone company to a customer's equipment (such as a router). It performs line encoding and conditioning functions, and it often has a loopback function for testing.

CURSOR A symbol on a display screen that indicates the position at which the next character entered will be displayed. The symbol often blinks so that it is more visible.

CYRIX Company that made CPUs in direct competition with Intel and AMD. Now owned by VIA Technologies.

DAILY BACKUP Also called a *daily copy backup*, this backup type makes a copy of all files that have been changed on that day without changing the archive bits of those files.

DAISY-CHAIN A method of connecting together several devices along a bus and managing the signals for each device.

DAT (DIGITAL AUDIO TAPE) Higher storage capacity tape recording system that uses digital recording methods. Used for digital audio and video as well as data backups.

DATABASE A collection of data that is organized in such a way that users can easily input and retrieve specific information. Users search databases via structured requests called *queries*. Examples of database programs include Microsoft Access, Microsoft SQL Server, dBase, and so on. *See* DBMS (Database Management System).

DATAGRAM Another term for *network packets* or *frames*. *See* Packets and Frames.

DATA LINK CONTROL (DLC) A network protocol used for many years to link PCs to mainframe computers. Because Hewlett-Packard adopted the DLC protocol for use by network printers, DLC enjoyed a much longer life than it probably should have—given the existence of so many alternatives. All versions of Windows, including Windows XP, still support DLC.

DATA LINK LAYER *See* OSI Seven-Layer Model.

DB-15 DB connector (female) used in 10Base5 networks. *See also* DIX and AUI.

DB CONNECTORS D-shaped connectors used for a variety of different connections in the PC and networking world. Can be either male or female, with a varying number of pins or sockets.

DBMS (DATABASE MANAGEMENT SYSTEM) A systematic approach to storing, updating, securing, and retrieving information stored as data files. Each data file contains any number of *records*, which in turn store specific data items in different *fields*. For example, Microsoft Active Directory uses a database file (NTDS.DIT) to store user account records. Each user account record contains individual fields such as the user name, password, group membership, and so on.

DEBUG To detect, trace, and eliminate errors in computer programs.

DEDICATED CIRCUIT A circuit that runs from a breaker box to specific outlets.

DEDICATED SERVER A machine that does not use any client functions, only server functions.

DEDICATED TELEPHONE LINE A telephone line that is an always open, or connected, circuit. Dedicated telephone lines usually do not have numbers.

DEFAULT A software function or operation that occurs automatically unless the user specifies something else.

DEFAULT GATEWAY In a TCP/IP network, the nearest router to a particular host. This router's IP address is part of the necessary TCP/IP configuration for communicating with multiple networks using IP.

DEFRAGMENTATION (DEFRAG) A procedure in which all the files on a hard disk are rewritten on disk so that all parts of each file are written in contiguous clusters. The

result is an improvement of up to 75 percent of the disk's speed during retrieval operations.

DENIAL OF SERVICE (DoS) ATTACKS Also known as *flooding attacks*. DoS attacks flood the network with so many requests that it becomes overwhelmed and ceases functioning.

DETERMINISTIC This means access to the wire is granted in a predictable way, rather than through a random process like CSMA/CD. Token passing is an example of a deterministic method to resolve which machine should have access to the wire at a given moment.

DEVICE DRIVER A subprogram to control communications between the computer and some peripheral hardware.

DHCP (DYNAMIC HOST CONFIGURATION PROTOCOL) A service that enables a DHCP server to set TCP/IP settings automatically for a network's DHCP clients.

DHCP LEASE When a system requests DHCP IP information, the DHCP server creates a DHCP lease for the requested IP information, which allows the client to use these settings for a certain amount of time.

DHCP SCOPE The pool of IP addresses that a DHCP server may allocate to clients requesting IP addresses, or other IP information like DNS server addresses.

DIFFERENTIAL BACKUP Similar to an incremental backup in that it backs up the files that have been changed since the last backup. This type of backup does not change the state of the archive bit.

DIGITAL CERTIFICATE A public encryption key signed with the digital signature from a trusted third party called a *certificate authority (CA)*. This key serves to validate the identity of its holder when that person or company sends data to other parties.

DIGITAL SIGNATURE A string of characters created from a private encryption key, which verifies a sender's identity to those who receive encrypted data or messages.

DIGITAL SUBSCRIBER LINE (DSL) A high-speed Internet connection technology that uses a regular telephone line for connectivity. DSL comes in several varieties, including Asynchronous (ADSL) and Synchronous (SDSL), and many speeds. Typical home-user DSL connections are ADSL with a download speed of up to 1.5 Mbps and an upload speed of up to 384 Kbps.

DIMM (DUAL IN-LINE MEMORY MODULE) A type of DRAM packaging, similar to SIMMs with the distinction that each side of each tab inserted into the system performs a separate function. Comes in 72- and 144-pin Small Outline (SO) as well as 144- and 168-pin versions.

DIRECT CABLE CONNECTION A direct serial-to-serial, parallel-to-parallel, or infrared-to-infrared port connection between two PCs.

DIRECT CURRENT (DC) A type of electricity where the flow of electrons is in a complete circle.

DIRECTORY A logical container of files and other directories; synonymous with *folder*. Typically implemented as a file that contains pointers (directions) to files or other directories.

DIRECTORY SERVICE A distributed database that contains all user, group, and security information for a network structure such as a *domain*. Microsoft Active Directory, Novell NetWare Directory Service (NDS, later called eDirectory), and Banyan Vines are examples of directory services.

DIRECT-SEQUENCE SPREAD-SPECTRUM (DSSS) A spread-spectrum broadcasting method defined in the 802.11 standard that sends data out on different frequencies at the same time.

DISK DRIVE CONTROLLER The circuitry that controls the physical operations of the floppy disks and/or hard disks connected to the computer.

DISK MANAGEMENT A snap-in available with the Microsoft Management Console that allows a user to configure the various disks installed on a system; available from the Administrative Tools area of the Control Panel.

DISK MIRRORING Process by which data is written simultaneously to two or more disk drives. Read and write speed is decreased but redundancy, in case of catastrophe, is increased. Considered RAID level 1.

DISK STRIPING Process by which data is spread among multiple (at least two) drives. It increases speed for both reads and writes of data. Considered RAID level 0, because it does *not* provide fault tolerance.

DISK STRIPING WITH PARITY Provides fault tolerance by writing data across multiple drives, and includes an additional drive, called a *parity drive*, that stores information to rebuild the data contained on the other drives. Disk Striping with Parity requires at least three physical disks: two for the data and a third for the parity drive. It provides data redundancy at RAID levels 3-5 with different options.

DISPLAY A device that enables information, either textual or pictorial, to be seen but not permanently recorded. Sometimes called the *monitor*, the most widely used kind is the cathode-ray tube, or CRT; liquid crystal diode, or LCD, displays are also popular.

DISTRIBUTED COORDINATION FUNCTION (DCF) One of two methods of collision avoidance defined by the 802.11 standard

and the only one currently implemented. DCF specifies much stricter rules for sending data onto the network media.

DITHERING A technique for smoothing out digitized images; using alternating colors in a pattern to produce perceived color detail.

DIX CONNECTOR (DIGITAL, INTEL, XEROX) The DIX standard was the original implementation of Ethernet. The DIX connector is the standard connector used with 10Base5 Ethernet, also known as the *AUI*.

DLC *See* Data Link Control (DLC).

DLL (DYNAMIC LINK LIBRARY) A file of executable functions or data that can be used by a Windows application. Typically, a DLL provides one or more particular functions, and a program accesses the functions by creating links to the DLL.

DLT (DIGITAL LINEAR TAPE) Huge data capacity tapes used for tape backups.

DMA (DIRECT MEMORY ACCESS) A technique that some PC hardware devices use to transfer data to and from the memory without requiring the use of the CPU.

DMZ (DEMILITARIZED ZONE) A lightly protected or unprotected network positioned between your firewall and the Internet.

DNS (DOMAIN NAME SERVICE OR SYSTEM) A TCP/IP name resolution service that resolves host names to IP addresses.

DNS DOMAIN A specific branch of the DNS name space. First-level DNS domains include .com, .gov, and .edu.

DNS RESOLVER CACHE A cache used by Windows workstation clients to keep track of previously-resolved DNS information.

DNS TREE A hierarchy of DNS domains and individual computer names organized into a tree-like structure. At the top of a DNS tree is the root.

DOCUMENT A medium and the data recorded on it for human use; for example, a report sheet or book. By extension, any record that has permanence and that can be read by a human or a machine.

DOCUMENTATION A collection of organized documents or the information recorded in documents. Also instructional material specifying the inputs, operations, and outputs of a computer program or system.

DOMAIN A term used to describe logical security boundaries that contain groupings of users, computers, or networks. In Microsoft networking, a domain is a group of computers and users that share a common account database and a common security policy. For the Internet, a domain is a group of computers that share a common element in their hierarchical name. Other types of domains also exist, such as collision domains.

DOMAIN CONTROLLER A Microsoft Windows NT/2000/2003 machine that stores the user and server account information for its domain in a central database. On a Windows NT domain controller, the database is called the *Security Accounts Manager*, or *SAM* database, and is stored as part of the registry. Windows 2000/2003 domain controllers store all account and security information in the *Active Directory* directory service.

DOMAIN USERS AND GROUPS Users and groups that are defined across an entire network domain.

DOS (DISK OPERATING SYSTEM) The set of programming that allows a program to interact with the computer. Examples of disk operating systems include Microsoft's MS-DOS, IBM's PC-DOS and OS/2, and Apple's MacOS System 7. Microsoft's Windows 3.1 is not technically an operating system because it still requires MS-DOS to work, but it is often referred to as one. Windows 95/98 and Windows NT are true disk operating systems.

DOSKEY A DOS utility that enables you to type more than one command on a line, store and retrieve previously used DOS commands, create stored macros, and customize all DOS commands.

DOS PROMPT A letter representing the disk drive, followed by the greater-than sign (>), which together inform you that the operating system is ready to receive a command.

DOT-MATRIX PRINTER A printer that creates each character from an array of dots. Pins striking a ribbon against the paper, one pin for each dot position, form the dots. The printer may be a serial printer (printing one character at a time) or a line printer.

DOUBLE WORD A group of 32 binary digits. Four bytes.

DOWNLOAD The transfer of information from a remote computer system to the user's system. Opposite of upload.

DOWNSTREAM NEIGHBOR A receiving node in a Token Ring network is the downstream neighbor to the sending node.

DPI (DOTS PER INCH) A measure of printer resolution that counts the dots the device can produce per linear inch.

DRAM (DYNAMIC RANDOM ACCESS MEMORY) The memory used to store data in most personal computers. DRAM stores each bit in a "cell" composed of a transistor and a capacitor. Because the capacitor in a DRAM cell can only

hold a charge for a few milliseconds, DRAM must be continually refreshed, or rewritten, to retain its data.

DRIVE DUPLEXING The process of writing identical data to two hard drives on different controllers at the same time, to provide data redundancy.

DRIVE MIRRORING The process of writing identical data to two hard drives on the same controller at the same time, to provide data redundancy.

DSL (DIGITAL SUBSCRIBER LINE) *See* Digital Subscriber Line (DSL).

DSP (DIGITAL SIGNAL PROCESSOR) A specialized microprocessor-like device that processes digital signals at the expense of other capabilities, much as the FPU is optimized for math functions. DSPs are used in such specialized hardware as high-speed modems, multimedia sound cards, MIDI equipment, and real-time video capture and compression.

DUMB TERMINAL A device that enables a user to access programs and data on mainframe computers. Dumb terminals resemble personal computers in that they have a monitor, keyboard, and possibly a mouse, but they are not stand-alone computing devices. All have some sort of networking device, such as a modem or network interface card (NIC).

DUPLEXING Also called *disk duplexing* or *drive duplexing*, duplexing is similar to mirroring, in that data is written to and read from two physical drives for fault tolerance. In addition, separate controllers are used for each drive, for both additional fault tolerance and additional speed. Considered RAID level 1.

DVI (DIGITAL VIDEO INTERFACE) While traditional CRT monitors are analog, LCD monitors are digital. DVI is the digital video interface that is most often seen on LCD flat-panel monitors.

DYNAMIC LINK A method of linking data so that it is shared by two or more programs. When data is changed in one program, the data is likewise changed in the other.

DYNAMIC LINK LIBRARY (DLL) *See* DLL (Dynamic Link Library).

DYNAMIC ROUTING Process by which routers in an internetwork automatically exchange information with all other routers, enabling them to build their own list of routes to various networks, called a *routing table*. Dynamic routing requires a dynamic routing protocol, such as OSPF or RIP.

DYNAMIC ROUTING PROTOCOL A protocol that supports the building of automatic routing tables, such as OSPF (Open Shortest Path First) or RIP (Routing Information Protocol).

EDB (EXTERNAL DATA BUS) The primary data highway of all computers. Everything in your computer is tied either directly or indirectly to the external data bus. *See also* Frontside Bus and Backside Bus.

EDO (ENHANCED DATA OUT) An improvement on FPM DRAM in that more data can be read before the RAM must be refreshed.

EEPROM (ELECTRICALLY ERASABLE PROGRAMMABLE READ-ONLY MEMORY) A type of ROM chip that can be erased and reprogrammed electrically. EEPROMs were the most common BIOS storage device until the advent of Flash ROM.

EIA/TIA (ELECTRONICS INDUSTRY ASSOCIATION/TELECOMMUNICATIONS INDUSTRY ASSOCIATION) The standards body that defines most of the standards for computer network cabling. Most of these standards are defined under the EIA/TIA 568 standard.

EIDE (ENHANCED IDE) A marketing concept by Western Digital that consolidated four improvements for IDE drives. These improvements included support for drives with capacity beyond 504 MB, four devices in a system, increase in drive throughput, and nonhard drive devices. *See* ATAPI, Parallel ATA, and PIO.

EISA (ENHANCED ISA) An improved expansion bus, based on the ISA bus, with a top speed of 8.33MHz, a 32-bit data path, and a high degree of self-configuration. Backwardly compatible with legacy ISA cards.

E-MAIL (ELECTRONIC MAIL) A service that enables users to communicate via written messages routed through the Internet. E-mail messages may contain HTML formatting and file *attachments*. E-mail applications include Microsoft Outlook, Pegasus, Eudora, and others. E-mail can be sent automatically to a large number of addresses, known as a *mailing list*.

E-MAIL SERVER Also known as *mail server*. Server that accepts incoming mail, sorts the mail for recipients into mailboxes, and sends mail to other servers using the Simple Mail Transfer Protocol (SMTP) and Post Office Protocol (POP) e-mail protocols.

EMERGENCY REPAIR DISK (ERD) This disk saves critical boot files and partition information and is our main tool for fixing boot problems in Windows 2000/XP/2003.

EMI (ELECTRO-MAGNETIC INTERFERENCE) An electrical interference from one device to another, resulting in poor performance in the device capabilities. This is similar to having static on your TV while running a hair dryer, or placing two monitors too close together and getting a "shaky" screen.

EMM386.EXE An expanded memory emulator that enables DOS applications to use the extended memory as if it were expanded memory. EMM386.EXE also enables the user to load device drivers and programs into the upper memory area.

ENCAPSULATION The process of putting the packets from one protocol inside the packets of another protocol. An example of this is TCP/IP encapsulation in NetWare servers, which places IPX/SPX packets inside TCP/IP packets. This encapsulation enables Novell NetWare to use TCP/IP for transport while still allowing the network operating system to gain the data it needs from IPX/SPX.

ENCRYPTION A method of securing messages by scrambling and encoding each packet as it is sent across an unsecured medium, such as the Internet. Each encryption level provides multiple standards and options.

EPROM (ERASABLE PROGRAMMABLE READ-ONLY MEMORY) A special form of ROM that can be erased by high-intensity ultraviolet light, and then rewritten or reprogrammed.

EQUIPMENT RACK A metal structure used in equipment rooms to secure network hardware devices and patch panels. Devices designed to fit in such a rack use a height measurement called *units*, or simply *U*.

EQUIPMENT ROOM A central location for computer or telephone equipment and, most importantly, centralized cabling. All cables will usually run to the equipment room from the rest of the installation.

ESD (ELECTRO-STATIC DISCHARGE) The movement of electrons from one body to another. ESD is a real menace to PCs as it can cause permanent damage to semiconductors.

ESDI (ENHANCED SMALL DEVICE INTERFACE) Second-generation hard drives, distinct from their predecessors, ST506, by greater data density and lack of dependence on CMOS settings. Completely obsolete.

ETHERNET Name coined by Xerox for the first standard of network cabling and protocols. Ethernet is based on a bus topology. The IEEE 802.3 subcommittee defines the current Ethernet specifications.

EVENT VIEWER A utility made available as an MMC snap-in in Windows 2000/XP/2003 that enables a user to monitor various system events, including network bandwidth usage and CPU utilization.

EXECUTABLE VIRUS Viruses that are literally extensions of executables and that are unable to exist by themselves. Once an infected executable file is run, the virus loads into memory, adding copies of itself to other EXEs that are subsequently run.

EXPANSION BUS Set of wires going to the CPU, governed by the Expansion Bus Crystal, directly connected to expansion slots of varying types (ISA, PCI, AGP, and so forth). Depending on the type of slots, the expansion bus runs at a percentage of the main system speed (8.33–66 MHz).

EXPANSION SLOT A receptacle connected to the computer's expansion bus, designed to accept adapters.

EXTENDED BASIC SERVICE SET (EBSS) A single wireless access point servicing a given area that has been extended by adding more access points.

EXTERNAL DATA BUS (EDB) The primary data highway of all computers. Everything in your computer is tied either directly or indirectly to the external data bus. *See also* Frontside Bus and Backside Bus.

EXTERNAL NETWORK ADDRESS A number added to the MAC address of every computer on an IPX/SPX network, which defines every computer on the network; this is often referred to as a *network number*.

EXTERNAL NETWORK NUMBER A special number, added to the MAC address of every computer on an IPX/SPX network, that provides each computer on the network with a unique identifier.

EXTERNAL THREATS Threats to your network through external means; examples include virus attacks and the exploitation of users, security holes in the OS, or the network hardware itself.

FAQ (FREQUENTLY ASKED QUESTIONS) Common abbreviation coined by BBS users and spread to Usenet and the Internet. This is a list of questions and answers that pertain to a particular topic, maintained so that users new to the group don't all bombard the group with similar questions. Examples are "What is the name of the actor who plays *X* on this show, and was he in anything else?" or "Can anyone list all of the books by this author in the order that they were published so that I can read them in that order?" The common answer to this type of question is "Read the FAQ!"

FAST ETHERNET Any of several flavors of Ethernet that operate at 100 megabits/second.

FAT (FILE ALLOCATION TABLE) A FAT is a hidden table of every cluster on a hard disk. The FAT records how files are stored in distinct clusters. The address of the first cluster of the file is stored in the directory file. In the FAT entry for the first cluster is the address of the second cluster used to store that file. In the entry for the second cluster for that file is the address for the third cluster, and so on. This table is the only way for DOS to know where to access files. There are two FATs created, mirror images of each other, in case one is destroyed or damaged.

FAT16 File allocation table that uses 16 bits for addressing clusters. Commonly used with DOS and Windows 95 systems.

FAT32 File allocation table that uses 32 bits for addressing clusters. Commonly used with Windows 98 and Windows Me systems. Some Windows 2000/XP systems also use FAT32, although most use the more robust NTFS.

FAULT TOLERANCE The capability of any system to continue functioning after some part of the system has failed. RAID is an example of a hardware device that provides fault tolerance.

FDDI (FIBER DISTRIBUTED DATA INTERFACE) A standard for transmitting data on optical fiber cables at a rate of around 100 million BPS.

FEDERAL COMMUNICATIONS COMMISSION (FCC) In the United States, the FCC regulates public airwaves and rates PCs and other equipment according to the amount of radiation emitted.

FIBER OPTICS A high-speed physical medium for transmitting data, which is made of high-purity glass fibers sealed within a flexible opaque tube. Much faster than conventional copper wire such as coaxial cable.

FILE A collection of any form of data that is stored beyond the time of execution of a single job. A file may contain program instructions or data, which may be numerical, textual, or graphical information.

FILE AND PRINT SHARING SERVICE A service running on Windows that enables the system to share its resources.

FILE FORMAT The type of file, such as picture or text; represented as a suffix at the end of the filename (text = TXT or .txt, and so forth).

FILE FRAGMENTATION The allocation of a file in a noncontiguous sector on a disk. Fragmentation occurs because of multiple deletions and write operations.

FILE NAME A name assigned to a file when the file is first written on a disk. Every file on a disk within the same folder must have a unique name. Prior to Windows 95, file names were restricted to 11 characters—8 characters for the file name and 3 characters for the extension—hence, the so-called 8.3 naming convention. Starting with Windows 95, you may use up to 255 characters for file names on a Windows machine. Macintosh file names are limited to 31 characters. File names can contain nearly any character (including spaces). The list of forbidden characters varies according to the operating system, but often include the following: \ / : * ? " < > |

FILE SERVER A computer designated to store software, courseware, administrative tools, and other data on a local or wide area network. It "serves" this information to other computers via the network when users enter their personal access codes.

FIRE RATING Ratings developed by Underwriters Laboratories and the National Electrical Code (NEC) to define the risk of network cables burning and creating noxious fumes and smoke.

FIREWALL A device or application that restricts traffic between a local network and the Internet based on the type of data transmitted.

FIREWIRE An IEEE 1394 standard to send wide-band signals over a thin connector system that plugs into TVs, VCRs, TV cameras, PCs, and so forth. This serial bus developed by Apple and Texas Instruments enables connection of 60 devices at speeds ranging from 100 to 800 megabits per second.

FLASH ROM A type of ROM technology that can be electrically reprogrammed while still in the PC. Flash is overwhelmingly the most common storage medium of BIOS in PCs today, because it can be upgraded without even having to open the computer on most systems.

FLAT NAME SPACE A naming convention that gives each device only one name that must be unique. NetBIOS uses a flat name space. TCP/IP's DNS uses a hierarchical name space.

FLOPPY DISK A removable and widely used data storage medium that uses a magnetically coated flexible disk of Mylar enclosed in a plastic envelope or case.

FONT A set of consistent size, shape, or style of printer characters, including alphabetic and numeric characters and other signs and symbols.

FORWARD LOOKUP ZONES Special storage areas that hold the IP addresses and names of systems for a particular domain or domains. Forward Lookup Zones are contained within authoritative DNS servers.

FPU (FLOATING POINT UNIT) A formal term for the math coprocessor (also called a *numeric processor*). This is a specialized processor that handles certain calculations faster than the CPU. A math coprocessor calculates using floating point math (which allows for decimals), whereas the CPU can only deal with integers. Intel's 486 and Pentium chips and Motorola's PowerPC have an FPU built into the CPU chip, whereas earlier designs, such as Intel's 80387, needed a separate chip to be installed.

FQDN (FULLY QUALIFIED DOMAIN NAME) The complete DNS name of a system, from its host name to the top-level domain name. For example, mikespc.houston.totalsem.com.

FRAME A defined series of binary data that is the basic container for a discrete amount of data moving across a network. Also commonly called a *packet*.

FRAME CHECK SEQUENCE (FCS) A sequence of bits placed in a frame that is used to check the primary data for errors.

FRAME RELAY An extremely efficient data transmission technique used to send digital information such as voice, data, LAN, and WAN traffic quickly and cost-efficiently to many destinations from one port. Frame relay switches packets end-to-end much faster than X.25 but with no guarantee of data integrity.

FREEWARE Software that is distributed for free, with no licensing fee.

FREQUENCY-HOPPING SPREAD-SPECTRUM (FHSS) A spread-spectrum broadcasting method defined in the 802.11 standard that sends data on one frequency at a time, constantly shifting (or *hopping*) frequencies.

FRONTSIDE BUS Name for the wires that connect the CPU to the main system RAM. Generally runs at speeds of 66–533 MHz. Distinct from the expansion bus and the backside bus, even though the frontside bus shares wires with the former.

FRU (FIELD REPLACEABLE UNIT) Any part of a PC that is considered to be replaceable "in the field," that is, a customer location. There is no official list of FRUs; it is usually a matter of policy by the repair center.

FTP (FILE TRANSFER PROTOCOL) A service that enables computers to quickly transfer and store data files to and from FTP servers using the FTP protocol. The FTP service is built into all modern network operating systems. Examples of third-party FTP clients include CuteFTP, WS-FTP, LeechFTP, and so on.

FULL CONTROL A standard NTFS permission that allows users full access over a file or folder.

FULL-DUPLEX Describes any device that can send and receive data simultaneously.

FUNCTION KEY A keyboard key that gives an instruction to a computer, as opposed to keys that produce letters, numbers, marks of punctuation, and so forth.

GATEWAY 1. A hardware or software setup that translates between two dissimilar protocols. For example, Prodigy has a gateway that translates among its internal, proprietary e-mail format, and Internet e-mail format. 2. Gateway is also used to describe any mechanism for providing access to another system; for example, AOL might be called a *gateway* to the Internet. *See* Default Gateway.

GIF (GRAPHICS INTERCHANGE FORMAT) A method of storing graphics developed for CompuServe in the early 1980s. Because GIF is a compressed format, it takes up much less disk space than conventional file formats and can, therefore, be transmitted faster over phone lines. GIF is a non-lossy format, meaning that no data is lost when an image is converted to GIF, but the format is limited to 8-bit graphics, or 256 colors.

GIGA- The prefix that generally refers to the quantity 1,073,741,824. One gigabyte would be 1,073,741,824 bytes. With frequencies, in contrast, giga- often refers to one billion. One gigahertz would be 1,000,000,000 hertz.

GIGABIT ETHERNET *See* 1000BaseT.

GIGABYTE 1024 megabytes.

GLOBAL USERS AND GROUPS Users and groups that are defined for an entire Windows domain.

GOPHER A widely successful method of making menus of material available over the Internet. Gopher is a client/server style program, which requires that the user have a Gopher Client program. Although Gopher spread rapidly across the globe in only a couple of years, it has been largely supplanted by HTTP, also known as the *World Wide Web*. Thousands of Gopher Servers are still on the Internet and they will probably be with us for a while.

GRAPHIC A computer-generated picture produced on a computer screen or paper, ranging from simple line or bar graphs to colorful and detailed images.

GREEN PC A computer system designed to operate in an energy-efficient manner.

GROUP POLICY A feature of Windows' Active Directory that allows an administrator to apply policy settings, such as desktop configuration or security settings, to network users *en masse.*

GROUP POLICY OBJECTS (GPOS) A Group Policy Object (GPO) enables network administrators to define multiple rights and permissions to entire sets of users all at one time.

GROUPS Collections of network users who share similar tasks and need similar permissions; defined to make administration tasks easier.

GROUPWARE Software that serves the group and makes the group as a whole more productive and efficient in group tasks, for example, Group Scheduling.

GUI (GRAPHICAL USER INTERFACE) The method by which a computer and a user interact. Early interfaces were text-based; that is, the user "talked" to the computer by typing and the computer responded with text on a CRT. A GUI, on the other hand, enables the user to interact with the computer graphically, by manipulating icons that represent programs or documents with a mouse or other pointing device.

HALF-DUPLEX Any device that can only send or receive data at any given moment. Most Ethernet transmissions are half-duplex.

HANDSHAKING A procedure performed by modems, terminals, and computers to verify that communication has been correctly established.

HANG When a computer freezes, so that it does not respond to keyboard commands, it is said to "hang" or to have "hung." Synonymous with *freeze* or *frozen,* and *halt* or *halted.*

HANG TIME Colloquially, the number of seconds a too-often-hung computer is airborne after you have thrown it out a second-story window.

HARD DRIVE A data-recording system using solid disks of magnetic material turning at high speeds.

HARDWARE Physical computer equipment such as electrical, electronic, magnetic, and mechanical devices. Anything in the computer world that you can hold in your hand. A floppy drive is hardware; Microsoft Word is not.

HARDWARE ABSTRACTION LAYER (HAL) A part of the Windows NT/2000/XP operating system that separates system-specific device drivers from the system hardware.

HARDWARE COMPATIBILITY LIST (HCL) A list that is maintained by Microsoft that names all the hardware that is supported by an operating system. This list is helpful to use when upgrading a system; with a quick glance, you can make sure that support is available for all the devices in a system before you begin the upgrade.

HARDWARE PROFILE A list of devices that Windows automatically enables or disables in the Device Manager, depending on what devices the system detects.

HARDWARE PROTOCOL A hardware protocol defines many aspects of a network, from the packet type to the cabling and connectors used.

HARDWARE TOOLS Physical tools used to configure a network, including cable testers, protocol analyzers, hardware loopback devices, and toners.

HAYES COMMAND SET A standardized set of instructions used to control modems. Examples are

AT Attention (used to start commands)
ATDT Attention Dial Tone
ATDP Attention Dial Pulse
ATH Attention Hang Up

HEX (HEXADECIMAL) Hex symbols based on a numbering system of 16 (computer shorthand for binary numbers), using ten digits and six letters to condense 0s and 1s to binary numbers. Hex is represented by digits 0 through 9 and alpha *A* through *F*, so that 09h has a value of 9, and 0Ah has a value of 10.

HIERARCHICAL NAME SPACE A naming scheme where the full name of each object includes its position within the hierarchy. An example of a hierarchical name is www.totalseminars.com, which includes not only the host name, but also the domain name. DNS uses a hierarchical name space scheme for Fully Qualified Domain Names (FQDNs).

HIGH RESOLUTION Using a sufficient number of pixels in display monitors or dots per inch when printing, to produce well-defined text characters and smoothly defined curves in graphic images.

HIMEM.SYS A DOS device driver that configures extended memory and high memory so that programs conforming to XMS can access it.

HMA (HIGH MEMORY AREA) The first 64K of memory above 1 megabyte. Programs that conform to XMS can use HMA as a direct extension of conventional memory. Most of the portions of DOS that must be loaded into conventional memory can be loaded into the HMA.

HOMEPAGE The web page that your browser is set to use when it starts up or the main web page for a business, organization, or person. Also, the main page in any collection of web pages.

HOME RADIO FREQUENCY (HOMERF) An implementation of the IEEE 802.11 wireless Ethernet standard that is intended for home use. Not for use in large business network environments.

HONEY POT An area of a network that an administrator sets up for the express purpose of attracting a computer hacker. If a hacker takes the bait, the network's important resources are unharmed and network personnel can analyze the attack to predict and protect against future attacks, making the network more secure.

HORIZONTAL CABLING Cabling that connects the equipment room to the work area.

HOST A single device (usually a computer) on a TCP/IP network that has an IP address; any device that can be the source or destination of a data packet. Also, in the mainframe world, a computer that is made available for use by multiple people simultaneously.

HOST ID The portion of an IP address that defines a specific machine.

HOSTS FILE A static text file that resides on a computer and is used to resolve DNS host names to IP addresses. The HOSTS file is checked before the machine sends a name resolution request to a DNS name server. The HOSTS file has no extension.

HTML (HYPERTEXT MARKUP LANGUAGE) An ASCII-based script-like language for creating hypertext documents like those on the World Wide Web.

HTTP (HYPERTEXT TRANSFER PROTOCOL) Extremely fast protocol used for network file transfers in the WWW environment.

HTTP OVER SSL (HTTPS) A secure form of HTTP, used commonly for Internet business transactions or any time where a secure connection is required. *See also* HTTP (HyperText Transfer Protocol) and SSL (Secure Sockets Layer).

HUB A hardware device that sits at the center of a star topology network, providing a common point for the connection of network devices. In a 10BaseT Ethernet network, the hub contains the electronic equivalent of a properly terminated bus cable; in a Token Ring network, the hub contains the electronic equivalent of a ring.

HYBRID A mix or blend of two different topologies. A star bus topology is a hybrid of the star and bus topologies.

HYPERTEXT A document that has been marked up to enable a user to select words or pictures within the document, click them, and connect to further information. The basis of the World Wide Web.

HYPERTEXT TRANSPORT PROTOCOL WITH SSL (HTTPS) SSL is a protocol developed by Netscape for transmitting private documents over the Internet. HTTPS is a file or web page that uses SSL to encrypt sensitive data.

IANA (INTERNET ASSIGNED NUMBERS AUTHORITY) The organization responsible for assigning public IP addresses.

IBM-TYPE DATA CONNECTOR/UNIVERSAL DATA CONNECTOR (IDC/UDC) A unique hermaphroditic connector designed by IBM for Token Ring networks.

ICF (INTERNET CONNECTION FIREWALL) A software firewall built into Windows XP that protects your system from unauthorized access from the Internet.

ICS (INTERNET CONNECTION SHARING) Also known simply as *Internet sharing*, a term used to describe the technique of enabling more than one computer to access the Internet simultaneously using a single Internet connection. When you use Internet sharing, you connect an entire LAN to the Internet using a single public IP address.

IDE (INTELLIGENT OR INTEGRATED DRIVE ELECTRONICS) A PC specification for small- to medium-sized hard drives in which the controlling electronics for the drive are part of the drive itself, speeding up transfer rates and leaving only a simple adapter (or *paddle*). IDE only supported two drives per system of no more than 504 megabytes each and has been completely supplanted by Enhanced IDE. EIDE supports four drives of over 8 gigabytes each and more than doubles the transfer rate. The more common name for PATA drives. *See* ATA (AT Attachment).

IEEE (INSTITUTE OF ELECTRONIC AND ELECTRICAL ENGINEERS) IEEE is the leading standards-setting group in the United States.

IEEE 802.1 IEEE subcommittee that defined the standards for Higher Layer LAN Protocols.

IEEE 802.2 IEEE subcommittee that defined the standards for Logical Link Control.

IEEE 802.3 IEEE subcommittee that defined the standards for CSMA/CD (a.k.a. *Ethernet*).

IEEE 802.4 IEEE subcommittee that defined the standards for token bus.

IEEE 802.5 IEEE subcommittee that defined the standards for Token Ring.

IEEE 802.6 IEEE subcommittee that defined the standards for MAN (metropolitan area network).

IEEE 802.7 IEEE subcommittee that defined the standards for broadband.

IEEE 802.8 IEEE subcommittee that defined the standards for fiber optic.

IEEE 802.9 IEEE subcommittee that defined the standards for isochronous LAN.

IEEE 802.10 IEEE subcommittee that defined the standards for security.

IEEE 802.11 IEEE subcommittee that defined the standards for wireless.

IEEE 802.12 IEEE subcommittee that defined the standards for demand priority/100BaseVG.

IEEE 802.14 IEEE subcommittee that defined the standards for cable modems.

IETF (INTERNET ENGINEERING TASK FORCE) The primary standards organization for the Internet.

IFCONFIG A command-line utility for Linux servers and workstations that displays the current TCP/IP configuration of the machine, similar to IPCONFIG and WINIPCFG for Windows systems.

IMAP (INTERNET MESSAGE ACCESS PROTOCOL) An alternative to POP3. IMAP retrieves e-mail from an e-mail server, like POP3; the main difference is that IMAP uses TCP/IP port 143.

IMPEDANCE The amount of resistance to an electrical signal on a wire. It is used as a relative measure of the amount of data a cable can handle.

INCREMENTAL BACKUP A type of backup that backs up all files that have their archive bits turned on, meaning they have been changed since the last backup. This type of backup turns the archive bits off after the files have been backed up.

INDEPENDENT BASIC SERVICE SET (IBSS) A basic unit of organization in wireless networks formed by two or more wireless nodes communicating in ad-hoc mode.

INFRASTRUCTURE MODE Wireless networks running in infrastructure mode use one or more wireless access points to connect the wireless network nodes centrally. This configuration is similar to the *star topology* of a wired network.

INHERITANCE A method of assigning user permissions, in which folder permissions flow downward into subfolders.

INSULATING JACKET The insulating jacket is the outside part of a fiber-optic cable that holds it all together.

INTERLACED TV/video systems in which the electron beam writes every other line, then retraces itself to a second pass to complete the final framed image. Originally, this reduced magnetic line paring, but took twice as long to paint, which added some flicker in graphic images.

INTERNAL NETWORK A LAN that resides behind a router, modem, or firewall.

INTERNAL NETWORK ADDRESS A number added to MAC addresses on an IPX/SPX network that define the servers on that network.

INTERNAL THREATS All the things that a network's own users do to create problems on the network. Examples include accidental deletion of files, accidental damage to hardware devices or cabling, and abuse of rights and permissions.

INTERNET CONNECTION FIREWALL (ICF) *See* ICF (Internet Connection Firewall).

INTERNET CONNECTION SHARING (ICS) *See* ICS (Internet Connection Sharing).

INTERNET CONTROL MESSAGE PROTOCOL (ICMP) ICMP messages consist of a single packet and are connectionless. ICMP packets determine connectivity between two hosts.

INTERNET PROTOCOL VERSION 4 (IPv4) IPv4 addresses consist of four sets of numbers, each number being a value between 0 and 255, using a period to separate the numbers. This is often called *dotted decimal* format. No IPv4 address may be all 0s or all 1s (255). Examples include 192.168.0.1 and 64.176.19.164.

INTERNET PROTOCOL VERSION 6 (IPv6) IPv6 addresses consist of eight sets of four hexadecimal numbers, each number being a value between 0000 and FFFF, using a colon to separate the numbers. An example is FEDC:BA98:7654:3210:0800:200C:00CF:1234.

InterNIC The organization that maintains the DNS services, registrations, and so forth run by Network Solutions, General Atomics, and AT&T.

INTERRUPT A suspension of a process, such as the execution of a computer program, caused by an event initiated by a device on the computer and performed in such a way that the process can be resumed. Events of this kind include sensors monitoring laboratory equipment or a user pressing an interrupt key.

INTRANET A private network inside a company or organization that uses the same kinds of software and services you find on the public Internet, but that is only for internal use.

I/O (INPUT/OUTPUT) A general term for reading and writing data to a computer. The term *input* includes data from a keyboard, pointing device (such as a mouse), and file from a disk. Output includes writing information to a disk, viewing it on a CRT, and printing it to a printer.

I/O DEVICE Pieces of hardware that enable a user to move data in to or out of the computer, such as a mouse or a keyboard.

IP (INTERNET PROTOCOL) The Internet standard protocol that provides a common layer over dissimilar networks used to move packets among host computers and through gateways if necessary. Part of the TCP/IP protocol suite.

IP ADDRESS The numeric address of a computer connected to a TCP/IP network, such as the Internet. The IP address is made up of 4 octets of 8-bit binary numbers that are translated by the computer into their shorthand numeric values; for example, 11000000.10101000.00000100.00011010 = 192.168.4.26. IP addresses must be matched with a valid subnet mask, which identifies the part of the IP address that is the network ID and the part that is the host ID.

IPCONFIG A command-line utility for Windows that displays the current TCP/IP configuration of the machine; similar to Windows 9x's WINIPCFG and UNIX/Linux's IFCONFIG.

IPSEC (IP SECURITY) A group of protocols used to encrypt IP packets. IPSec is most commonly seen on Virtual Private Networks. *See* VPN (Virtual Private Network).

IPX/SPX (INTERNETWORK PACKET EXCHANGE/SEQUENCE PACKET EXCHANGE) Protocol suite developed by Novell, primarily for supporting Novell NetWare-based networks.

IRC (INTERNET RELAY CHAT) A live online group discussion. IRC uses centralized IRC servers that manage all discussions for IRC clients. Usually shortened to simply *chat*.

IRQ (INTERRUPT REQUEST) A signal from a hardware device, such as a modem or a mouse, indicating that it needs the CPU's attention. In PCs, IRQs are sent along specific IRQ channels associated with a particular device. Therefore, it is important to ensure that two devices do not share a common IRQ channel.

ISA (INDUSTRY STANDARD ARCHITECTURE) A design found in the original IBM PC for the sockets on the motherboard that allowed additional hardware to be connected to the computer's motherboard. An 8-bit, 8.33-MHz expansion bus that was designed by IBM for its AT computer and released to the public domain. An improved 16-bit bus was also released to the public domain. Various other designs, such as IBM's MicroChannel and EISA bus, tried to improve on the design without much popularity. ISA only supports 8- and 16-bit data paths, so 32-bit alternatives such as PCI and AGP have become popular. Although ISA slots linger on a few motherboards, they are almost never seen in new systems.

ISDN (INTEGRATED SERVICES DIGITAL NETWORK) The CCITT (Comité Consutatif Internationale Téléphonique et Télégraphique) standard that defines a digital method for communications to replace the current analog telephone system. ISDN is superior to telephone lines because it supports up to 128 Kbps transfer rate for sending information from computer to computer. It also allows data and voice to share a common phone line.

ISP (INTERNET SERVICE PROVIDER) An institution that provides access to the Internet in some form, usually for a fee.

ISV (INDEPENDENT SOFTWARE VENDOR) Firms that develop and market software.

IT (INFORMATION TECHNOLOGY) The business of computers, electronic communications, and electronic commerce.

JAVA A network-oriented programming language invented by Sun Microsystems and specifically designed for writing programs that can be safely downloaded to your computer through the Internet and immediately run without fear of viruses or other harm to your computer or files. Using small Java programs (called *applets*), web pages can include functions such as animations, calculators, and other fancy tricks.

JPEG (JOINT PHOTOGRAPHIC EXPERTS GROUP) A method of formatting images for efficient storage and transfer across phone lines; JPEG files are often a factor of ten or more times smaller than non-compressed files. JPEG is a *lossy* format, meaning that some data is lost when an image is converted. Most JPEG conversion software allows the user to decide between more or less compression at the cost of image quality. JPEG supports 24-bit images (up to 16.8 million colors). Because computers running MS-DOS are limited in their file names, this format is also referred to as *JPG*.

JUMPER A series of pairs of small pins that can be shorted with a *shunt* to configure many different aspects of PCs. Usually used in configurations that are rarely changed, such as master/slave settings on IDE drives.

JUST A BUNCH OF DISKS (JBOD) An array of hard drives that are simply connected with no RAID implementations.

K- (OR KB) Most commonly used as the suffix for the binary quantity 1024. 640 K means 640 ? 1024 or 655360. Just to add some extra confusion to the IT industry, *K* is often misspoken as "kilo," the metric value for 1000. 10 KB, for example, spoken as "10 kilobytes," means 10240 bytes rather than 10000 bytes.

KBPS (KILOBITS PER SECOND) Data transfer rate of 1,000 bits per second. Note that this is not synonymous with KB, or 1,024.

KERBEROS An authentication standard designed to allow different operating systems and applications to authenticate each other.

KERMIT A communications protocol that enables you to transfer files between your computer and online network systems. Kermit has built-in error correction and can handle binary (non-text) files.

KERN The amount of distance between characters in a particular font.

KERNEL The core portion of a program that resides in memory and performs the most essential operating system tasks.

KILOHERTZ (KHZ) A unit of measure that equals a frequency of one thousand cycles per second.

KNOWLEDGE BASE A large collection of documents and FAQs that is maintained by Microsoft. Found on Microsoft's web site, the Knowledge Base is an excellent place to search for assistance on most operating system problems.

LAN (LOCAL AREA NETWORK) A group of PCs connected together via cabling, radio, or infrared that use this connectivity to share resources such as printers and mass storage.

LASER PRINTER An electrophotographic printer in which a laser is used as the light source.

LAST KNOWN GOOD CONFIGURATION An option on the Advanced Startup Options menu in Windows NT/2000/XP/2003 that enables your system to revert to a previous configuration in order to troubleshoot and repair any major system problems.

LAYER A grouping of related tasks involving the transfer of information. Also, a particular level of the OSI reference model, for example, Physical layer, Data Link layer, and so forth.

LAYER 2 SWITCH Also known as a *bridge*. Filters and forwards data packets based on the MAC addresses of the sending and receiving machines.

LAYER 3 SWITCH Also known as a *router*. Filters and forwards data packets based on the network addresses of the sending and receiving machines.

LBA (LOGICAL BLOCK ADDRESSING) A translation (algorithm) of IDE drives promoted by Western Digital as a standardized method for breaking the 504-megabyte limit in IDE drives. Subsequently, LBA was universally adopted by the PC industry and is now standard on all PATA drives. Allows drives up to 8.4 gigabytes.

LCD (LIQUID CRYSTAL DISPLAY) A display technology that relies on polarized light passing through a liquid medium, rather than on electron beams striking a phosphorescent surface.

LED (LIGHT EMITTING DIODES) Solid state devices that light up when charged with electrical current.

LIMITED ACCOUNT A type of user account that has limited access to a system. Accounts of this type cannot alter system files, install new programs, and edit settings using the Control Panel.

LINE PRINTER DAEMON (LPD) A TCP/IP function running on a UNIX/Linux system that works as a server and shares a local printer.

LINE PRINTER REMOTE (LPR) A TCP/IP function running on a UNIX/Linux system that wants to access a printer under the control of LPD.

LINK LIGHT An LED on NICs, hubs, and switches that lights up to show good connection between the devices.

LINK SEGMENTS Segments that link other segments together but are unpopulated or have no computers directly attached to them. *See* 5-4-3 Rule.

LINK STATE The state describing whether a wireless device is connected.

LINUX Open-source, graphical UNIX-clone operating system invented by Linus Torvalds.

LMHOSTS FILE A static text file that resides on a computer and is used to resolve NetBIOS names to IP addresses. The LMHOSTS file is checked before the machine sends a name resolution request to a WINS name server. The LMHOSTS file has no extension.

LOCAL 1. Refers to systems connected to the same network segment, usually in the same physical site. Systems that are outside the local network segments are considered *remote*. 2. Refers to user accounts stored on a single computer system on a network.

LOCAL BUS A high-speed data path that directly links the computer's CPU with one or more slots on the expansion bus. This direct link means signals from an adapter do not have to travel through the computer expansion bus, which is significantly slower.

LOCALHOST An alias for the loopback address of 127.0.0.1, referring to the current machine.

LOCALTALK A network protocol created by Apple computers to add networking to their computers. LocalTalk uses a bus topology, with each device daisy-chained to the next device on the segment, and a proprietary cabling with small round DIN-style connectors.

LOCAL USER ACCOUNTS The accounts for each local system on a Windows NT/2000/XP/2003 network. These accounts are stored in the local system's Registry.

LOCAL USERS AND GROUPS The users and groups defined on each individual Windows NT/2000/XP/2003 system.

LOGICAL ADDRESS An address that describes both a specific network and a specific machine on that network.

LOGICAL DRIVES Sections of a hard drive that are formatted and assigned a drive letter, each of which is presented to the user as if it is a separate drive.

LOGICAL UNIT NUMBERS (LUNs) A specialized SCSI configuration that enables multiple devices to share a single SCSI ID. This type of arrangement is found most commonly in high-end servers that have large hard disk arrays.

LOOPBACK ADDRESS Sometimes called the *localhost*, the loopback address is a reserved IP address used for internal testing: 127.0.0.1.

LOOPBACK TEST A special test often included in diagnostic software that sends data out of the NIC and checks to see if it comes back.

LOW-LEVEL FORMAT Defining the physical location of magnetic tracks and sectors on a disk.

LUMINESCENCE The part of the video signal that controls the luminance/brightness of the picture. Also known as the Y portion of the component signal.

MAC (MEDIA ACCESS CONTROL) 1. Unique 48-bit address assigned to each network card. IEEE assigns blocks of possible addresses to various NIC manufacturers to help ensure that each address is unique. 2. The sublayer of the data-link layer of the OSI model uses MAC addresses for locating machines.

MACHINE LANGUAGE A programming language or instruction code that is immediately interpretable by the hardware of the machine concerned.

MAC OS The operating system used on Apple Macintosh computers.

MACRO VIRUS A specially written application macro (collection of commands) that performs the same functions as a virus. These macros normally autostart when the application is run and then make copies of themselves, often propagating across networks.

MAILBOX Special holding areas on an e-mail server that separates out e-mail for each user.

MAIL SERVER *See* E-mail Server.

MAINFRAME Extremely powerful (and in most cases, physically large) computers that support thousands of user sessions simultaneously. Users access applications on the mainframe through dumb terminals. Mainframes typically have multiple CPUs, large amounts of RAM and disk storage space, and layers of hardware redundancy that enable hot-swapping of most hardware components. Mainframes are used extensively in industrial and scientific settings, banking, and in the military.

MAN (METROPOLITAN AREA NETWORK) Defined as an IEEE 802.6 network, a MAN is a group of computers connected via cabling, radio, leased phone lines, or infrared, that use this connectivity to share resources such as printers and mass storage. Usually the distance is between that of a LAN and a WAN: different buildings, but within the same city. A typical example of a MAN is a college campus. No firm dividing lines dictate what is considered a WAN, MAN, or LAN.

MAPPED DRIVE A virtual drive set up on a computer that, in reality, links to a folder or drive on another computer.

MAPPING The process that links a shared folder or drive on another computer to the local one with a persistent link.

MASS STORAGE Hard drives, CD-ROMs, removable media drives, and so forth.

MATH COPROCESSOR Also called *math unit, floating point unit,* or *FPU.* A secondary microprocessor whose function is the handling of floating point arithmetic. Although originally a physically separate chip, math coprocessors are now built into today's CPUs.

MAU (MULTISTATION ACCESS UNIT) A hub used in Token Ring networks. Also abbreviated as *MSAU.*

MB (MEGABYTE) 1,048,576 bytes.

MCA (MICROCHANNEL ARCHITECTURE) Expansion bus architecture developed by IBM as the (unsuccessful) successor to ISA. MCA had a full 32-bit design and was self-configuring.

MCC (MEMORY CONTROLLER CHIP) The chip that handles memory requests from the CPU. Although once a special chip, it has been integrated into the chipset on all PCs today.

MEDIA CERTIFIER TOOL A device used by professional installers that can test the electrical characteristics of a cable and then generate a certification report to prove that your cable runs pass EIA/TIA standards.

MEGA- A prefix that usually stands for the binary quantity 1,048,576. One megabyte is 1,048,576 bytes. One megahertz, however, is a million hertz. Sometimes shortened to *meg,* as in "a 286 has an address space of 16 megs."

MEMORY A device or medium that serves for temporary storage of programs and data during program execution. The term is synonymous with storage, although it is most frequently used for referring to the internal storage of a computer that can be directly addressed by operating instructions. A computer's temporary storage capacity is measured in kilobytes (KB) or megabytes (MB) of RAM (random access memory). Long-term data storage on disks is also measured in kilobytes, megabytes, gigabytes, and terabytes.

MESH TOPOLOGY Each computer has a dedicated connection to every other computer in a network.

MHz (MEGAHERTZ) A unit of measure that equals a frequency of 1 million cycles per second.

MICROCOMPUTER A computer system in which the central processing unit is built as a single tiny semiconductor chip or as a small number of chips. The term is synonymous with personal computer (PC.)

MICROPROCESSOR Main computer chip that provides speed and capabilities of the computer. Also called a *CPU.*

MICROSOFT MANAGEMENT CONSOLE (MMC) The MMC provides a unified interface for a variety of configuration tools called *snap-ins.* Windows comes with a number of pre-defined consoles such as Computer Management, Users and Groups, and so on. Administrators can also create custom consoles that include snap-ins used to perform a specific task.

MICROSOFT PRODUCT ACTIVATION (MPA) Introduced by Microsoft with the release on Windows XP, Microsoft Product Activation prevents unauthorized use of Microsoft's software by requiring a user to "activate" the software via the Internet or an automated phone system.

MIDI (MUSICAL INSTRUMENT DIGITAL INTERFACE) MIDI is a standard that describes the interface between a computer and a device for simulating musical instruments. Rather than sending large sound samples, a computer can simply send "instructions" to the instrument describing pitch, tone, and duration of a sound. MIDI files are, therefore, much more efficient. Because a MIDI file is made up of a set of instructions rather than a copy of the sound, it is easy to modify each component of the file. It also is possible to program many channels or *voices* of music to be played simultaneously, creating symphonic sound.

MIME (MULTIPURPOSE INTERNET MAIL EXTENSIONS) A standard for attaching binary files, such as executables and images, to the Internet's text-based mail (24-Kbps packet size).

MINICOMPUTER Minicomputers are similar to mainframe computers in that they are very powerful, multiprocessor systems with lots of hardware redundancy and hot-swapping capability. However, instead of handling thousands of simultaneous user sessions, they handle hundreds and are smaller in size. Minicomputers are used extensively in the telecommunications industry.

MIPS (MILLIONS OF INSTRUCTIONS PER SECOND) A measurement of CPU performance used for processor benchmarks.

MIRRORING Also called *drive mirroring.* Reading and writing data at the same time to two drives for fault-tolerance purposes. Considered RAID level 1.

MLA (MULTI-LETTERED ACRONYM) The abbreviation for any object or thought that can be condensed to an abbreviation.

MMU (MEMORY-MANAGEMENT UNIT) A chip or circuit that translates virtual memory addresses to physical addresses and may implement memory protection.

MODEM (MODULATOR/DEMODULATOR) A device that converts both digital bit streams into analog signals (modulation) and incoming analog signals back into digital signals (demodulation). The analog communications channel is typically a telephone line and the analog signals are typically sounds.

MONITOR An electronic display device that shows text, graphics, and other functions performed by the computer.

MOTHERBOARD The primary circuit board that holds all the core components of the computer.

MOUNTING RACK Racks used in equipment rooms to mount servers, monitors, and other network hardware, thereby conserving space.

MP3 (MPEG-1 AUDIO LAYER 3) An audio compression scheme used extensively on the Internet.

MPEG (MOTION PICTURE EXPERTS GROUP) A sophisticated video standard that enables digital video to be compressed using a form of JPEG image compression and a technique called *differencing*, in which only the differences between frames are recorded, rather than the frame itself.

MSAU (MULTISTATION ACCESS UNIT) A hub used in Token Ring networks. Also abbreviated as *MAU*.

MS-CHAP Microsoft's variation of the CHAP protocol. It uses a slightly more advanced encryption protocol.

MSCONFIG A utility found in Windows that enables a user to configure a system's boot files and critical system files.

MULTIMEDIA A single work assembled using elements from more than one medium, such as high-resolution color images, sounds, video, and text that contains characters in multiple fonts and styles.

MULTIPLEXER A device that merges information from multiple input channels to a single output channel.

MULTI-SPEED HUB Any hub that supports more than one network speed for otherwise similar cabling systems. Multi-speed hubs come in two flavors: one has mostly dedicated slower ports, with a few dedicated faster ports, while the other has only special autosensing ports that automatically run at either the faster or the slower speed.

MULTITASKING The process of running multiple programs or tasks on the same computer at the same time.

NAME RESOLUTION A method that enables one computer on the network to locate another to establish a session. All network protocols perform name resolution in one of two ways: *broadcasting* or by providing some form of *name server*.

NAME SERVER A computer whose job is to know the name of every other computer on the network.

NAT (NETWORK ADDRESS TRANSLATION) NAT works hand-in-hand with DHCP to mask the IP address of network clients behind a single public IP address. NAT devices (either dedicated hardware devices such as routers, or a PC with two NICs running the software NAT service) have two interfaces: one that connects to the Internet via an ISP-supplied IP address, and another that connects to the LAN. The NAT service converts (or *translates*) the IP addresses and TCP/UDP port numbers of data packets forwarded from the LAN interface from an address in the private IP address range to the public IP address. NAT enables multiple network clients to share a single Internet connection, and provides a level of firewall-like security.

NBTSTAT A command-line utility used to check the current NetBIOS name cache on a particular machine. The utility compares NetBIOS names to their corresponding IP addresses.

NDS (NOVELL DIRECTORY SERVICES) Novell's directory service, supplied with NetWare versions 4.*x* and later. Administrators use NDS to organize users, servers, and groups into a hierarchical tree structure. Also called eDirectory.

NETBEUI (NETBIOS EXTENDED USER INTERFACE) NetBEUI is an extended version of the NetBIOS protocol that operates at the Transport layer of the OSI model. NetBEUI has been overshadowed by other protocols, such as IPX/SPX, mainly because NetBEUI is not routable and therefore unsuitable for connecting to the Internet. Microsoft is phasing support for NetBEUI out of their products, starting with Windows XP.

NETBIOS (NETWORK BASIC INPUT/OUTPUT SYSTEM) The NetBIOS protocol creates and manages connections based on the names of the computers involved. NetBIOS operates at the Session layer of the OSI seven-layer model.

NETBIOS NAME A computer name that identifies both the specific machine and the functions that machine performs. A NetBIOS name consists of 16 characters: the first 15 are an alphanumeric name, and the 16th is a special suffix that identifies the role the machine plays.

NETBIOS OVER TCP/IP (NETBT) A process used by Microsoft to transform NetBIOS into an application-layer function on a TCP/IP network, which added the flexibility of TCP/IP to NetBIOS support.

NETSTAT A command-line utility used to examine the sockets-based connections open on a given host.

NETWORK A collection of two or more computers interconnected by telephone lines, coaxial cables, satellite links, radio, and/or some other communication technique. A computer *network* is a group of computers that are connected together and communicate with one another for a common purpose. Computer networks support "people and organization" networks, users who also share a common purpose for communicating.

NETWORK ID A number that identifies the network on which a device or machine exists. This number exists in both IP and IPX protocol suites.

NETWORK INTERFACE CARD (NIC) A hardware device that connects the PC to a network. NICs come as internal component cards that install onto the PC's motherboard, or as external devices that use the PC's USB or PC Card ports. NICs may have connections for coax, STP, UTP, or fiber optic cabling, or 802.11- or Bluetooth-based wireless technology.

NETWORK LAYER *See* OSI Seven-Layer Model.

NETWORK NAMES A 32-bit identification string that's inserted into the header of each data packet processed by a wireless access point. Usually known as the *Service Set Identification* (SSID). When properly configured, only wireless clients whose SSID matches that of the wireless access point are able to gain access to the wireless network.

NETWORK PROTOCOL 1. The rules and standards that define how computers communicate over a network. 2. The software applications and services that enable computers to access a network and establish sessions with remote computers. Examples of network protocols include TCP/IP, IPX/SPX, NetBEUI, DLC, and others.

NETWORK SHARE Network shares are logical representations of resources on a network. A single resource, such as a printer, disk drive, or folder, may have numerous network shares configured under numerous names and with different access security settings.

NETWORK THREATS Anything that endangers the integrity and security of data available on a network. Examples of network threats include unauthorized access, virus infection, deletion or manipulation of data, loss of network services, etc.

NETWORK TOPOLOGY 1. Describes the physical structures that connect PCs, cabling, routers, hubs, patch panels, and other pieces of hardware to one another. 2. Describes the logical organization of a network, such as domains and workgroups.

NEWSGROUP Discussion groups on public or private USENET networks.

NFS (NETWORK FILE SYSTEM) A file system that enables UNIX systems to treat files on a remote UNIX machine as though they were local files.

NODE 1. A member of a network. 2. A point where one or more functional units interconnect transmission lines. 3. In the Windows MMC, a container object that enables access to snap-in consoles.

NOISE Undesirable signals bearing no desired information and frequently capable of introducing errors into the communication process.

NON-DISCOVERY MODE A setting for Bluetooth devices that prevents them from broadcasting their presence, effectively hiding them from other Bluetooth devices.

NORMAL BACKUP A full backup of every selected file on a system. This type of backup turns off the archive bit after the backup.

NORTHBRIDGE The Northbridge is the chip or chips that connect a CPU to memory, the PCI bus, Level 2 cache, and AGP activities. The Northbridge chips communicate with the CPU through the FSB.

NOS (NETWORK OPERATING SYSTEM) An operating system that provides basic file and supervisory services over a network. While each computer attached to the network does have its own OS, the NOS describes which actions are allowed by each user and coordinates distribution of networked files to the users who request them.

NOVELL NETWARE A popular and powerful network operating system, providing network services ranging from simple file storage and sharing to World Wide Web, e-mail, VPN, and other services. Novell NetWare is the only NOS that adheres to the strict definition of client/server.

NOVELL STORAGE SERVICES (NSS) A file format used in NetWare servers.

NS (NANOSECOND) A billionth of a second. Light travels a little over 11 inches in one nanosecond.

NSLOOKUP A handy tool that advanced techs use to query the functions of DNS servers.

NTFS (NT FILE SYSTEM) Microsoft's proprietary file system for hard drives that enables object-level security, long filename support, compression, and encryption. NTFS 4.0 debuted with Windows NT 4.0. Windows 2000/XP/2003 come with NTFS 5.0.

NTFS PERMISSIONS Settings, or groups of settings, that enable administrators to control levels of access to files and folders on a per-user basis. There are two sets of NTFS permissions, special permissions and standard permissions. Special permissions include things such as Traverse Folders, Read Attributes, and Take Ownership (to name just a few) that enable or deny granular control over what a user or group can do to an NTFS resource. Standard permissions are pre-configured groupings of special permissions that are used to grant or deny more general access to resources, such as Modify, Read, and Write. Special permissions are rarely used, as standard permissions encompass the majority of actions that a user will ever need to take.

NTLDR A Windows NT/2000/XP/2003 boot file. Launched by the MBR or MFT, NTLDR looks at the BOOT.INI configuration file for any installed operating systems.

NWLink Also known as *IPX/SPX-compatible protocol*, this is Microsoft's implementation of IPX/SPX. *See also IPX/SPX* (Internetwork Packet Exchange/Sequence Packet Exchange).

Object A system component that is given a set of characteristics and can be managed by the operating system as a single entity.

OCR (Optical Character Recognition) The process of converting characters represented in a graphical format into ASCII. This is usually done in conjunction with a scanner to allow for editing of printed material.

OEM (Original Equipment Manufacturer) Contrary to the name, an OEM does not create original hardware, but rather purchases components from manufacturers and puts them together in systems under its own brand name. Dell Computers and Gateway 2000, for example, are for the most part OEMs. Apple Computers, which manufactures most of the components for its own Macintosh-branded machines, is not an OEM. Also known as *VARs (value-added resellers)*.

Ohm Electronic measurement of a cable's or an electronic component's impedance.

OLE (Object Linking and Embedding) The Microsoft Windows specification that enables objects created within one application to be placed, or embedded, in another application. The two applications are *linked*, meaning that when the original object is modified, the copy is updated automatically.

Open Shortest Path First (OSPF) An interior gateway routing protocol developed for IP networks based on the *shortest path first* or *link-state algorithm*.

Open Source Applications and operating systems that offer access to their source code; this enables developers to modify applications and operating systems easily to meet their specific needs.

Organizational Unit Also *OU*. A type of container used in Windows and NetWare network operating systems to enable grouping of user accounts for the purpose of administrative control.

OS (Operating System) The set of programming that enables a program to interact with the computer and provides an interface between the PC and the user. Examples are Microsoft Windows XP, Apple Macintosh OS X, and SUSE Linux.

Oscilloscope A device that gives a graphical/visual representation of signal levels over a period of time.

OSI (Open Systems Interconnection) An international standard suite of protocols defined by the International Organization for Standardization (ISO) that implements the OSI reference model for network communications between computers.

OSI Seven-Layer Model An architecture model based on the OSI protocol suite, which defines and standardizes the flow of data between computers. The following lists the seven layers:

> **Layer 1** The **Physical layer** defines hardware connections and turns binary into physical pulses (electrical or light). Repeaters and hubs operate at the Physical layer.
> **Layer 2** The **Data Link layer** identifies devices on the Physical layer. MAC addresses are part of the Data Link layer. Bridges operate at the Data Link layer.
> **Layer 3** The **Network layer** moves packets between computers on different networks. Routers operate at the Network layer. IP and IPX operate at the Network layer.
> **Layer 4** The **Transport layer** breaks data down into manageable chunks. TCP, UDP, SPX, and NetBEUI operate at the Transport layer.
> **Layer 5** The **Session layer** manages connections between machines. NetBIOS and Sockets operate at the Session layer.
> **Layer 6** The **Presentation layer**, which can also manage data encryption, hides the differences between various types of computer systems.
> **Layer 7** The **Application layer** provides tools for programs to use to access the network (and the lower layers). HTTP, FTP, SMTP, and POP3 are all examples of protocols that operate at the Application layer.

Overclocking To run a CPU or video processor faster than its rated speed.

Overdrive Generic name given to processors designed as aftermarket upgrades to computer systems.

Overscanning Displaying less than the complete area of an image to the viewer. Most monitors may slightly overscan. Also of value when using a Twain scanner to capture 2K ? 2K images, and allowing playback in a smaller window, but moving beyond the normal borders to view close-up detail of portions of the image controlled by the mouse pointer.

PACKET Basic component of communication over a network. A group of bits of fixed maximum size and well-defined format that is switched and transmitted as a complete whole through a network. It contains source and destination address, data, and control information. *See also* Frame.

PACKET FILTERING Packet filters, also known as *IP filters*, will block any incoming or outgoing packet from a particular IP address or range of IP addresses. Packet filters are far better at blocking outgoing IP addresses, because the network administrator knows and can specify the IP addresses of the internal systems.

PAD Extra data added to an Ethernet frame to bring the data up to the minimum required size of 64 bytes.

PAP (PASSWORD AUTHENTICATION PROTOCOL) The oldest and most basic form of authentication, it's also the least safe because it sends all passwords in clear text.

PARALLEL ATA (PATA) A disk drive implementation that integrates the controller on the disk drive itself. *See also* ATA (AT Attachment).

PARALLEL PORT A connection for the synchronous, high-speed flow of data along parallel lines to a device, usually a printer.

PARAMETER A value used to modify a routine or command. Synonymous with *argument*.

PARITY A method of error detection in which a small group of bits being transferred is compared to a single *parity* bit, which is set to make the total bits odd or even. The receiving device reads the parity bit and determines whether the data is valid based on the oddness or evenness of the parity bit.

PARTITION A section of the storage area of a hard disk. A partition is created during initial preparation of the hard disk, before the disk is formatted.

PASSWORD A series of characters that enable a user to gain access to a file, a folder, a PC, or a program.

PASSWORD RESET DISK A special type of floppy disk that can allow a user to recover a lost password without losing access to any encrypted, or password-protected, data.

PATCH CABLES Short UTP cables that connect patch panels to the hubs.

PATCH PANEL A panel containing a row of female connectors (ports) that terminate the horizontal cabling in the equipment room. Patch panels facilitate cabling organization and provide protection to horizontal cabling.

PATH The route the operating system must follow to find an executable program stored in a subdirectory.

PBX (PRIVATE BRANCH EXCHANGE) A private phone system used within an organization.

PC (PERSONAL COMPUTER) A more popular phrase than the more correct term *microcomputer*, PC means a small computer with its own processor and hard drive, as opposed to a dumb terminal connected to a central mainframe computer. Used in this fashion, the term *PC* indicates computers of many different manufacturers, using a variety of processors and operating systems. Although the term *PC* was around long before the original IBM PC was released, it has come to be almost synonymous with IBM-compatible computers, hence, the incorrect but common question, "Are you a Mac or a PC person?"

PCI (PERIPHERAL COMPONENT INTERCONNECT) A design architecture for the sockets on the computer motherboard that enable system components to be added to the computer. PCI is a "local bus" standard, meaning that devices added to a computer through this port will use the processor at the motherboard's full speed (up to 33 MHz), rather than at the slower 8 megahertz speed of the regular bus. In addition to moving data at a faster rate, PCI moves data 32 or 64 bits at a time, rather than the 8 or 16 bits that the older ISA busses supported.

PCMCIA (PERSONAL COMPUTER MEMORY CARD INTERNATIONAL ASSOCIATION) A consortium of computer manufacturers who devised the standard for credit card-sized adapter cards that add functionality in many notebook computers, PDAs, and other computer devices. The simpler term *PC Card* has become more common in referring to these cards.

PDA (PERSONAL DIGITAL ASSISTANT) Sometimes called *palmtop computers*, PDAs are computers small enough to fit into the palm of your hand. Early PDAs were used mainly as digital organizers, keeping track of contact lists, task lists, calendar events, and so on. Modern PDAs are much more powerful, and support chopped-down versions of productivity software such as Microsoft Office, multimedia, wireless networking, and telephone functions. PDAs run specialized operating systems, such as Palm OS or Microsoft Windows CE, Pocket PC, or Windows Mobile Edition. Popular PDAs include the various Palm models, HP's iPAQ, Sony Clie, and others. Most PDAs accept input via a *stylus* and special handwriting recognition software. Some come equipped with tiny keyboards.

PEER-TO-PEER NETWORKS A decentralized network in which each machine acts as both a client and a server, and maintains its own security over its own shared resources.

PENTIUM Name given to the fifth generation of Intel microprocessors, distinct with 32-bit address bus, 64-bit external data bus, and dual pipelining. Also used for subsequent generations of Intel processors: Pentium Pro, Pentium II, Pentium II Xeon, Pentium III, and Pentium III Xeon.

PERIPHERAL Any device other than the motherboard components of the computer. The floppy drive is a peripheral; the CPU is not a peripheral.

PERMISSIONS Sets of attributes that network administrators assign to resources to define what users and groups can do with them.

PERSISTENT CONNECTION A connection to a shared folder or drive that the computer immediately reconnects to at logon.

PERSONAL AREA NETWORKS (PAN) The network created among Bluetooth devices such as PDAs, printers, keyboards, mice, and so on.

PHOSPHOR An electrofluorescent material used to coat the inside face of a Cathode Ray Tube (CRT). After being hit with an electron, phosphors glow for a fraction of a second.

PHYSICAL ADDRESS A way of defining a specific machine without referencing its location or network. A MAC address is an example of a physical address.

PHYSICAL LAYER *See* OSI Seven-Layer Model.

PIM (PERSONAL INFORMATION MANAGER) A software application designed to hold and manage personal information such as phone numbers, contact notes, schedules, and to-do lists.

PING (PACKET INTERNET GROPER) Network utility that sends a small network message (ICMP ECHO) to a remote computer to check for presence and response time.

PIO (PROGRAMMABLE INPUT/OUTPUT) Using the address bus to send communication to a peripheral. The most common way for the CPU to communicate with peripherals.

PIO MODE A series of speed standards created by the Small Form Factor committee for the use of PIO by hard drives. The PIO modes range from PIO mode 0 to PIO mode 4.

PIXEL (PICTURE ELEMENT) In computer graphics, the smallest element of a display space that can be independently assigned color or intensity.

PLATEN The cylinder that guides paper through an impact printer and provides a backing surface for the paper when images are impressed onto the page.

PLATFORM Hardware environment that supports the running of a computer system.

PLENUM 1. The space between a building's false ceiling and the floor above it. Most of the wiring for networks is located in this space. 2. Plenum is also the fire rating of the grade of cable allowed to be installed in this location.

PLUG AND PLAY Also known as *PnP*. A combination of smart PCs, smart devices, and smart operating systems that automatically configure all the necessary system resources and ports for peripheral devices.

POINT COORDINATION FUNCTION (PCF) A method of collision avoidance defined by the 802.11 standard, which has yet to be implemented.

POINT-TO-MULTIPOINT These devices can communicate with more than one other network segment.

POP (POST OFFICE PROTOCOL) Also known as *Point Of Presence*, this refers to the way e-mail software such as Eudora gets mail from a mail server. When you obtain a SLIP, PPP, or shell account, you almost always get a POP account with it; and it is this POP account that you tell your e-mail software to use to get your mail. The current standard is called POP3.

POPULATED SEGMENT A segment that has one or more nodes directly attached to it.

PORT 1. A logical endpoint through which computers send specific types of network or data traffic. For example, port 80 is reserved for HTTP communication. 2. A physical connector used to attach network or I/O device cabling to the PC, such as a parallel or USB port.

PORT FILTERING Preventing the passage of any IP packets through any ports other than the ones prescribed by the system administrator.

PORT NUMBER Number used to identify the requested service (such as SMTP or FTP) when connecting to a TCP/IP host. Some example port numbers include 80 (HTTP), 20 (FTP), 69 (TFTP), 25 (SMTP), and 110 (POP3).

POSTSCRIPT A language defined by Adobe Systems, Inc. for describing how to create an image on a page. The description is independent of the resolution of the device that will create the image. It includes a technology for defining the shape of a font and creating a raster image at many different resolutions and sizes.

POWER USERS A user account that has the capability to do many, but not all, of the basic administrator functions.

PPP (POINT-TO-POINT PROTOCOL) A protocol that enables a computer to connect to the Internet through a dial-in connection and to enjoy most of the benefits of a direct connection. PPP is considered to be superior to SLIP because of its error detection and data compression features, which SLIP lacks, and the capability to use dynamic IP addresses.

PPPoE (PPP OVER ETHERNET) A specialized implementation of PPP, specifically designed to allow Ethernet connections to enjoy some of the benefits of PPP, such as encryption. Used exclusively by ADSL.

PPTP (POINT-TO-POINT TUNNELING PROTOCOL) A protocol that works with PPP to provide a secure data link between computers using encryption.

PREAMBLE A 64-bit series of alternating ones and zeroes ending with 11 that begins every Ethernet frame. The preamble gives a receiving NIC time to realize a frame is coming and to know exactly where the frame starts.

PRESENTATION LAYER *See* OSI Seven-Layer Model.

PROGRAM A set of actions or instructions that a machine is capable of interpreting and executing. Used as a verb, it means to design, write, and test such instructions.

PROMISCUOUS MODE A mode of operation for a network interface card in which the NIC processes all packets that it sees on the cable.

PROMPT A character or message provided by an operating system or program to indicate that it is ready to accept input.

PROPRIETARY Term used to describe technology that is unique to, and owned by, a particular vendor.

PROTECTED MODE The operating mode of a CPU to allow more than one program to be run while ensuring that no program can corrupt another program currently running.

PROTOCOL An agreement that governs the procedures used to exchange information between cooperating entities; usually includes how much information is to be sent, how often it is sent, how to recover from transmission errors, and who is to receive the information.

PROTOCOL STACK The actual software that implements the protocol suite on a particular operating system.

PROTOCOL SUITE A set of protocols that are commonly used together and operate at different levels of the OSI seven-layer model.

PROXY SERVER A device that fetches Internet resources for a client without exposing that client directly to the Internet. Most proxy servers accept requests for HTTP, FTP, POP3, and SMTP resources. The proxy server will often cache a copy of the requested resource for later use.

PSTN (PUBLIC SWITCHED TELEPHONE NETWORK) Also known as *POTS (Plain Old Telephone Service)*. Most common type of phone connection that takes your sounds, translated into an analog waveform by the microphone, and transmits them to another phone.

PUNCHDOWN TOOL *See* 110-Punchdown Tool.

PVC (POLYVINYL CHLORIDE) A material used for the outside insulation and jacketing of most cables. Also a fire rating for a type of cable that has no significant fire protection.

QIC (QUARTER-INCH TAPE OR CARTRIDGE)/TRAVAN TAPE Tape backup cartridges that use quarter-inch tape.

QUEUE The waiting area for things to happen, or, as we say in America, the *line*. An example is the print queue, where print jobs wait until it is their turn to be printed.

RAID (REDUNDANT ARRAY OF INDEPENDENT [OR INEXPENSIVE] DEVICES [OR DISKS]) A way of creating a fault-tolerant storage system. There are six levels. Level 0 uses byte-level striping and provides no fault tolerance. Level 1 uses mirroring or duplexing. Level 2 uses bit-level striping. Level 3 stores error correcting information (such as parity) on a separate disk, and uses data striping on the remaining drives. Level 4 is level 3 with block-level striping. Level 5 uses block-level and parity data striping. Other configurations are possible, such as RAID 10 (a mirrored set of two RAID 5 arrays), but these are uncommon.

RAM (RANDOM ACCESS MEMORY) Expandable system memory in which any address can be written to or read from as easily as any other address. Typical system RAM is dynamic memory, meaning that RAM doesn't retail data after powering down the system.

RASTER The horizontal pattern of lines that forms an image on the monitor screen.

REAL MODE The original 64K segmented memory, single-tasking operating mode of the Intel 8086 and 8088 CPUs.

REAL-TIME The processing of transactions as they occur, rather than batching them. Pertaining to an application in which response to input is fast enough to affect subsequent inputs and guide the process and in which records are updated immediately. Real-time systems are those with a response time of milliseconds; interactive systems respond in seconds, and batch systems may respond in hours or days.

RECOVERY CONSOLE A DOS-like interface, accessed using Windows 2000/XP/2003 boot disks or CD-ROM, that can be used to repair a system that is suffering from massive operating system corruption or other problems.

RECYCLE BIN When files are deleted from a modern Windows system, they are moved to the Recycle Bin. To permanently remove files from a system, they must be removed from the Recycle Bin.

REFRESH The process of repainting the CRT screen, causing the phosphors to remain lit (or change). Also refers to the process of recharging RAM.

REGEDIT.EXE A 16-bit program used to edit the Windows 9x registry.

REGEDT32.EXE 32-bit version of the program used to edit the registry on Windows NT/2000/XP systems.

REMOTE Any system that is non-local (i.e., another system on the same network segment, or a system that is on a different network segment).

REMOTE ACCESS The capability to access a computer from outside a building in which it is housed. Remote access requires communications hardware, software, and actual physical links.

REMOTE ACCESS SERVER (RAS) Refers to both the hardware component (servers built to handle the unique stresses of a large number of clients calling in) and the software component (programs that work with the operating system to allow remote access to the network) of a remote access solution.

REMOTE INSTALLATION SERVICES (RIS) A service introduced with Windows 2000 used to initiate an image-based installation of the Windows operating system onto a PC via a network.

REPEATER A device that takes all of the data packets it receives on one Ethernet segment and re-creates them on another Ethernet segment. This allows for longer cables or more computers on a segment. Repeaters operate at Level 1 (Physical) of the OSI seven-layer model.

REPLICATION A fancy word meaning *copy*. During the replication process, data is copied from one PC to another. In the case of Windows 2000 Server/Server 2003 Active Directory domains, the AD database is replicated among all domain controllers (DCs), thus ensuring that each DC has a current and consistent copy of the database. Windows can also be configured to replicate user data files between file servers via the Distributed File Service (DFS) to ensure fault tolerance.

RESISTANCE The tendency for physical medium to impede electron flow. It is classically measured in a unit called *ohms*.

RESOLUTION A measurement expressed in horizontal and vertical dots or pixels for CRTs and/or printers. Higher resolutions provide sharper details, thus displaying better-looking images.

RESOURCE 1. Any object, service, or device that can be shared with other PCs and users on a network. 2. Components of functions of a system used to perform tasks (i.e., memory addresses, channels to the CPU, and so on).

RESTORE POINT A system snapshot created by the System Restore utility that is used to restore a malfunctioning system. *See also* System Restore.

REVERSE LOOKUP ZONES A DNS setting that resolves IP addresses to FQDNs. In other words, it does exactly the reverse of what DNS normally accomplishes using Forward Lookup Zones.

RG-6 A type of cable that is virtually never installed in networks these days, but still has enough of an installed base that you should at least know about it. The cable used for cable TV is RG-6.

RG-8 Often referred to as *Thick Ethernet*, RG-8 is the oldest and least-used cabling type still in use. It gets the name Thick Ethernet because it is used exclusively for 802.5 Thick Ethernet networks. RG-8 is rated at 50 ohms and has a distinct yellow or orange/brown color.

RG-58 A type of cable that works with the still quite popular Thin Ethernet network technology. It is rated at 50 ohms.

RIGHTS Novell NetWare's term for resource permissions.

RING IN The Ring In port on a Token Ring MAU is used to connect to the Ring Out port on a second MAU, and vice versa, to form a single logical ring.

RING OUT The Ring Out port on a Token Ring MAU is used to connect to the Ring In port on a second MAU, and vice versa, to form a single logical ring.

RING TOPOLOGY A network topology in which all the computers on the network attach to a central ring of cable.

RJ (REGISTERED JACK) Connectors used for UTP cable for both telephone and network connections.

RJ-11 Type of connector with 4-wire UTP connections; usually found in telephone connections.

RJ-45 Type of connector with 8-wire UTP connections; usually found in network connections and used for 10BaseT networking.

ROM (READ-ONLY MEMORY) The generic term for non-volatile memory that can be read from but not written to. This means that code and data stored in ROM cannot be corrupted by accidental erasure. Additionally, ROM retains its data when power is removed, which makes it the perfect medium for storing BIOS data or information such as scientific constants.

ROOT DIRECTORY The top-level directory that contains all other sub-directories.

ROUTER A device connecting separate networks, which forwards a packet from one network to another based only on the network address for the protocol being used. For example, an IP router looks only at the IP network number. Routers operate at Layer 3 (Network) of the OSI seven-layer model.

ROUTING TABLE A list of paths to various networks required by routers. This can be built either manually or dynamically via one of the routing protocols, such as RIP or OSPF.

RS-232C A standard port recommended by the Electronics Industry Association for serial devices.

RUN The length of cable that connects nodes to the equipment room.

SAMBA A service that enables UNIX-based systems to communicate using SMB (Server Message Blocks). This, in turn, enables them to act as Microsoft clients and servers on the network.

SCALABILITY The capability to support system or network growth.

SCANNER A device that senses alterations of light and dark. It enables the user to import photographs, other physical images, and text into the computer in digital form.

SC CONNECTOR One of two special types of fiber-optic cable used in 10BaseFL networks.

SCSI (SMALL COMPUTER SYSTEM INTERFACE) A powerful and flexible peripheral interface popularized on the Macintosh and used to connect hard drives, CD-ROM drives, tape drives, scanners, and other devices to PCs of all kinds. Because SCSI is less efficient at handling small drives than IDE, it did not become popular on IBM-compatible computers until price reductions made these large drives affordable. Normal SCSI enables up to seven devices to be connected through a single bus connection, whereas Wide SCSI can handle 15 devices attached to a single controller.

SCSI CHAIN A SCSI host adapter and all of the devices attached to it.

SDRAM (SYNCHRONOUS DRAM) DRAM that is tied to the system clock and, thus, runs much faster than traditional FPM and EDO RAM.

SECTOR A segment of one of the concentric tracks encoded on the disk during a low-level format. A sector holds 512 bytes of data.

SECURE SOCKETS LAYER (SSL) See SSL (Secure Sockets Layer).

SEGMENT The network bus that network clients connect to. See 5-4-3 rule.

SEQUENTIAL A method of storing and retrieving information that requires data to be written and read sequentially. Accessing any portion of the data requires reading all the preceding data.

SERIAL ATA (SATA) A hard drive technology that offers many advantages over PATA (Parallel ATA) technology, including thinner cabling, keyed connectors, and lower power requirements. Current SATA drives transfer data at 150 megabytes per second. Future SATA drives will be much faster, while PATA drives are at the top speed the technology enables.

SERVER A computer that shares its resources, such as printers and files, with other computers on the network. An example of this is a Network File System Server that shares its disk space with a workstation that has no disk drive of its own.

SERVER-BASED NETWORK A network in which one or more systems function as dedicated file, print, or application servers, but do not function as clients.

SERVICE SET IDENTIFICATION (SSID) A 32-bit identification string, sometimes called a *network name*, that's inserted into the header of each data packet processed by a wireless access point.

SESSION A networking term used to refer to the logical stream of data flowing between two programs and being communicated over a network. Many different sessions may be emanating from any one node on a network.

SESSION LAYER See OSI Seven-Layer Model.

SESSION SOFTWARE Session software handles the process of differentiating between various types of connections on a PC.

SHARE LEVEL SECURITY A security system in which each resource has a password assigned to it at the network level, but not the local level. Access to the resource is typically password-based. See Share Permissions.

SHARE PERMISSIONS Permissions that only control the access of other users on the network with whom you share your resource. They have no impact on you (or anyone else) sitting at the computer whose resource is being shared.

SHAREWARE Software that is distributed freely, enabling potential users to "try before they buy." Shareware typically has a pre-configured "trial period," after which it will cease to function unless the user opts to purchase a license. Most shareware is distributed with full functionality, but some vendors may disable advanced functions until a license is purchased.

SHELL A term that generally refers to the user interface of an operating system. A shell is the command processor that is the actual interface between the kernel and the user.

SHORT CIRCUIT Allows electricity to pass between two conductive elements that weren't designed to interact together. Also called a *short*.

SHUNT A tiny metal connector enclosed in plastic that creates an electrical connection between two posts of a jumper. Often incorrectly referred to as the jumper itself.

SIGNAL STRENGTH A measurement of how well your wireless device is connecting to other devices.

SIMM (SINGLE IN-LINE MEMORY MODULE) A type of DRAM packaging distinct by having a number of small tabs that install into a special connector. Each side of each tab is the same signal. SIMMs come in two common sizes: 30-pin and 72-pin.

SIMPLE VOLUME A type of volume created when setting up dynamic disks. A simple volume acts like a primary partition on a dynamic disk.

SL ENHANCED A type of CPU that has the capability to turn off selected peripherals as well as run on low (3.3v or less) power. *See also* SMM (System Management Mode).

SLIP (SERIAL LINE INTERFACE PROTOCOL) A protocol that enables a computer to connect to the Internet through a dial-in connection and enjoy most of the benefits of a direct connection. SLIP has been almost completely replaced by PPP, which is considered superior to SLIP because of its error detection and data compression—features that SLIP lacks—and the capability to use dynamic IP addresses.

SMB (SERVER MESSAGE BLOCKS) Protocol used by Microsoft clients and servers to share file and print resources.

SMM (SYSTEM MANAGEMENT MODE) A special CPU mode that enables the CPU to reduce power consumption via the selective shutdown of peripherals.

SMTP (SIMPLE MAIL TRANSFER PROTOCOL) The main protocol used to send electronic mail on the Internet.

SNAP-INS Small utilities that can be used with the Microsoft Management Console.

SNEAKERNET The term used for saving the file on a portable medium and physically walking it over to another computer.

SNMP (SIMPLE NETWORK MANAGEMENT PROTOCOL) A protocol that enables communication and management of remote network hardware devices such as hubs, routers, and switches. The remote device in question must be SNMP-capable.

SOCIAL ENGINEERING Methods of convincing network users to perform tasks on your behalf, such as revealing passwords or launching applications, that may compromise the network. Examples include impersonation of authority figures (law enforcement officers, network administrators, vendor support personnel), threats of punishment, promises of rewards, misdirection, and so on.

SOCKET A virtual endpoint for a network session. A combination of a port number and an IP address that uniquely identifies a connection.

SOFTWARE Programmatic instructions used to perform tasks on a PC. Examples of software include application programs, such as Microsoft Office, device drivers, protocol suites, client services, and the network operating system itself, among many others.

SOLID CORE A cable that uses a single solid wire to transmit signals.

SONET (SYNCHRONOUS OPTICAL NETWORK) A standard for connecting fiber-optic transmission systems. SONET defines interface standards at the Physical layer of the OSI seven-layer model.

SOURCE CODE The program in a language prepared by the programmer. This code cannot be directly executed by the computer and must first be translated into executable object code. Also, the building blocks of an operating system or application.

SOUTHBRIDGE The Southbridge is part of a motherboard chipset. It handles all the inputs and outputs to the many devices in the PC.

SPOOL A temporary storage area in memory that caches pending print jobs.

SPREADSHEET A software program that enables users to perform mathematical calculations in a tabular format, such as budgeting, keeping track of investments, or tracking grades.

SPS (STAND-BY POWER SUPPLY OR SYSTEM) A device that supplies continuous clean power to a computer system immediately following a power failure. *See also* UPS (Uninterruptible Power Supply).

SQL (STRUCTURED QUERY LANGUAGE) 1. A language created by IBM that relies on simple English statements to perform database queries. SQL enables databases from different manufacturers to be queried using a standard syntax. 2. A Microsoft database application, *SQL Server*.

SRAM (STATIC RAM) A type of RAM that uses a flip-flop type of circuit, rather than the typical transistor/capacitor of DRAM, to hold a bit of information. SRAM does not need to be refreshed and is faster than regular DRAM. Used primarily for cache.

SSL (Secure Sockets Layer) A protocol developed by Netscape for transmitting private documents over the Internet. SSL works by using a public key to encrypt sensitive data. This encrypted data is sent over an SSL connection, and then decrypted at the receiving end using a private key.

ST506 A model of hard drive developed by Seagate. This drive, as well as the WD1003 controller developed by Western Digital, created the standard for the first generation of hard drives and controllers. As a result, drives that copied the connections and BIOS commands of the ST506 came to be known as ST506 drives.

Stackable Hub Hubs with a special proprietary connection that enables them to function in groups, called *stacks*, as a single device.

Star Bus Topology This is a hybrid of the Star and Bus topologies. This topology uses a physical star, where all nodes connect to a single wiring point such as a hub, and a logical bus that maintains the Ethernet standards. One benefit of a Star Bus topology is fault tolerance.

Star Ring Topology A star ring is a hybrid of the Token Ring topology and the physical star.

Star Topology A network topology in which all computers in the network connect to a central wiring point.

Static Routing A process by which routers in an internetwork obtain information about paths to other routers. This information must be configured manually.

ST Connector One of two special types of fiber-optic cable used in 10BaseFL networks.

Storage A device or medium that can retain data for subsequent retrieval.

STP (Shielded Twisted Pair) A popular cabling for networks composed of pairs of wires twisted around each other at specific intervals. The twists serve to reduce interference (also called *crosstalk*). The more twists, the less interference. The cable has metallic shielding to protect the wires from external interference. Token Ring networks are the only common network technology that uses STP, although Token Ring more often now uses UTP.

Stranded Core A cable that uses a bundle of tiny wire strands to transmit signals. Stranded core is not quite as good a conductor as solid core, but it will stand up to substantial handling without breaking.

Stripe Set A group of two or more disk drives that store data sequentially. Striped sets perform faster read and write operations than a single disk, but the threat of data loss is increased because no one disk in a striped set contains all pieces of file data.

Structured Cable The practice of organizing the cables in a network for ease of repair and replacement.

Subnet Sections of a TCP/IP network sharing a common IP addressing scheme. *See* Subnet Mask.

Subnet Mask The value used in TCP/IP settings to divide the IP address of a host into its component parts: network ID and host ID.

Super User Account A colloquial term that refers to the default administrator user account in Windows NT/2000/XP, and 2003. The administrator account, appropriately named *Administrator*, has complete authority to perform any tasks on the system, including accessing, moving, copying, and deleting files and folders, reconfiguring system settings, creating and disabling user accounts, installing programs, and so on.

SVGA A graphics standard that specifies a monitor resolution of 800 ? 600 at 256 colors.

Switch 1. A hardware device that filters and forwards data packets between network segments. 2. Synonymous with *parameter* or *argument*. 3. A hardware device that completes or terminates an electrical circuit.

Switched Ethernet A network setup in which some devices are placed into their own collision domains. Logically, an Ethernet switch puts each device plugged into one of its switched ports into its own collision domain.

Synchronous Describes a connection between two electronic devices where neither must acknowledge (ACK) when receiving data.

SYSCON An ancient, but completely functional, program used to set up trustee rights, and create users and groups in NetWare 3.*x*.

Sysop (System Operator) Anyone responsible for the physical operations of a computer system or network resource. A System Administrator decides how often backups and maintenance should be performed, and the System Operator performs those tasks.

System BIOS The primary set of BIOS stored on an EPROM or Flash chip on the motherboard. Defines the BIOS for all the assumed hardware on the motherboard, such as keyboard controller, floppy drive, basic video, RAM, and so forth.

System Monitor A utility that can be used to evaluate and monitor system resources, like CPU usage and memory usage.

System Resources System resources are I/O addresses, IRQs, DMA channels, and memory addresses.

System Restore A utility in Windows Me and XP that enables you to return your PC to a recent working configuration when something goes wrong. System Restore returns your computer's system settings to the way they were the last time you remember your system working correctly—all without affecting your personal files or e-mail.

T-1 A leased-line connection capable of carrying data at 1,544,000 bits per second.

T-3 A leased-line connection capable of carrying data at 44,736,000 bits per second.

T-Connector A connector used in 10Base2 networks that is designed in a T shape. The stem of the T-connector plugs into the female connector on the Ethernet NIC, and the two pieces of coaxial cable are plugged into either end of the top bar.

TCP (Transmission Control Protocol) Part of the TCP/IP protocol suite, TCP operates at Layer 4 (Transport) of the OSI seven-layer model. TCP is a connection-oriented protocol.

TCP/IP (Transmission Control Protocol/Internet Protocol) A set of communication protocols, including TCP, IP, UDP, and others, developed by the U.S. Department of Defense that enables dissimilar computers to share information over a network.

TDR (Time Domain Reflectometer) Advanced cable tester that tests the length of cables and their continuity or discontinuity, and identifies the location of any discontinuity due to a bend, break, unwanted crimp, and so on.

Telephony The science of converting sound into electrical signals, moving those signals from one location to another, and then converting those signals back into sounds. This includes modems, telephone lines, the telephone system, and any products used to create a remote access link between a remote access client and server.

Telnet A service that enables users on the Internet to log on to remote systems from their own host systems.

Tera- A prefix that usually stands for the binary number 1,099,511,627,776, which is 2 to the 40th power. When used for mass storage, often shorthand usage for a trillion bytes.

Terabyte 1,099,511,627,776 bytes.

Terminal A "dumb" device connected to a computer network that acts as a point for entry or retrieval of information.

Terminal Emulation Software that enables a PC to communicate with another computer or network as if it were a specific type of hardware terminal.

Terminating Resistors Any device that absorbs excess electrical signals off a wire. Examples include the device used at each end of a coaxial cable to absorb the excess electrical signals, which helps avoid signal bounce or reflection. The level of resistance in RG-58 coaxial cables requires them to have 50 ohm impedance. Another device with the same name is used to terminate the ends of a SCSI chain.

Terminator 1. *See* Terminating Resistors. 2. In a machine-dominated future, a type of cyborg designed to infiltrate groups of human resistance fighters. May be sent into the past to prevent the resistance leader from being born, thus ensuring the successful destruction of mankind.

Thick Ethernet (Thicknet) Thick Ethernet, or Thicknet, also goes by the name *RG-8*. This is the oldest coax cabling type still in use.

Thin Ethernet (Thinnet) Thin Ethernet, or Thinnet, is known also as *RG-58*. It stands alone as the only coax cable type still widely used in networks.

TIFF (Tagged Image File Format) A graphical file format in which images are divided into discrete blocks or strips called *tags*. Each tag contains formatting information, such as width and number of colors, for the entire image. The TIFF format is useful because it can describe many different types of images, but it is also complex and writing software for it is difficult.

TLA (Three-Letter Acronym) Any acronym of three letters, such as FAT (File Allocation Table) and GIF (Graphics Interchange Format).

Token The token is a frame that enables the systems on a Token Ring network to effectively "take turns" sending data. The rule is that no device can transmit data unless it's currently holding the token.

Token Passing The system used by Token Ring networks to control access to the ring. A node receives a token from its upstream neighbor and, when it is finished transmitting data, passes the token on to its downstream neighbor.

Token Ring A LAN and protocol in which nodes are connected together in a ring, and a special packet called a token, passed from node to node around the ring, controls communication. A node can send data only when it receives the token and the token is not in use. This avoids the collision problems endemic to Ethernet networks.

Tone Generator *See* Toners.

Tone Probe *See* Toners.

Toners Generic term for two devices used together— a tone generator and a tone locator (probe)—to trace cables by sending an electrical signal along a wire at a particular frequency. The tone locator then emits a sound when it distinguishes that frequency. An example of a tone generator/tone locator device is Triplett Corporation's *Fox and Hound*.

TOPOLOGY 1. The pattern of interconnections in a communications system among devices, nodes, and associated input and output stations. 2. Also describes how computers connect to each other without regard to how they actually communicate. *See* Network Topology.

TRACERT (ALSO TRACEROUTE) A command-line utility used to follow the path a packet takes between two hosts.

TRANSCEIVER The devices that transmit and receive signals on a cable.

TRANSPORT LAYER *See* OSI Seven-Layer Model.

TRIVIAL FILE TRANSFER PROTOCOL (TFTP) A protocol that transfers files between servers and clients. Unlike FTP, TFTP requires no user login. Devices that need an operating system, but have no local hard disk (for example, diskless workstations and routers), often use TFTP to download their operating systems.

TROJAN VIRUS A virus that masquerades as a file with a legitimate purpose, so that a user will run it intentionally. The classic example is a file that runs a game, but also causes some type of damage to the player's system.

TRUSTEE RIGHTS NetWare lingo for user and group permissions to a shared folder. Any user or group with rights to a certain shared folder is said to have trustee rights to that folder.

TSR (TERMINATE AND STAY RESIDENT) A DOS program that mostly closes immediately after starting up, but leaves a tiny piece of itself in memory. TSRs are used to handle a broad cross-section of DOS-level system needs, such as running hardware (MOUSE.COM) or applying higher-level functionality to hardware already under the control of device drivers. MSCDEX.EXE, for example, assigns a drive letter to a CD-ROM drive after the CD-ROM driver has loaded in CONFIG.SYS.

TWAIN (TECHNOLOGY WITHOUT AN INTERESTING NAME) A programming interface that enables a graphics application, such as a desktop publishing program, to activate a scanner, frame grabber, or other image-capturing device.

TWISTED PAIR The most overwhelmingly common type of cabling used in networks consists of twisted pairs of cables. The two types of twisted pair cabling are UTP (Unshielded Twisted Pair) and STP (Shielded Twisted Pair). The twists serve to reduce interference, called *crosstalk*; the more twists, the less crosstalk.

TYPE 1 CONNECTOR Another name for the IBM-designed hermaphroditic connector called either an *IBM-type Data Connector (IDC)* or a *Universal Data Connector (UDC)*.

UART (UNIVERSAL ASYNCHRONOUS RECEIVER/TRANSMITTER) A device that turns serial data into parallel data. The cornerstone of serial ports and modems.

UDP (USER DATAGRAM PROTOCOL) Part of the TCP/IP protocol suite, UDP is an alternative to TCP. UDP is a connectionless protocol.

UNC (UNIVERSAL NAMING CONVENTION) Describes any shared resource in a network using the convention \\<*server name*>\<*name of shared resource*>.

UNITS (U) The unique height measurement used with network equipment racks, expressed as U. One U equals 1.75 inches.

UNIX A powerful, open source network operating system originally developed by Bell Laboratories in the 1970s. UNIX is widely used on many types of server systems.

UPS (UNINTERRUPTIBLE POWER SUPPLY) A device that supplies continuous clean power to a computer system the whole time the computer is on. Protects against power outages and sags. The term *UPS* is often used mistakenly when people mean SPS (Stand-by Power Supply or System).

UPLINK PORT Special port in a hub used to connect to another hub by crossing the sending and receiving wires. *See* Crossover Port.

UPSTREAM NEIGHBOR The computer right before a node on a Token Ring network.

URL (UNIFORM RESOURCE LOCATOR) A Uniform Resource Locator is an address that defines the location of a resource on the Internet and World Wide Web. URLs use the format *protocol://IP address or domain name/resource name*. For example, http://www.totalsem.com/mikespc/mikesstuff/stuff.doc, ftp://63.31.12.159/srv/lovestruck.mp3.

USB (UNIVERSAL SERIAL BUS) A 12-Mbps serial interconnect for keyboards, printers, joysticks, and many other devices. Enables hot-swapping and daisy chaining of devices. USB 2.0 devices transfer data at up to 480 Mbps.

USENET Started by Duke University and UNC-Chapel Hill. An information cooperative linking around 16,000 computer sites and millions of people. Usenet provides a series of "news groups" analogous to online conferences.

USER Anyone who uses a computer. You. Me, too, for that matter.

USER ACCOUNT A container that identifies a user to the application, operating system, or network, including name, password, user name, groups to which the user belongs, and other information based on the user and the OS or NOS being used. Usually defines the rights and roles a user plays on a system.

USER DATAGRAM PROTOCOL (UDP) A protocol used by some older applications, most prominently TFTP (Trivial FTP), to transfer files. UDP packets are both simpler and smaller than TCP packets, and they do most of the behind-the-scenes work in a TCP/IP network.

USER LEVEL SECURITY A security system in which each user has an account, and access to resources is based on user identity.

USER PROFILES A collection of settings that corresponds to a specific user account and may follow the user, regardless of the computer at which he or she logs on. These settings enable the user to have customized environment and security settings.

UTP (UNSHIELDED TWISTED PAIR) A popular cabling for telephone and networks composed of pairs of wires twisted around each other at specific intervals. The twists serve to reduce interference (also called *crosstalk*). The more twists, the less interference. The cable has no metallic shielding to protect the wires from external interference, unlike its cousin, *STP*. 10BaseT uses UTP, as do many other networking technologies. UTP is available in a variety of grades, called categories, as defined in the following:

> **Category 1 UTP** Regular analog phone lines, not used for data communications.
> **Category 2 UTP** Supports speeds up to 4 megabits per second.
> **Category 3 UTP** Supports speeds up to 16 megabits per second.
> **Category 4 UTP** Supports speeds up to 20 megabits per second.
> **Category 5 UTP** Supports speeds up to 100 megabits per second.
> **Category 5e UTP** Supports speeds up to 100 megabits per second with two pairs and up to 1000 megabits per second with four pairs.
> **Category 6 UTP** Improved support for speeds up to 1000 megabits per second.

V STANDARDS Standards established by CCITT for modem manufacturers to follow (voluntarily) to ensure compatible speeds, compression, and error correction.

VESA (VIDEO ELECTRONICS STANDARDS ASSOCIATION) A consortium of computer manufacturers that standardized improvements to common IBM PC components. VESA is responsible for the Super VGA video standard and the VLB bus architecture.

VGA (VIDEO GRAPHICS ARRAY) The standard for the video graphics adapter that was built into IBM's PS/2 computer. It supports 16 colors in a 640 ? 480 pixel video display, and quickly replaced the older CGA (Color Graphics Adapter) and EGA (Extended Graphics Adapter).

VIRTUAL Pertaining to a device or facility that does not physically exist, yet behaves as if it does. Examples include *virtual memory, virtual device drivers, virtual private network,* and so on.

VIRTUAL DEVICE DRIVER (VxD) A special type of driver file used to support older Windows programs. Windows protection errors take place when VxDs fail to load or unload. This usually occurs when a device somehow gets a device driver in both CONFIG.SYS and SYSTEM.INI or the Registry.

VIRTUAL LAN (VLAN) A LAN that, using smart, VLAN-capable switches, can place some (or any on the more expensive VLANs) systems on whatever collision domain you want.

VIRUS A type of program containing malicious executable code. Viruses are designed to install themselves onto systems without the user's knowledge or permission, and cause varying degrees of damage to the system when executed. Some viruses cause no significant damage, while others may destroy data, corrupt the OS, render the system unbootable, or enable remote users to take control of the PC. Viruses are typically designed to propagate by creating copies of themselves and transmitting the copies to other PCs via open network shares, e-mail, and unsecured ports.

VIRUS DEFINITION OR DATA FILE These files are also called *signature files*, depending on the virus protection software in use. These files enable the virus protection software to recognize the viruses on your system and clean them. These files should be updated often.

VLB (VESA LOCAL BUS) A design architecture for the sockets on the computer motherboard that enable system components to be added to the computer. VLB was the first *local bus* standard, meaning that devices added to a computer through this port would use the processor at its full speed, rather than at the slower 8-megahertz speed of the regular bus. In addition to moving data at a faster rate, VLB moves data 32 bits at a time, rather than the 8 or 16 bits that the older ISA busses supported. Although VLB was common on machines using Intel's 486 CPU, modern computers now use PCI busses instead.

VOLATILE Memory that must have constant electricity to retain data. Alternatively, any "programmer" six hours before deadline after a nonstop 48-hour coding session, running on nothing but caffeine and sugar.

VOLTS (V) The pressure of the electrons passing through a wire is called *voltage* and is measured in units called volts (V).

Volume 1. A physical unit of a storage medium, such as a tape reel or disk pack, that is capable of having data recorded on it and subsequently read. 2. A contiguous collection of cylinders or blocks on a disk that are treated as a separate unit.

VPN (Virtual Private Network) A network configuration that enables a remote user to access a private network via the Internet. VPNs employ an encryption methodology called *tunneling*, which protects the data from interception.

VRAM (Video RAM) A type of memory in a video display adapter that's used to create the image appearing on the CRT screen. VRAM uses dual-ported memory, which enables simultaneous reads and writes, making it much quicker than DRAM.

WAN (Wide Area Network) A geographically dispersed network created by linking various computers and LANs over long distances, generally using leased phone lines. There is no firm dividing line between a WAN and a LAN.

Warm Boot A system restart performed after the system has been powered and operating. This clears and resets the memory, but does not stop and start the hard drive.

Wattage (Watts or W) The amount of amps and volts needed by a particular device to function is expressed as how much wattage (watts or W) that device needs.

WAV (Windows Audio Format) The default sound format for Windows.

WB (Write Back) Defines a certain type of SRAM cache where instructions from the CPU to write changes are held in the cache until time is available to write the changes to main memory.

Web Server A server that enables access to HTML documents by remote users using the HTTP protocol.

Well-Known Ports Port numbers from 0 to 1204 that are used primarily by client applications to talk to server applications in TCP/IP networks.

Wi-Fi Protected Access (WPA) A wireless security protocol that addresses the weaknesses and acts as a sort of upgrade to WEP. WPA offers security enhancements such as dynamic encryption key generation (keys are issued on a per-user and per-session basis), an encryption key integrity-checking feature, user authentication through the industry-standard Extensible Authentication Protocol (EAP), and other advanced features that WEP lacks.

WIN32 A programming interface or API for an early PC 32-bit mode fully supported by Windows NT. Many functions are supported in Windows 3.*x*, and written to the Win32 subset to gain improved performance on a 386. Windows 3.*x* translates the 32-bit calls in an application into its native 16-bit calls.

Windows A powerful and flexible network operating system developed by Microsoft in the 1980s. Windows comes in a variety of desktop and server versions, including Windows 9*x* (95, 98, 98SE, ME), Windows NT Workstation and Server, Windows 2000 Professional and Server, Windows XP Home and Professional Editions, and Windows Server 2003. Many of these versions also have their own variations, such as Windows Server 2003 Small Business Edition, Terminal Server, Enterprise Edition, DataCenter, and so on.

WINIPCFG A graphical program used on Windows 95, Windows 98, and Windows Me machines to display the current TCP/IP configuration of the machine; similar to Windows NT/2000/XP's IPCONFIG and UNIX/Linux's IFCONFIG.

WINS (Windows Internet Name Service) A name resolution service that resolves NetBIOS names to IP addresses.

Winsock (WINdows SOCKets) Microsoft Windows implementation of the TCP/IP Sockets interface.

WINS Relay Agent A WINS relay agent forwards WINS broadcasts to a WINS server on the other side of a router to keep older systems from broadcasting in place of registering with the server.

Wireless Access Point Connects wireless network nodes to wireless or wired networks. Many wireless access points are combination devices that act as high-speed hubs, switches, bridges, and routers, all rolled into one.

Wireless Equivalency Privacy (WEP) A wireless security protocol that uses a 64-bit encryption algorithm to scramble data packets.

Wireless Fidelity (Wi-Fi) The most widely adopted wireless networking type in use today. Technically, only wireless devices that conform to the extended versions of the 802.11 standard—802.11a, 802.11b, and 802.11g—are Wi-Fi certified.

Wireless Network *See* Wireless Fidelity (Wi-Fi).

Word A group of 16 binary digits or 2 bytes.

Word Processor A program used to enter or edit text information in personal computers, often used to create a file before it is uploaded to a network. May also be used to process text after it has been downloaded.

Work Area The work area in a basic structured cabling network is often simply an office or cubicle that potentially contains a PC attached to the network.

WORKGROUP A convenient method of organizing computers under Network Neighborhood/My Network Places in Windows operating systems. Workgroups have "flat" namespaces, and contain no method for applying security.

WORKSTATION 1. A term used to differentiate a network client system from a server system. 2. A specialized type of high-end PC that has very powerful CPU(s), massive amounts of RAM, and other high-performance hardware making it suitable for advanced mathematical, scientific, or graphical applications. Sun and Silicon Graphics Inc. are two popular manufacturers of workstation-class PCs.

WORM A worm is a very special form of virus. Unlike other viruses, a worm does not infect other files on the computer. Instead, it replicates by making copies of itself on other systems on a network by taking advantage of security weaknesses in networking protocols.

WWW (WORLD WIDE WEB) The system of servers supporting graphics and multimedia via HTTP. The WWW is a specialized use (some call it a layer) of the Internet, but is not synonymous with the Internet at large.

X.25 A type of Packet Switched network that enables remote devices to communicate with each other across high-speed digital links without the expense of individual leased lines.

XGA (EXTENDED GRAPHICS ARRAY) IBM video display to bring 1,024 ? 768 resolution to monitors. Can display 65,536 colors at low resolution, and 256 at high resolution.

XMODEM A file transfer protocol (FTP) that provides error-free asynchronous communications through telephone lines.

XMS (EXTENDED MEMORY SERVICES) The RAM above 1 megabyte that is installed directly on the motherboard, and directly accessible to the microprocessor. Usually shortened to simply "extended" memory.

YMODEM A file transfer protocol (FTP) that is more robust than Xmodem; it features a time and date stamp transfer, as well as batch file transfers.

ZIF SOCKET (ZERO INSERTION FORCE SOCKET) A type of socket for CPUs that enables insertion of a chip without much pressure. Intel promoted the ZIF socket with its overdrive upgrades. The chip is dropped into the socket's holes and a small lever is turned to lock it in. Somewhat replaced in modern motherboards by Slot 1 and Slot A architecture, ZIF is still in style in Super Socket 7 and Socket 370 motherboards.

ZMODEM Streaming asynchronous file transfer protocol (FTP) used by communication software. Popular for downloading.

ZOMBIE ATTACK A method of launching Denial of Service (DoS) attacks or spreading spam. Instigators of zombie attacks take over the function of numerous remote computers (via virus or worm), and use the remote systems to run malicious programs that flood the target system with requests or send mass e-mails. Zombie attacks make it difficult to trace the attack back to the original instigator.

Index

References to illustrations are in *italics*.

INTERNATIONAL CONTACT INFORMATION

AUSTRALIA
McGraw-Hill Book Company
Australia Pty. Ltd.
TEL +61-2-9900-1800
FAX +61-2-9878-8881
http://www.mcgraw-hill.com.au
books-it_sydney@mcgraw-hill.com

CANADA
McGraw-Hill Ryerson Ltd.
TEL +905-430-5000
FAX +905-430-5020
http://www.mcgraw-hill.ca

**GREECE, MIDDLE EAST, & AFRICA
(Excluding South Africa)**
McGraw-Hill Hellas
TEL +30-210-6560-990
TEL +30-210-6560-993
TEL +30-210-6560-994
FAX +30-210-6545-525

MEXICO (Also serving Latin America)
McGraw-Hill Interamericana Editores
S.A. de C.V.
TEL +525-1500-5108
FAX +525-117-1589
http://www.mcgraw-hill.com.mx
carlos_ruiz@mcgraw-hill.com

SINGAPORE (Serving Asia)
McGraw-Hill Book Company
TEL +65-6863-1580
FAX +65-6862-3354
http://www.mcgraw-hill.com.sg
mghasia@mcgraw-hill.com

SOUTH AFRICA
McGraw-Hill South Africa
TEL +27-11-622-7512
FAX +27-11-622-9045
robyn_swanepoel@mcgraw-hill.com

SPAIN
McGraw-Hill/
Interamericana de España, S.A.U.
TEL +34-91-180-3000
FAX +34-91-372-8513
http://www.mcgraw-hill.es
professional@mcgraw-hill.es

**UNITED KINGDOM, NORTHERN,
EASTERN, & CENTRAL EUROPE**
McGraw-Hill Education Europe
TEL +44-1-628-502500
FAX +44-1-628-770224
http://www.mcgraw-hill.co.uk
emea_queries@mcgraw-hill.com

ALL OTHER INQUIRIES Contact:
McGraw-Hill Technology Education
TEL +1-630-789-4000
FAX +1-630-789-5226
http://www.mhteched.com
omg_international@mcgraw-hill.com